Social work sex offenders

Making a difference

Malcolm Cowburn and
Steve Myers

First published in Great Britain in 2016 by

Policy Press
University of Bristol
1-9 Old Park Hill
Bristol BS2 8BB
UK
t: +44 (0)117 954 5940
pp-info@bristol.ac.uk
www.policypress.co.uk

North America office:
Policy Press
c/o The University of Chicago Press
1427 East 60th Street
Chicago, IL 60637, USA
t: +1 773 702 7700
f: +1 773-702-9756
sales@press.uchicago.edu
www.press.uchicago.edu

British Library Cataloguing in Publication Data
A catalogue record for this book is available from the British Library.

Library of Congress Cataloging-in-Publication Data
A catalog record for this book has been requested.

ISBN 978-1-4473-0119-6 paperback
ISBN 978-1-4473-0120-2 hardcover
ISBN 978-1-4473-0121-9 ePub
ISBN 978-1-4473-1245-1 Mobi

Cover design by Policy Press
Front cover: image kindly supplied by istock
Printed and bound in Great Britain by CMP, Poole
Policy Press uses environmentally responsible print partners

SOCIAL WORK IN PRACTICE series

Series editors: **Viviene Cree**, University of Edinburgh and
Steve Myers, University of Salford

This important series sets new standards in introducing social workers to
the ideas, values and knowledge base necessary for professional practice.
These core texts are designed for students undertaking professional training
at all levels as well as fulfilling the needs of qualified staff seeking to update
their skills or move into new areas of practice.

Editorial advisory board:

Suzy Braye, University of Sussex

Jim Campbell, Goldsmith's University of London

Gina Hardesty, Independent Consultant

Ravi Kohli, University of Bedfordshire

Jill Manthorpe, King's College London

Kate Morris, University of Nottingham

Joan Orme, University of Glasgow

Alison Shaw, Policy Press

Charlotte Williams, RMIT University, Australia

Contents

List of tables and figures

Tables

Figures

Acknowledgements

Both authors owe their thanks to Professor Viv Cree for her comments and suggestions on an earlier draft of this book.

Malcolm Cowburn would like to thank the following people for reading early drafts of parts of this book: Gary Gunby, Safeguarding coordinator of Buckfast Abbey; Professor Michael Hauskeller, Exeter University; Dr Sarah Nelson, Edinburgh University; Dr Steve Riley, Faculty of Humanities, University of Utrecht; Anne Robinson, Sheffield Hallam University; and Professor Kim Stevenson, Plymouth University. In addition, immeasurable thanks go to his partner Hilary Pengelly for her support, for reading and commenting on many drafts, and for enduring a houseguest that had long outstayed its welcome.

Steve Myers would like to thank all at The Junction project in Rotherham for their creative practice over the years. Thanks also go to Judith Milner for her support and ideas, David Bottomley for patience beyond usual expectations, and those colleagues at the University of Salford and further afield who have provided critical perspectives on the complexities of social work practice.

Introduction: constructing sex crimes and sex offenders

Introduction

Social work with people who sexually harm others is complex and demanding. It involves feelings, thoughts and actions, and is imbued with values. It occurs in a range of settings and is undertaken by qualified, trainee and unqualified social workers. A social work approach incorporates values, psychological perspectives and consideration of sexual violence as part of a social context. Social work is not an activity undertaken by isolated workers; it takes place within agencies that have policies and procedures to guide practice. This book is not a replacement for official guidance; rather, it seeks to provide an in-depth exploration of issues that make up social work practice. Practice issues are located in the social, political, administrative and welfare context of the UK, primarily focusing on England and Wales; while policy and procedural issues may remain geographically specific, other matters have a wider currency.

Social work is currently undergoing radical change in the UK due to central government initiatives designed to address perceived (albeit contested) shortcomings in education and practice. This means that any description of how social work is delivered is contingent and subject to significant caveats, including the increasing tendency for the four constituent nations (England, Wales, Scotland and Northern Ireland) to develop their own health and welfare services and structures. In addition to this, there is a move to more regionalised approaches to welfare delivery within England itself, devolving increased public service financial responsibility to newly constituted political bodies that will take localised decisions on what is the best model to meet their needs. Inevitably, there will be a fragmentation of structures that social workers find themselves practising in, which may lead to the development of very different approaches and job expectations.

Social workers currently work in what can be broadly termed as 'statutory' services (local government and some charitable organisations with legal mandates to provide specific services, as well as criminal justice agencies) and private, voluntary or independent (PVI) organisations. The former tend to have duties placed on them for delivering core elements of policy, whereas the PVI sector provides services that are contracted or seen as complementary, although this distinction has become increasingly blurred with a decrease in state-delivered services and an increase in contracting out services to the PVI sector.

Social workers have tended to specialise in working either with children (and their families) or working with adults, a distinction that has grown over the previous 30 years and looks likely to continue through, for example, the appointment of separate chief social workers for children and for adults in England (Department of Health, 2014).

The landscape is further complicated by those who focus on mental health and learning disability, which constitute separate fields of practice. Criminal justice is also a separate social work domain in England, although it is seen as a core social work activity in Scotland. Increasingly, adult services in England are being organised and delivered within overall health provision and it is likely that social workers with adults will be part of an integrated health and community social care framework.

Wherever social workers are located, they work in multidisciplinary structures to deliver their service, and this is often supported by explicit policy recommendations. A range of professionals with different skills is encouraged to work in complementary ways in order to enhance welfare and to safeguard vulnerable people. This recognises that people have multiple needs that are best met by applying appropriate skills and knowledge, and social workers are often at the forefront of making assessments and judgements about the required level of intervention and resources. As we see in later chapters, responses to sexual offending and the safeguarding of vulnerable people require social workers to collaborate with criminal justice, health, education and other welfare professionals. Throughout the book, we explore the particular skills, values and knowledge that social workers utilise to ensure that individual and community safety is enhanced.

The aims of this book are:

■ to recognise the emotional context of working with people who sexually harm others;
■ to consider values and ethics underpinning practice;
■ to reflect critically on current theories, research, policy and practice in relation to people who have sexually harmed others; and
■ to explore the role and practices of social workers in working with sexual offenders in order to safeguard vulnerable people.

While these aims address the theory, methods and organisational practices of social work, they also recognise the importance of emotions in practising social work. As Olive Stevenson (2013, p 1) notes: 'To be an effective social worker, there has to be a dynamic interplay between emotion and intellect'. This chapter considers the intricate interplay between feelings and knowledge in the practice of social work with people who sexually offend. The first area we consider relates to our values and the language used throughout the book. This involves recognising the *constructive* nature of language. The language we choose to use embodies our view of social work, sexual violence and the people that harm others sexually. We outline the values that inform the shape and content of the book, and we establish how key terms are used. In the next section, we explore popular knowledge about sex crimes and sex offenders as presented in the news media. The news media is a key source of (mis)information that shapes popular understandings of social and political issues. Using the framework of 'folk devils' and 'moral panics', we encourage a critical attitude to media reportage and raise some questions about social reactions to sex crimes. A key social reaction linked to popular knowledge is *denial*. Denial in relation to sex crimes has many manifestations; we explore personal, societal and professional forms of not recognising sexual violence, its prevalence or its impacts. Denial is both a cognitive and an emotional response to uncomfortable information; in the penultimate section of this chapter, we explore the emotional impacts of working with sex offenders. The final section of this chapter addresses issues of race, ethnicity and sex offending. These issues evoke strong feelings and social prejudices, and present distinctive challenges for social workers. We explore issues of representation, racism and the difficulties of engagement with criminal justice services.

Values and terminologies

'Value(s)' is a nebulous term potentially covering areas as diverse as economics, theology, philosophy, business studies, medicine and all of the social sciences, to name but a few. It is a slippery concept to engage with and can leave more confusion and less clarity in its wake. However, Sarah Banks (2006, p 6) provides a gentle introduction: '"values" can be regarded as particular types of belief that people hold about what is regarded worthy or valuable'. This section clarifies the terms we use throughout the book and why we use them. Gregory and Holloway (2005) have shown how language socially *constructs* social work, the social worker and the people that social workers are required to professionally engage with. This means that the language used in legislation, social work texts, social work reports and social work records *creates*, through description and analysis, the social work role, tasks and methods. It also constructs the social worker and the different groups of people s/he engages with (eg some people are portrayed as being vulnerable, some as alienated and some as criminal). Gregory and Holloway (2005) identify three forms of language through which this occurs: 'moral', 'therapeutic' and 'managerial'. Social work is variously described in terms that highlight its moral, therapeutic or managerial purpose. We explore these (and other) perspectives in the next chapter; however, it is important to recognise that the language we use is never value-free. Clarifying terminology is therefore not merely a process of using the 'right' language; rather, it is a *constructive* process that embodies particular value orientations of social work.

Underpinning value base of the book

Social work values are concerned with respect for the individual; these values recognise the equal moral worth of every human being. Social work practice seeks to respect and sustain individual dignity. Closely linked to this is social work's commitment to social justice; unlike most professions, social work explicitly includes the social context in its statement of values (IFSW and IASSW, 2004). Social justice in the context of sex crimes is a central concern of this book. This has implications for the language we use and the way in which we construct not only social work and the social worker, but also sex crimes, the people that commit them and the people that are harmed by them.

To aspire to social justice requires scrutiny of the knowledge(s) that underpin the formulation of social policy and the development of penal practices. Most sex crimes are never reported and most people who inflict sexual harm on others are unconvicted, yet public concern about 'sex offenders' is high. Social and penal policy is shaped around what is known about *convicted* sex offenders. This knowledge is necessarily partial and limited, yet these limitations are rarely acknowledged.

A commitment to social justice carries a requirement to *understand* sexual harm through a range of academic disciplines, including sociology, anthropology and psychology. Our understanding of sexual harm is summarised thus:

■ Men and/or boys commit most, but not all, sex crimes. In most societies, and communities, culture and values privilege male power and denigrate women and girls (patriarchy). Such cultures are supportive of sex crimes and minimise both the extent and the harm caused by sex crimes.

■ People who sexually harm others can be male, female or have indeterminate gender. They can be of any ethnicity, social class or faith group. Many offenders may not have a faith. They can have any sexuality. Sexually harmful behaviour can be demonstrated by children and young people even when they are below the age where this is legally a crime. Intellectual and physical ability is no determinant of whether or not someone becomes a sexual offender.

■ Victim–survivors of sexual harm can be male, female or have indeterminate gender. They can be of any ethnicity, social class or faith group. Many victim–survivors may not have a faith. They can be of any age or sexuality. They can be of various learning and physical abilities.

This book adopts a challenging approach in relation to some of the conventional forms of knowledge surrounding sex offending and sex offenders. Throughout the book, we highlight the importance of critically examining the values that underpin both knowledge of, and practice with, sex offenders; nowhere is this more important than in the language we use to discuss sexual harm, the people that perpetrate it and the people who are hurt.

Naming the person committing sexual harm

The use of the phrase 'sexual offences' needs qualification, as does the term 'sex offender'. Offences are acts that are both defined and proscribed by law. Legal definitions of (sex) crimes embody the values of dominant groups in particular societies at specific times. Behaviours defined in law as sexual offences vary significantly across time and culture. However, legally defining sexual offences does not guarantee that a person will feel able to report the sexual harm they have experienced. A study by Percy and Mayhew (1997), using a number of international victim self-report surveys, estimated that there are 15 times more unreported sex offenders than reported ones; in 2011, Rape Crisis South London (2011) suggested that only 11% of women who are victims of serious sexual assault report the crime. Therefore, under-reporting remains a constant problem.

However, once an offence has been reported, the vast majority of reports do not result in anyone being convicted of an offence. Court processes differ across countries, but attrition is an international phenomenon. Approximately 10% of cases reported to the police result in a criminal conviction (for further details, see Figure 2.2, p 37). Thus, to write or speak of 'sex offenders', with the implication that these people are defined by a criminal conviction, is problematic insofar as this excludes many people who may have harmed others but not been convicted.

Conversely, some innocent people may be convicted of sexual offences (see Locke, 2013; Falselyaccused.co.uk, 2015). This is a very difficult area because social workers may be required to engage with people *on the basis of their conviction* and a person who maintains his/her innocence will be unable to engage in any formal risk assessment process because this requires her/him to reflect on their offending behaviour. While issues related to this group of people are not centrally considered in this book, we suggest that social workers should advise 'offenders' who maintain their innocence to seek legal representation in order to challenge their conviction.

The aforementioned complexities pose challenges for the sensitive, but economic, use of language in this book. A person who contravenes the law relating to sexual offences is a 'sex offender', so named because they have been convicted of the offence in a criminal court. However, many people sexually harm others without their actions being reported and the offender being convicted; in such cases, the harmful person is known as the 'perpetrator'. Social workers work with both offenders and perpetrators. In some cases, a person accused of a sexual offence may be innocent and yet be convicted; unless the conviction is overturned by a court, this person remains (technically) an 'offender'. The word 'offender' is, however, problematic for (at least) two reasons: it dehumanises the person referred to and it describes her/him solely in terms of their past actions. Yet, completely avoiding the use of the word 'offender' in this book is stylistically problematic. We use the term consciously, recognising its shortcomings. Throughout the book, we also use other phrases, as we have done in this introduction, to dilute the impact of the 'offender' word.

Naming the person harmed by sex offences

When referring to the person harmed by sex offences, we use the words 'victim' and 'victim-survivor'. We are aware that the former term is resisted or rejected by many people who have experienced sexual harm. Many prefer the term 'survivor' or 'thriver', or, indeed, choose not to name themselves in relation to the sexual harm they have experienced. However, for the purposes of this book, it is important that we identify the person that is harmed as a victim. Many offenders deny that there is a victim involved in their actions, and potentially this denial may be inadvertently adopted by social workers.

Naming acts of sexual harm

We use a variety of terms to name acts of sexual harm, including 'sexual violence'; we take the view that whether an offence involves physical contact or not, it is *violating*, and can thus be regarded as being sexually *violent*. We do not engage in the semantic niceties of 'How violent is violent?' A victim's personal experience of violation/violence is not personally comparable with any other violence; to make such comparison fails to understand the harm experienced by individual victims. We also use the terms 'sexual coercion' and 'sexual harm'.

Social worker identities

When we refer to 'social workers', we do not assume a homogeneous identity, common type of work placement or qualified status. We recognise that workers have a range of intersecting identities, for example, gender, ethnicity, class, age, sexuality, (dis)ability and faith. These will variously affect how they engage in social work. We ask readers not to make assumptions as to the identities of social workers in the case studies and the practice-based learning exercises, but to consider the exercises firstly from their own identifications and then secondly from other positions.

Author identities

While we recognise the potential diversity of our readership, it is appropriate to say something about ourselves as authors of this book. We are white men who qualified to practice as social workers. Malcolm worked with sex offenders as a probation officer for 12 years and then managed a therapy unit for young victim-survivors of sex crimes before becoming a university academic. Much of his teaching and research has focused on issues related to sex offenders, identities (including masculinities and ethnicities) and diversity. Steve worked with children and young people with sexually harmful behaviours as a social worker in both statutory and voluntary agencies for seven years before also becoming a university academic. His teaching and research has been about working with difficult behaviours and developing creative ways of doing this. Our identities, work experience and education influence how we respond, as erstwhile practitioners and academics, to people who sexually harm others. As such, we recognise the importance of critical reflection to ensure that we are aware of the complexities of practice in this area.

The influence of the news media: seeing through the folk devil and the moral panic

Popular responses towards sex offenders ignore their humanity and are generated and sustained by 'common-sense' aspects of most cultures. In most societies, the sex offender is a pariah, a social outcast. Social workers may take on many of these attitudes without giving them critical scrutiny. These attitudes are not a sound basis for professional social work. The first reflective exercise helps readers explore and understand how they feel and what they think about sex offenders.

Reflective exercise: What do you know about sex offenders, victims and sex crimes?

This exercise is designed to help you identify what you know and what you feel about all parties involved in sex crimes. It does not need any prior preparation, but it does require you to answer the questions quickly and honestly. Use a blank piece of paper.

1. Using all types of language to capture how you feel about sex offenders and what you know about them, complete this sentence as many times as you can in 60 seconds: 'Sex offenders are ...'
2. Using all types of language to capture how you feel about victims of sex offenders and what you know about them, complete this sentence as many times as you can in 60 seconds: 'Victims of sex offenders are ...'
3. Using whatever language seems to be appropriate to capture how you feel and what you know about sex violence, complete this sentence as many times as you can in 60 seconds: 'Sexual violence is ...'
4. Where do you find information about sex offenders?

We will return to this piece of work later in the book, when we will ask you to begin to analyse your attitudes and knowledge.

Most people start to develop an understanding of sex crimes and sex offenders from the media (social media, newspapers and television). However, this may be problematic because of how the media, predominantly, represent these issues. Willis et al (2010, p 551), in their study of how public attitudes help or hinder sex offenders refrain from offending, note that the less aware people were of relevant issues, the more likely they were to subscribe to stereotypical beliefs disseminated by news media. In a US study of the attitudes and beliefs of lawmakers, Sample and Kadleck (2008) found that US politicians' main source of information about sex crimes was the media. Clearly, the news media is both powerful and influential, and requires further consideration.

Since 1991, when Soothill and Walby published *Sex Crime in the News*, there has been regular academic interest in how sex crimes are reported in the media (Jenkins, 1998; Kitzinger, 1999, 2004; Cowburn and Dominelli, 2001; Critcher, 2002, 2003; Silverman and Wilson, 2002; Greer, 2003; Jewkes, 2011). A common theme in these studies is how the use of stereotypical images, whether the 'rapist' of the 1980s or, more recently, the 'paedophile', obscures considered discussion of sexual harm and how to reduce it. Academic critique of media representations can be understood through what Garland (2008) calls the 'study of social reaction'. A key contribution to this considers 'Folk devils and moral panics'. The concepts 'folk devil' and 'moral panic' were first coined and brought together by Stan Cohen in 1972. A 'folk devil' is 'A condition, episode, person or group of persons [that] ... become defined as a threat to societal values and interests' (Cohen, 1972, p 9).

A key phrase here is 'societal values and interests'; Rohloff et al (2013, p 8) point to 'the deployment of morality to obfuscate dominant ideological interests; to act as a veil over the workings of power'. Society is not homogeneous, but the social construction of the 'folk devil' is part of the 'veil'. The 'folk devil' is construed as 'other', as apart from and a threat to respectable (middle-class) society. A recent edited collection (Cree et al, 2015a) following an Economic and Social Research Council (ESRC) (2012) seminar series identifies a range of folk devils. Here, we select a few: the 'spatial folk devil', defined as problematic because of where they originate from and live (Mannay, 2015); 'feral families' – welfare-dependent, prone to violence and predominantly Maori (Beddoe, 2015); 'teenage mothers' (Brown, 2015); child traffickers (Westwood, 2015); 'radicalised' minority groups (McKendrick, 2015); 'Chavs' (Le Grand, 2015); and Roma people (Clark, 2015). Additionally, 'paedophiles' of various types (Furedi, 2015; Quayle, 2015) are identified. While these groups are diverse, they share the following characteristics in media reportage: they are outsiders; they lack moral worth; they do not subscribe to 'societal' values; and they are negatively portrayed. Such 'folk devils' are represented as marginal and threatening to 'society'. 'Society's' response to these groups is orchestrated through the deployment of a 'moral panic', which is presented 'in a stylised and stereotypical fashion by the mass media; the moral barricades are manned by editors, bishops, politicians and other right thinking people' (Cohen, 1972, p 9).

Garland (2008, p 9) offers this succinct summary of the term moral panic: it is a 'way of saying "no" to the forces of hyperbole'. To characterise a social reaction (eg media reportage of sex crimes) as moral panic is to question the seriousness of the reaction. Thus, Cree et al (2015b, p xii) comment:

> The lens of moral panic highlights the ways in which social issues that begin with real concerns may lead to labeling and stigmatizing of certain behaviours and individuals; they may precipitate harsh and disproportionate legislation; they may make people more fearful and society a less safe place.

The concepts of folk devil and moral panic, used analytically, highlight oppressive social dynamics in relation to marginalised and oppressed groups by challenging both how these groups are described (as 'folk devils') and the social reaction to them ('moral panic'), which, in some cases, is used to justify draconian laws, and sometimes the denial of human rights.

Reflective exercise: Reflections on media portrayals of sex offenders

1. What type of news media do you engage with (eg newspapers, television, internet, Twitter, etc)?
2. In the next month, note how often sex offenders are reported on and how they are described.
3. What information does this provide you and how does this influence how you think about sex offenders and sex crimes?
4. How does this information relate to your responses to the first reflective exercise earlier in this chapter?

In considering media representations of the sex offender, we note that he is generally an atypical man who is discovered to have a range of 'deviant' and sexually dangerous preoccupations. Where the offender is a woman, they are also portrayed as being 'odd', 'abnormal' and deviant. Offences discussed are outside of the home – in public space or within institutions (Greer, 2003; Kitzinger, 2004; Jewkes, 2011). In recent years, representations have changed slightly to accommodate the 'celebrity sex offender', the 'institutional' sex offender (particularly members of organisations with responsibilities for children, eg, churches and residential schools) and the South Asian sex offender. The offenders remain 'outsiders': they operate outside of domestic space, but they use their status as a vehicle for both committing and concealing their offences (Terry and Ackerman, 2008; Cowburn, 2012; Gill and Harrison, 2015).

Hayes and Baker (2014) identified six ways in which female sex offenders (FSOs) were described through media reporting: demonisation; sensationalism and titillation; minimisation and mitigation; medicalisation and psychologising; romanticising; and women as nurturers. FSOs were demonised through language that was extreme and rejecting, using emotionally charged phrases to describe both them and their behaviour. Linked to this was a sensationalism in the reporting that seemed designed to entertain the audience through explicit descriptions of the behaviours in ways that were almost pornographic in their emphasis. The rarity of these cases added to the novelty of the described behaviours. Where the abuse was same-sex, there were high levels of anger and anxiety about transgressing roles. Within the reporting, there was a theme of viewing women as accomplices of men, either coerced or emotionally dependent, which minimised their responsibility and was seen as making them less culpable. The same outcome was seen in the description of the women as having emotional or psychological problems, usually stereotypically gendered, such as depression or maladjustment. They were 'ill' and this was linked to their offending, including reports that these adult women were so damaged that their male child victims were viewed as the powerful ones in the abuse. Abusive incidents were also reconfigured with a 'romantic' angle, particularly where the victim was a male adolescent, using terms such as 'lover' and 'affair' that would be hard to imagine in contemporary descriptions if the genders were reversed. This had the effect of making the male victim complicit in his abuse, minimising any harm that may have been done to him. This was not the case where the victim was female, where anxieties about the damaging impact were heightened due to homophobia. Hayes and Baker (2014) found that descriptors of the women emphasised traditional and essentialised gender roles, such as mother and carer, which emphasised nurturing and trust. These roles were challenged by the sexually abusive behaviour and compounded the response: the women were castigated for their behaviour *and* for transgressing their expected roles.

Media-constructed sex offenders are outsiders, deviant and social pariahs who threaten not only potential victims, but also the domestic structures of social life (Jewkes, 2011; Galeste et al, 2012). However, this way of presenting the sex offender as a folk devil has some flaws: it does nothing to develop understanding of sex offenders or the safety of individuals and communities in relation to sex crimes. Galeste et al (2012, p 4) note that media representation of child sex offenders in the US:

> fuels the public's morbid fascination with sex offenders who target children.... Such media reports have led to national moral panics surrounding the safety of children ... that has, in turn, perpetuated the acceptance of myths that run contrary to empirical knowledge about sex crimes and sex offenders.

'Empirical knowledge about sex crimes and sex offenders' points to most sex offenders as being 'ordinary' members of many communities (eg workplace, faith and geographical). Most victims of sex crimes know the person who harms them (Home Office, 2007; Bonnycastle, 2012). Sex offenders are not a group of alien beings that stand outside 'society' posing a threat that 'right thinking people' must defend. They are part of communities and, in some cases, achieve national prominence within their chosen fields of work; they are an ever-changing and disparate group of people. We explore issues relating to knowledge about people who commit sex offences in Chapter Two.

There are many ways in which to understand sexually harmful behaviours. However, in this case, a moral panic perspective does not offer greater insights. Moreover, the 'folk devil' sex offender is clearly a 'hyperbolic' construction that conceals the more commonplace sex offender. Building penal policies and social work practice on the basis of moral panics caused by the sex offender as folk devil ignores the need for wider community safety/public health approaches to preventing sex crimes. In the chapters that follow, we show that 'moral panic'–driven penal policies, such as the sex offender register and public notification, are not making much of a contribution to challenging the underlying causes of sex crimes and, thus, developing safer communities. Without critical interrogation, folk devil mythologies and moral panics in relation to sex crimes will continue to contribute to wider societal denial of the commonplace nature of sex crimes. It is to the phenomenon of denial that we now turn.

Understanding denial

This section focuses on three different types of denial that while they may be interlinked, also have their own distinctive characteristics; all of them, in various ways, affect how we understand and respond to sex offenders. They are: worker denial, societal denial and offender denial. Before exploring each of these aspects, it is helpful to consider a wider definition of denial. The online Oxford English dictionary (OED, 2015) offers (among others) this definition of denial: 'Refusal to acknowledge a person or thing as having a certain character or certain claims; a disowning, disavowal'.

While this definition is general in character, it captures the essence of denial across all three types; all of them would reject the 'certain character' of a sex offender or the threat of sexual danger. The OED (2015) also offers another pertinent definition: '*Psychoanal.* The suppression (usu. at an unconscious level) of a painful or unacceptable wish or of experiences of which one is ashamed. Now also in more general use, esp. in phr. *in denial*'. This particular focus is relevant to both workers and offenders; it acknowledges psychological ways of coping with difficult and painful experiences through suppressing any recognition of them.

Worker denial

We suggest that worker denial (of abuse, of harm to children, vulnerable adults and to self) may be rooted in both the anticipation and the actuality of direct work. It has two dimensions: cognitive and emotive. Cognitively, some social work assessments may ignore signs of abuse and trauma or reinterpret them. Emotively, denial represents a failure to recognise the emotional impact of the work. Listening to and/or reading graphic descriptions of sexual harms inflicted upon victims, children and adults is an intellectually and emotionally challenging task (see later). Perhaps the most serious consequence of worker denial is that victims may be left in vulnerable situations and offenders and offending may be ignored.

Societal denial

Societal denial of sexual offending is the failure of governments to recognise the extent of sexually harmful behaviours in the wider population and the harmful impacts of such crimes on victims, families and communities. Cohen (2001, p 1) identifies three forms of denial: literal denial (nothing happened), interpretive denial (something happened but it is not what you think) and implicatory denial (what happened was not really bad and can be justified). A common aspect to all three forms is:

> people, organisations, governments or whole societies are presented with information that is too disturbing, threatening or anomalous to be fully absorbed or openly acknowledged. The information is therefore somehow repressed, disavowed, pushed aside or reinterpreted. Or else the information 'registers' well enough, but its implications – cognitive, emotional or moral – are evaded, neutralised or rationalised away. (Cohen, 2000, p 1)

In relation to sex crimes, a key aspect of denial is the social construction of the sex offender as the 'dangerous outsider'. Having neither family nor community, the sex offender and the threat s/he poses represent a denial of the fact that offenders and victims are most likely to know one another and, in many cases, be related to each other. This fact is 'disturbing' and 'threatens' the sanctity of the family as a place of safety, love and care.

Offender denial

There is a long history in the literature relating to practice[1] with sex offenders of considering denial (see Salter, 1988; Briggs et al, 1998). Such has been the central importance given to denial and taking responsibility for offending that it has had a high profile in treatment programmes, both in the US (McGrath et al, 2010) and the UK (Beech and Fisher, 2004). However, recently, its relevance to sex offender treatment has been questioned (Yates, 2009; Ware and Mann, 2012). Nevertheless, while the centrality of denial and responsibility within treatment programmes may be contested, it remains an issue for social workers, who frequently encounter sex offenders outside of formal therapeutic settings.

Reflective exercise: Identifying and analysing minimisations

Ware and Mann (2012, p 281, emphasis added) 'use the term *denial* to mean categorical rejection of the conviction, and the term *minimization* to refer to the common tendency to omit or underplay certain aspects of the offending or its consequences'.

In this exercise, we would like you to reflect on something that you have done that you feel ashamed of.

1. Can you identify ways in which you minimise your responsibility for this action? Write out things that you say to yourself and/or other people.
2. Can you identify ways in which you minimise the consequences of the action? Write out things that you say to yourself and/or other people.

Having written out these phrases, you can begin to identify patterns in what you are saying to yourself or to others (eg blaming others for what you have done [external attributions] or blaming something inside you [internal attributions]).

3. How do these phrases help you to cope with your day-to-day life? (What function do they serve?)

If you have some experience in working with sex offenders, repeat the exercise while thinking of how an offender spoke of his offences.

For social workers, encountering denial and minimisations from a sex offender can be difficult. A key issue is to listen to what is being said and to check that it has been recorded accurately. In this way, the worker dispassionately collects detailed information. These data are particularly important in assessing sex offenders and the risks that they may pose (see Chapter Five). The emotional impacts of listening and recording without challenging must be acknowledged and discussed in supervision, peer support, therapy or in other supportive relationships (see Chapter Seven).

Recognising the emotional impacts of working with sex offenders

The impacts of working with sex offenders may be different in degree, depending on whether the worker is engaging with the offender in relation to his/her offending behaviour, or whether they are in emotionally charged situations where (sexual) abuse is not yet formally identified but may be a strong possibility. However, there are commonalities across the work spectrum.

The literatures in relation to the effects of working directly with sex offenders, engaging in safeguarding social work and, more generally, social work in stressful situations point to the *reductive* impact of this work. This occurs in three areas: physical resilience, interpersonal abilities to engage positively in human relationships and professional capacities to observe, to interpret and to act. Although they often overlap, we consider them individually.

Physical resilience

Two areas of impact are highlighted: vicarious trauma (VT) and post-traumatic stress disorder (PTSD). VT is the taking on by the therapist/social worker of the symptoms (of trauma) experienced and described by the person they are working with. People who sexually harm others not only impose trauma on their victims, but, in many cases, have also been victimised themselves, with female offenders having higher rates of victimisation than men (see Ogloff et al, 2012). VT is experienced through a range of bodily symptoms, for example, alterations to workers' sex lives, headaches and nausea (Leicht, 2008; Pack, 2011; NSPCC, 2013). Symptoms of PTSD include disordered sleep (Ellerby, 1997; Jackson et al, 1997), recurrent and intrusive dreams, an inability to concentrate, fear (experienced somatically through a range of symptoms), and extreme tiredness (Farrenkopf, 1992). While the impacts may be experienced physically, it is more common that they are felt psychologically and emotionally. This directly affects a person's ability to relate to others, whether in a personal or in a professional capacity.

Interpersonal abilities to engage positively in human relationships

Listening to graphic details of offences and hearing personal histories of abuse and neglect may adversely affect a worker's wider view of the world and personal relationships, particularly in relation to issues of personal safety, trust, power, esteem and intimacy (McCann and Pearlman, 1990). This can involve workers imagining (potential) abusers everywhere, and feeling personally unsafe (Farrenkopf, 1992; Scheela, 2001; Leicht, 2008). Such insecurities may generate increased irritability (Bird Edmunds, 1997), as well as anger and frustration (Farrenkopf, 1992).

In response to these feelings, some workers numb their emotional response to day-to-day experiences and their abilities to respond empathically to harm caused by sexual and interpersonal violence (Farrenkopf, 1992; Bird Edmunds, 1997; Scheela, 2001). Such desensitising inevitably impacts on workers' professional lives.

Professional capacities to observe, to interpret and to act

The boundary between personal and professional lives is permeable; the impacts of work on interpersonal relations also affect relations with service users. This, however, changes as workers become more experienced. Farrenkopf's (1992) 'Phases of Impact' model identifies four separate phases of adjustment. In the first phase, workers suffer from shock and feelings of vulnerability; they are unable to understand what they were hearing and feeling. In the second phase, workers are immersed in their professional task, characterised by non-judgemental work ethics, empathy for the sex offender and hope that their work will prove to be effective. In the third phase, repressed emotions re-emerge, particularly anger and resentment, leading to cynicism. The final impact phase is either *negative*, where workers become disenchanted with their task and their client group, or one of *accommodation*, where workers adopt less idealistic goals for their work.

Scheela (2001) suggests a six-stage 'remodelling process'. The stages are: falling apart, taking on, tearing out, rebuilding, doing the upkeep and moving on. These phases capture how working with sex offenders initially challenges workers on both emotional and cognitive levels, but how through processes of change or adaptation, this is managed. These models are useful because they emphasise that worker reactions to working with sex offenders are not fixed, but change and develop through the acquisition of both knowledge and skills, and through developing appropriate support mechanisms.

In emotionally charged areas of social work, there is always an impact on the worker(s). The most serious consequence of this is that workers may not be able to engage with the difficult situation(s) they face (McFadden et al, 2015). This has recently been highlighted in cases where social workers have been found unable to engage with issues of sexual exploitation that have involved intra-racial sexual abuse (Jay, 2014; Bedford, 2015; Casey,

2015). This is a complex area that has ramifications across all of the chapters in this book. It relates to emotions, knowledge and values in practice.

Race, ethnicity and social work with sex offenders: towards confident social work practice

In this section, we address issues relating to race, ethnicity and social work practice with people who sexually harm others. We noted earlier in this chapter that the language we use constructs how we understand the issues. The terms 'race' and 'ethnicity' carry a wide range of assumptions and values, most of which vary according to who is using the term. The word 'race' is historically rooted in an essentialist, biological viewpoint that considers humanity to comprise of a number of 'races' defined, primarily, by skin colour and physiognomy. Within the term, which has had currency in Europe since the 18th century, there is an explicit hierarchy, with white people at the top and black people at the bottom (Phillips, 2012, p 35). In the US, Davis (1981, pp 94–5) cites the 1918 work of American scholar Dr Winfield Collins, which accepts this hierarchy as a given and highlights what he considers to be the essential (racial) nature of the 'negro' as an inability to control his sexuality and to tell the truth. Davis and others (eg Collins, 1991) argue that these white 'myths' have provided the justification for harsh racist criminal justice policies and practice. Thus, 'race' is a socio-biological construct that was used to provide ostensible justification for a (white) social hierarchy based on skin colour.

Interestingly, using the folk devil and moral panic framework, we can see that the white media construction of the black rapist as threatening white women and children led to the moral panic that was used to justify the oppression of black men – of the 455 men executed in the US between 1930 and 1967 on the basis of rape convictions, 405 of them were black (Davis, 1981, p 172). Although she did not use the moral panic framework, Davis (1981, p 199) unflinchingly describes the ideological impact of this 'folk devil' in creating a particular form of knowledge about sex crimes and sex offenders:

> The myth of the Black rapist continues to carry out the insidious work of racist ideology. It must bear a good portion of the responsibility for the failure of the anti-rape theorists to seek the identity of the enormous numbers of anonymous rapists who remain unreported, untried and unconvicted. As long as their analyses focus on accused rapists who are reported and arrested, thus on only a fraction of the rapes committed, Black men – and other men of colour – will inevitably be viewed as the villains responsible for the

current epidemic of sexual violence. The anonymity surrounding the vast majority of rapes is consequently treated as a statistical detail – or else a mystery whose meaning is inaccessible.

Racially constructed sex offender 'folk devils' continue to feature in popular discourse. In Australia, early this century, there was a spate of rapes committed by 'Lebanese' gangs; media reportage highlighted ethnicity and faith (Islam). Two issues were emphasised: the failure of national immigration policies and the likelihood that rape was culturally acceptable to the racial group committing the crimes (Warner, 2004; Humphrey, 2007). In the UK, there are similar racial sexual 'folk devils'. Following a series of convictions of groups of South Asian men for sexual offences against white children, the South Asian sex offender is being portrayed in terms that emphasise 'South Asian' race and ignore similar white offenders (Cockbain, 2013; Gill and Harrison, 2015). Racially based accounts of sex crimes are misleading and generally serve other ideological purposes. At extremes, racist groups use racially presented data to further their own toxic agendas (see, eg, British National Party, 2013).

Ashley-Montagu (1942), writing at the time of Second World War Nazi racism, was one of the first commentators to recognise the dangerous implications of the term 'race', and it was he who suggested using the alternative phrase 'ethnic group'. Phillips (2012, p 37) offers this definition of ethnicity: 'a self-ascribed collectivity with origins sharing symbolic attributes relating to culture, ancestry, religion, nationality, territory and language'. She further notes that the concept does not have the implicit hierarchies of the word 'race'. However, we recognise that ascribing a race or an ethnicity to a person, or group of persons, is a dynamic process involving the person giving the name, and the person, or persons, receiving (or refusing) the name (Phillips, 2010).

In this book, we use the terminologies of the sources we cite. When describing racial or ethnic dynamics, we are mindful of the implications of such terminology. For example, we recognise that in most 'Western'[2] countries, the dominant racial group is white; in the UK, a collective term for people not encompassed by the term 'white' is 'black and minority ethnic' (BME). This is a crude racial term, clustering together a diverse range of people solely by skin colour. It is, however, a term that has been used in government publications when discussing the discriminatory effects of government policies (Aspinall, 2002). Aspinall (2002) describes BME as 'panethnic terminology', and suggests that such terms are useful in that they can be used to identify discriminatory practices towards groups who share one characteristic (their skin is not white). However, it also carries an assumption that whiteness is a homogeneous category, and this is clearly not the case (Phillips, 2010). In this book, we use panethnic terminology when discussing issues relating to discrimination – recognising that some white groups (eg Irish people) may also be subject to discriminatory practice. When referring to particular ethnicities or cultural practices, we endeavour to be specific.

An area where 'racial monitoring' is helpful is in identifying the involvement of BME people in the processes of criminal justice. It appears that they are less involved in reporting sex crimes (eg Gilligan and Akhtar, 2006), that more alleged offenders plead 'not guilty' before the courts (Robinson, 2011) and that there is an under-representation of BME offenders on prison-based sex offender programmes (Cowburn and Lavis, 2009). There is low usage by BME communities of the Violent and Sex Offender Register (Kemshall and Weaver, 2012). Very few BME sex offenders are involved in the community-based initiative Circles of Support and Accountability (Cowburn et al, 2015). In attempting to understand this phenomenon, and considering the implications for social work practice, we must look at both racial and ethnic issues. Racial issues establish a foundation for BME mistrust of criminal justice systems. BME groups across the white Western world are over-represented as offenders in criminal justice systems and as prisoners (Gabbidon, 2010; Institute of Race Relations, 2015); such over-representation leads to suspicion that the criminal justice system does not operate equitably.

However, mistrust may only play a part in the disengagement of BME communities from criminal justice provision. In relation to BME people reporting crimes (to white authorities), there are suggestions that to do so would be a betrayal of the ethnic community. Andrew Norfolk (a journalist employed by the UK newspaper *The Times*), in his evidence to a House of Commons inquiry, stated that young Asian men had told him that they would not report community members who they knew to be sexually harming others (Great Britain, 2013, para 114). Droisen (1989) makes similar observations in relation to ethnicity and community betrayal.

Apart from mistrust and community loyalty, there are questions about the cultural appropriateness of the therapy programmes for sex offenders, not least because they operate from a Western understanding of the individual that ignores the cultural power of family and community commitments (Owusu-Bempah and Howitt, 2000; Cowburn et al, 2008). Moreover, the programmes are delivered in group format, and the management of both racial and ethnic dynamics is a serious challenge for programme providers (Doel and Kelly, 2014, pp 121–3). Also, BME sex offenders have expressed concerns about white group leaders' abilities to manage therapeutic groups in ways that ensure their safety and show knowledge and sensitivity to their cultures (Patel and Lord, 2001).

Anti-racist social work has a long history (eg Dominelli, 1988), and has adopted a range of theoretical perspectives concerning race and ethnicity.

Recent inquiry reports into the sexual exploitation of young people point to social worker fears of being considered racist (Jay, 2014; Bedford, 2015; Casey, 2015). These fears, the reports suggest, inhibit white workers' attempts to protect vulnerable children. It is not within the scope of this book to explore fully the practice of anti-racist social work, but we recognise its complexity and its relevance to social work with sex offenders. Many years ago, Ahmad (1992) and Robinson (1995) recognised the importance of (white) workers being confident in addressing issues related to diversity, particularly when challenging people of different ethnicities. Components of confidence are self-knowledge, awareness of values, ongoing professional knowledge (Bhatti-Sinclair, 2011) and an ability to engage with both the intellectual and emotional aspects of social work practice. By the end of this book, we hope that readers' confidence in working with all sex offenders will have developed, and that their professional confidence will have grown.

Structure of book

The book is structured, first, to provide a context for social work practice with sex offenders and then to address specific practice-related issues. Chapter Two introduces readers to theoretical approaches to understanding sex crimes and sex offenders. In Chapter Three, we consider issues relating to sentencing sex offenders and highlight contrasting approaches to punishment and associated penal responses. Chapter Four provides an overview of policies relating to safeguarding and managing sex offenders in the community. Chapters Five and Six address assessment and interventions, respectively. The final chapter draws the themes of the book together by presenting an account of reflexive social work practice with sex offenders.

Summary

- Language, through the expression of values and various forms of knowledge, creates different ways of understanding sex crimes and the people who commit them.
- The value base of the book and how language is to be used throughout the book was clarified.
- News media create distorted and inaccurate understandings of sex offenders (folk devils); social work knowledge extends beyond media representations.
- Denial of the nature and extent of sex crimes is to be found at individual worker, individual offender and societal levels.
- Working with sex offenders affects workers emotionally, physically and psychologically. Potentially, it can affect workers' personal and professional relationships. Awareness of these impacts is a key component in developing strategies for effective work with sex offenders.
- White constructs of black and Asian sex offenders potentially create racial folk devils. Racial folk devils potentially prevent (white) social workers from engaging constructively with BME communities.
- BME offenders', victims' and communities' engagement with processes of criminal justice appears to be minimal.
- Social work engagement with BME offenders, victims and communities is complex. There are cultural inhibitors that may make it difficult for some social workers to engage with their own ethnic community. Sensitive engagement with the nuances of these issues is essential.

Notes

[1] By 'practice' in this instance, we are primarily referring to psychologically oriented therapy, but it also crosses over into social work with sex offenders.
[2] This term requires some explanation; we use it to refer to Western Europe, North America and Australasia.

Understanding sex crimes and sex offenders

Introduction

The aim of this chapter is to outline and explore the contribution of key academic disciplines to understanding sex crimes and sex offenders. Sociological, biomedical, theological, legal and psychological perspectives are considered. In identifying individual disciplines, we recognise that each discipline is heterogeneous, and that forms of knowledge may be contested within each discipline. Moreover, knowledge within each discipline may be developed from differing epistemological positions (eg an evolutionary psychology account of sex crime differs significantly from a feminist psychological account).

The chapter initially considers *victim perspectives*. Victims' experiences are individual, and although a range of studies identify common impacts of violation, no systematised knowledge of sex crimes has been generated from such experiences. These accounts, however, make an important contribution to understanding sex crime and developing law and penal practices via victims' organisations. This has been particularly important in articulating and asserting victims' experiences of sex crime. We then move on to academic accounts of *sex crimes*. Sociological understandings of sex crime move beyond legal definitions (eg feminist accounts of sex crimes, which focus on patriarchy and the problem behaviours of the general population of men), but also analyse the behaviour of convicted populations (eg in studying what helps sex offenders *desist* from offending). The term 'theological' is used to recognise that, through history, various (theocentric) religions in different parts of the world have made statements about the nature of various sexual behaviours; proscribed behaviours are defined as sins. In secular societies, crimes are defined by law, which is often influenced by dominant theological frameworks and, according to one's epistemological position, either represents the 'moral consensus' or the interests of dominant groups (eg think about the criminalising and decriminalising of 'homosexual' activity). Biomedical understanding of 'sexual deviation' is independent of the law, defining some sex offences as the result of (mental) illness. However, as with the law, the viewpoint generally embodies dominant moral values but uses 'scientific' language to define a variety of sexual predilections, including those that inflict harm on non-consenting victims. These definitions focus on the acts deemed to be wrong, illegal or deviant. Psychological perspectives tend not to define particular acts (other than to recognise that they may be illegal and harmful) within an overall schema; rather, the focus is on individuals manifesting problematic behaviours (as defined by themselves or the criminal justice system). Forensic psychology has developed a range of classificatory systems for people who have sexually harmed children and adults; these systems carry implicit or explicit aetiological assumptions about the behaviours.

Figure 2.1 illustrates the interrelated nature of these perspectives, with individualised concerns nearer the centre of the circle. Societal responses to sex crimes are embodied in penal policy and the practices of the criminal justice system; it is within (and beyond) these that social workers primarily operate.

The third part of the chapter is concerned with exploring issues relating to *sex offenders*. We register three caveats. First, we recognise and discuss 'unconvicted' sex offenders in the second part of this chapter; in the third

Figure 2.1: Understandings of sex crimes

part of the chapter, the discussion focuses on convicted sex offenders. Second, the generic term 'sex offender' conceals the heterogeneity of the sex-offending population; in our statement of values in Chapter One, we recognise that sex offenders are a diverse population, and, where appropriate, we highlight and discuss issues of difference. The final caveat recognises that discussion of the 'individual' sex offender potentially ignores group offences (eg gang rapes, paedophile rings, 'sex' trafficking and rape in conflict and post-conflict settings). The making and viewing of child pornography is both an individual *and* a group offence (see Henshaw et al, 2015). Group offending dynamics are largely beyond the scope of this book and we refer readers to the following sources as starting points for further study: on gang rapes, see Chambers et al (2013); on females in gangs, see Wijkman et al (2015); on trafficking, see Breuil et al (2011); and on rape in conflict and post-conflict settings, see Sexual Violence Research Initiative (2014).

A note on epistemology

It is important to recognise epistemological influences on how knowledge is shaped. Foucault (1977, 1984) highlights the relationship between power and knowledge, and suggests that in late 19th-century Europe, scientific (medicine and psychology) and social-scientific (criminology, social work and psychology) forms of knowledge replaced religion as the dominant way of understanding both sexuality and social responses to deviance. In his analysis, Foucault did not, however, utilise a structuralist perspective. Structuralist understandings of the operation of power identify hierarchical 'divisions' of societies, such as class, gender, race and sexuality (Lukes, 2005). Early feminist theory particularly focuses on the social division of gender and analyse(s) how men have maintained power in most global societies. Feminist epistemologists (eg Harding, 1991, 2006; Code, 2006; Fricker, 2007) focus attention on how male knowledge, specifically 'scientific' knowledge, has both embodied and maintained the hierarchy of gender while adopting methodologies predicated on 'objectivity' (Harding, 1991, p 81). Other structuralist critiques referred to in Chapter One highlight the privileging of 'white' forms of knowledge; black feminists in the US insisted on the importance of race in seeking to understand sex crimes. The strength of feminist analysis of sex crimes is that it locates the discussion in a wider analysis of women's oppression; this ideological orientation, however, may have delayed the full recognition of females who sexually harm others and male victims of sexual harm. In scrutinising underlying epistemological assumptions of ways of understanding sex crime and sex offenders, we adopt a critical approach to the forms of knowledge we explore and describe.

Victim perspectives

The perspectives of victim-survivors of sex crimes are primarily concerned with the impact of offending on them personally. There are an increasing number of accounts of being groomed available on the internet (eg Surviving Therapist Abuse, 2009). Briere and Elliott (2003), in a study of 935 subjects, identified that 49.6% were male and 50.4% were female, and the mean subject age was 46 years, with a range of 18 to 90. They found that childhood sexual abuse is a significant risk factor for a range of psychological and psychiatric disorders and problems, including depression, phobias, obsessive-compulsive disorder, panic disorder, post-traumatic stress disorder, sexual disorders and both suicidal ideation and suicide attempts. The nature of the abuse – intrafamilial or extrafamilial – did not affect psychological outcome, neither did the sex of the abuser. Similarly, Deering and Mellor (2011) note that the consequences of sexual abuse by women on their victims are similar to when the offender is a man, including depression, substance abuse (Tsopelas et al, 2012) and self-harm (Denov, 2004). Deering and Mellor (2011), talking with both male and female survivors of female sexual abuse, found high levels of self-reported anger and aggression, difficulties with intimate relationships, and psychosexual malfunctioning, all of which are similar to the consequences of being abused by a man.

However, it is important to recognise that not all victims speak about their experiences. Kenny and McEachern (2000) and Futa et al (2001) have noted that 'sexual abuse' remains a concept constructed through discourses that have usually been in English, and that have generally explored the experiences of white children in North America, Western Europe and Australasia, rather than those of children in Asia, Africa and South America, or in minority communities in the West. Additionally, cultural notions of shame and modesty have been shown to inhibit South Asian victims from speaking about their experiences (Gilligan and Akhtar, 2006). Moreover, Valentine (2008) has noted that language is a gendered phenomenon, and in South Asian languages, it reproduces the gendered social order, thus restricting or preventing some victims from speaking authentically about their experiences. The challenge in understanding sex offending is to consider the many academic disciplinary perspectives alongside the authentic language of victim-survivors.

Understanding sex crimes

Sociological understandings

At the outset of this section, we recognise that we use the term 'sociological' to include criminological and social-anthropological work. We address three areas that locate sex crimes within a social context: identities, the construction of risk and understanding desistance.

Identities: problematic men, invisible women and the young sex offender

The term 'identity/ies' opens up a complex area of social theory that disputes the nature of identity: is it an innate aspect of a person that is fixed and unchanging, or is it contingent on time and place, and therefore changeable? Similarly, there are debates about the various strands of identity, for example, gender, ethnicity, sexuality, (dis)ability and so on. These debates explore whether there is a dominant identity to which others are subordinate. These explorations, while important, potentially deflect from the focus of this section. However, the sociological concept of 'intersectionality' is useful here (see Crenshaw, 1991; Grabham et al, 2009; Walby et al, 2012), in that it looks at the different dimensions of identity and how they intersect with one another across place and time. For example, in understanding and responding to sex offenders, it may be important to consider not only 'race' in its crudest form, but also issues related to masculinity, ethnicity and faith. Moreover, these issues have to be considered within a dynamic context involving time, location and (social) situation. Thus, in sociological terms, an understanding of offending that considers intersectionality offers a nuanced appreciation of the dynamics of identities. In Chapter One, we explored issues relating to race and ethnicity, and how the over-representation of BME people in criminal justice systems can lead to a racialised version of 'sex crime'; here, we address gender and age.

Thinking about gender in relation to understanding sex crime requires critical reflection on the wider social context. Feminist theories originate from structuralist accounts of social divisions and highlight patriarchal practices as supportive of sexual coercion and harm (eg Brownmiller, 1975; Kelly, 1988; Donat and D'Emilio, 1992; Gavey, 2005). While not homogeneous, feminist theories have made an important epistemological and political contribution to both understanding sex crimes and informing a social response to them. According to feminist activists, the laws surrounding sexuality and sexual behaviours favour the interests of the heterosexual man; this is largely achieved by using narrow definitions of sex crimes and stringent evidential requirements (Howe, 2008). A key theme in feminist writing is that sexually harmful behaviours are commonplace, but not all of them are identified in law. Gavey (2005), for example, refers to the 'cultural scaffolds' of rape, located in commonplace social attitudes, values and behaviours. Sanday's (1979, 2003, 2007) social-anthropological work, spanning three decades, draws attention to the characteristics of 'rape-free' and 'rape-prone' societies and communities, including rape-prone university campuses in the US. In all 'rape-prone' contexts, she found 'an ideology of male dominance enforced through the control and subordination of women' (Sanday, 2003, p 337). Feminist theories view male values and behaviours as underpinning and perpetuating sex crimes, and point out that social policy, not individual therapies, is the way to reduce sex crimes.

The critique of ordinary male behaviours prompted a range of studies of non-convicted male populations, particularly looking at the 'proclivity' to rape. Studies, mostly undertaken with male student populations, asked men to indicate their likelihood of raping if there would be no negative consequences for themselves (eg criminal prosecution). A consistent finding of between 25% and 30% of respondents indicates that they would rape (Stermac et al, 1990). More recently, two British studies of young people found significant support (particularly from male respondents) for attitudes that endorsed both rape and partner violence (Burton et al, 1998; Burman and Cartmel, 2006). Alleyne et al (2014) found that 66% of a sample of 'community males' did not emphatically reject an interest in 'multiple perpetrator rape'. A symposium at the Association for the Treatment of Sexual Abusers (ATSA) annual conference in 2015 considered studies exploring attitudes to rape in unconvicted male populations (ATSA, 2015). The issue of 'proclivity to rape' remains an international political concern; Bruenig (2015) describes the Obama administration's campaign against sexual assault ('It's On Us'[1]), which challenges social attitudes dynamically and endeavours to make sexual assault socially unacceptable in all sections of society. There are similar campaigns internationally, for example, the White Ribbon Campaign exists in many countries, including the UK.[2] These initiatives seek to challenge sexual violence as a social phenomenon, and not (only) as individual acts defined by the processes of the criminal justice system.

In feminist analyses of sex crimes, located in a wider analysis of women's oppression in which women are construed as victims of male society, recognising women as sex offenders becomes problematic (Harris, 2010). It is generally accepted that female sex offenders are an under-researched phenomenon, with large gaps in knowledge about why women offend, whom they offend against and how often they do this (Williams and Bierie, 2015). The dominant image (both lay and professional) is that such offending is uncommon, and that when it does happen, it is less serious than offending by men (Mellor and Deering, 2010). Indeed, in his book

Physical and Sexual Abuse of Children: Causes and Treatment, Walters (1978) felt able to categorically deny that women were capable of sexually offending against children, and asserted that the problem did not exist. Perceptions have changed, but slowly. There have been reports in the press of adult women school teachers sexually abusing their young male students where this has been presented almost as a 'rite of passage' of masculine socialisation through 'seduction', rather than abuse through breach of trust. This narrative makes it very difficult for victims to recognise that they have been abused.

Sexual coercion by women appears to be subject to processes of social denial and minimisation. Essentialist explanations of women's violence have tended to start with the premise that women are non-violent (except in extreme circumstances, where they are using self-defence against their abusive male partners), and that women who perpetrate aggression outside the stereotype are either 'mad', 'bad', 'evil' or 'victimised'; all of which deny and minimise personal agency and culpability (Allen, 1998). In short, both traditionalists and some feminists take the view that the violent behaviour of women deviates from expected 'normal' gender characteristics, whereas non-essentialised, postmodern feminist explanations stress that violence is neither inherently masculine nor feminine; it exists in a context of politics, economics, power relations and gender dynamics of the specific act of violence (Renzetti, 1999).

We now consider the issue of age in relation to sex offending, in particular, those crimes committed by young people, defined by the UK Ministry of Justice as people under 18. More refined definitional issues related to this population are addressed later in the chapter when we consider the offenders themselves. In England and Wales in 2013–15, there were 1,653 sexual offences for which a young person was convicted; this was 2% of all youth offences (Ministry of Justice and Youth Justice Board, 2015). In relation to the sentenced prison population of young offenders, sex offenders made up approximately 5% of the under-18 population from 2009 to 2014 (Ministry of Justice and Youth Justice Board, 2015). As with the adult sex offender population, this group has a low reconviction rate, with young sex offenders having a 're-offending rate of 15.0 per cent, compared with those with robbery offences which have a 41.5 per cent re-offending rate' (Ministry of Justice and Youth Justice Board, 2015, p 57). It is noteworthy that in these statistics relating to the overall young offender population, BME groups are over-represented in relation to the proportion of their ethnic group in the overall national population (Ministry of Justice and Youth Justice Board, 2015, p 28).

In the US, using data from the National Incident Based Reporting System (NIBRS), Finkelhor et al (2009, pp 1–2) found that:

- Juveniles account for more than one third (35.6%) of those known to the police to have committed sex offences against minors.
- Juveniles who commit sex offences against other children are more likely than adult sex offenders to offend in groups and at schools and to have more male victims and younger victims.
- The number of youth coming to the attention of police for sex offences increases sharply at age 12 and plateaus after age 14. Early adolescence is the peak age for offences against younger children. Offences against teenagers surge during mid to late adolescence, while offences against victims under 12 decline.
- A small number of juvenile offenders – 1 out of 8 – are younger than 12.
- Females constitute 7 per cent of juveniles who commit sex offences.
- Females are found more frequently among young youth than older youth who commit sex offences. This group's offences involve multiple-victim and multi-perpetrator episodes, and they are more likely to have victims who are family members or males.

In seeking to understand, sociologically, the phenomenon of sex offending by young people, the work of James Messerschmidt (1993, 2000, 2011, 2012) is of central importance. Messerschmidt's work is based on a series of 30 life history interviews conducted with 'thirty 15–18 year old White working class boys and girls: 20 violent (10 assaultive and 10 sexual offenders, each equally divided by sex) and 10 nonviolent (likewise equally divided by sex)' (Messerschmidt, 2011, p 207). The methodology here is important; he spent time listening to young people talk about their lives. The data was not gathered using 'validated' questionnaires, he allowed the young people to talk and subsequently analysed the data. He comments: 'Through these life history interviews, I have uncovered detailed accounts of embodied gender interaction in three distinct "sites": the family, the school and the peer group' (Messerschmidt, 2011, p 207).

Throughout all of his work, he is concerned to understand the people that he speaks to as socially located human beings. He analysed the data using grounded theory and identified specific emergent themes and patterns relating to the experience of being bullied and the transition into being a sex offender.

Messerschmidt is critical of most conventional criminology for its failure to address gender and embodiment in its account of (sex) crimes. His 'structured action theory' (Messerschmidt, 2000, 2012) draws on insights from symbolic interactionism and structural and post-structural theory.

His analysis (of life history transcripts and the committing of crimes) is based on the *situated* dynamic *performing* of gender (Messerschmidt, 2000). Gender is not a fixed element in social identity; it is *enacted* in different ways, at different times. Moreover, Messerschmidt recognises that gender interacts with other strands of identity (eg race and social class), which may be emphasised in different situations. His work strongly links with intersectional theory (referred to earlier). However, he is particularly keen to see identity as situational and fluid. In thinking about sexual and violent crime, he notes that 'theory that connects social action (micro) with social structure (macro) is essential to the comprehension of adolescent ... violence' (Messerschmidt, 2000, p 8). Individual violence is not different from the ways of being a young man or woman; it is shaped by dominant *social* ways of being. The implications of this analysis are distinctly sociological and have significance for social policy; from his study of adolescent female sex offenders, for example, Messerschmidt (2011, pp 229–30) suggests that educational/school policies are needed to help prevent young people from committing sex crimes:

> The suggested policies – school policy statements, gender-relevant and gender specific curriculum, and emphasis on empathy and pluralism in schools – obviously neither exhaustive nor comprehensive – argue persuasively that the topic of embodied heterogender is highly relevant to debates on bullying and eventual violent offending by victims. What these policies essentially aim to do is to 'reembody' youth by allowing them to recognise alternative and different ways of acting and through their body, thereby helping to develop embodied capacities other than those associated with bullying and interpersonal violence.

Understanding risk

Risk of being sexually harmed features in popular understandings of sex crime (as discussed in Chapter One). Sex crime is described as pervasive, and thus risks to particular populations (women and children) are portrayed as commonplace. Sociological perspectives on the nature of risk and risk assessment provide a counterbalance to news media perspectives by drawing attention to the limitations of the activity. Social anthropologist Mary Douglas (1985, 1992) suggests that risk is a political vehicle, used widely to legitimate the policies and practices of particular groups at specific times. This process of legitimation is achieved through utilising a quantitative paradigm in order to give risk a specious appearance of solidity. Mythen and Walklate (2006, p 1) comment: 'In theoretical terms, risk has conventionally been approached as an objective entity, to be mastered by calculation, assessment and probability'. Bauman (1993, pp 199–200) suggests that 'In the concept of "risk society", "risks" enter the stage already appropriated and managed by science and technology – as their unquestionable domain'. The 'risk analysis professional' (Douglas, 1992) plays a significant part in sociological analyses; s/he operates within specialist sub-disciplines that develop their own technical language (ie inaccessible to the general public). Bauman (1993, pp 200–8) highlights how risk discourses, through technologised approaches to knowledge, create a self-perpetuating, highly technical form of knowledge as the only valid way to approach, understand, assess and manage risk. This has the effect of prioritising certain forms of intellectual activity (calculative and mathematical) and certain subjects for inquiry:

> Technology's miraculous powers are intimately related to the stratagem of close focusing: a 'problem' to become a 'task', is first cut out from the tangle of its multiple connections with other realities, while the realities with which it is connected are left out of account and melt into the indifferent 'backdrop' of action. (Bauman, 1993, p 194)

In reflecting on this analysis in seeking to understand sex crime, we can see how the activities of forensic disciplines contribute to the construction of risk. Much of the psychological literature on risk and risk assessment is expressed in esoteric and inaccessible (to the lay reader) language. The terminologies are derived from medical, psychological and statistical vocabularies, and together create a discourse that embodies what may be considered to be 'expert' knowledge. The names of some of the instruments of assessment imply an abstracted technical world, with processes and procedures only to be understood by technical 'experts' (eg Static-99, Static-2002 and Risk Matrix-2002, cited in Bengtson and Långström, 2007, p 138). This technical endeavour may be located in a context of knowledge, derived from meta-analysis, which indicates that:

> most sexual offenders do not re-offend sexually, that first-time sexual offenders are significantly less likely to sexually re-offend than those with previous sexual convictions, and that offenders over the age of 50 are less likely to re-offend than younger offenders. In addition, it was found that the longer offenders remained offence-free in the community the less likely they are to re-offend sexually. (Harris and Hanson, 2004, p ii)

Sociological perspectives on the nature of risk and risk assessment draw attention to the limitations of the activity. Silver and Miller (2002, p 138) suggest that the main concern of an actuarial approach is the efficient management of resources, and that by focusing on aggregate populations identified on the basis of data from criminal justice systems, it contributes to further stigmatising populations that are already marginalised. The purely actuarial task potentially ignores both the socio-political context of risk assessment (eg remember Davis's [1981] comments, cited in Chapter One, on the sentencing and execution of black men) and the significant population of people who perpetrate sexual harms that do not come into contact with the criminal justice system (see the discussion of attrition later in this chapter). The implications of this analysis of risk for social work have been highlighted by Pollack (2010), who sees the calculation of risk as a part of the neoliberal agenda designed to control socially marginal populations. Pollack (2010, p 1276) notes that Ferguson and Lavalette (2006) call for a 'social work of resistance' to neoliberal agendas: 'Integral to developing such a framework is challenging standardized technologies of "managing risky behaviours", since "a 'what works' agenda that does not address issues of process, relationship and structural oppression often simply does not work"' (Ferguson and Lavalette, 2006, p 313). Sociological perspectives allow for a wider consideration of the socio-political implications of activities that are commonplace and rarely examined.

Understanding desistance

Much psychological research explores those issues that may prompt sex offenders to reoffend. An alternative way of looking at things is to consider what *helps* sex offenders to *avoid* reoffending – what helps them to 'desist' from offending. Willis, Levenson and Ward (2010, p 545, emphasis in original) note: 'The process of ceasing sexual and general offending and becoming a productive member of society is called *desistance*'. In recent years, there has developed a considerable body of criminological research in relation to general desistance from crime. The available research indicates that if sex offenders released from prison are provided with the resources to access stable housing, establish pro-social support networks and create intimate relationships, and are presented with opportunities for employment, then they are less likely to reoffend (Willis et al, 2010, p 545). However, Farrall (1995, p 56) notes 'that very few people actually desist as a result of intervention on the part of the criminal justice system or its representatives'. Ward and Maruna (2007, p 14) comment that it 'makes considerable sense to develop models of rehabilitation on the basis of what is known about how reintegration works in the "natural" environment outside of the criminal justice system'. Research clearly indicates that desistance is not an introverted psychological process, but a social activity; again, Willis et al (2010, p 548) locate the importance of social and psychological strengths in achieving aspirations: 'All human beings require help from other people to acquire and utilize the psychological capabilities and social resources necessary to realize their aspirations whether this involves completing job training, participating in social activities, or remaining crime free'.

McNeill (2012) identifies three separate perspectives on desistance that are increasingly becoming integrated in desistance theory: (1) the significance of age and maturation; (2) life transitions and social bonds; and (3) personal and social identity. Key for the sex offender in making this transition away from offending is community support because, as Willis et al (2010, p 548) note, the move from a treatment environment into the community is difficult. Desistance-based research has informed the development of the Good Lives Model of rehabilitation that is discussed elsewhere in this book (see Chapter Six).

Theological understandings

In the 'West', the (Christian) Church defined and dealt with sex crimes until the 19th century (Thomas, 2011, pp 39–59). Kirby (2013) describes the relevant biblical law (*Leviticus*, ch 20, verses 13–16) concerning sexual behaviour. A prime concern of 19th-century legislators in the UK was 'vice' and 'social purity' (Thomas, 2011); concerns with obscene publications (Act of 1857) and prostitution (campaigns of the Social Purity Movement) featured prominently. The language of the Bible and Christian morality defined and framed the laws relating to sex crimes in the 19th and 20th centuries; sex offences were seen as acts that contravened the dominant moral code. Acts were criminal because they contravened biblical stipulations about family relations (incest) or other men's 'property' (rape), or because they contravened heteronormative standards of 'decency' (indecent assault and gross indecency). Perhaps, partly, because of the harsh sanctions stipulated against victims in *Leviticus* chapter 20, there was no victim perspective involved in the framing of this legislation. In England and Wales, 'indecent assault' and 'gross indecency' remained sex crimes until the Sexual Offences Act 2003 (SOA). In many ways, such nomenclature implies that 'decency' is the main victim of the crime – decency has been offended – and that the people who were sexually harmed by these acts (the real victims) were an incidental element in the offence. In England and Wales, the SOA revised the terminology and gave victims an active presence in the proceedings.

The law

This section refers to the law as it applies to England and Wales; it does not pretend to provide an exhaustive account (for such an account, see Stevenson et al, 2004; Gerry et al, 2014). Furthermore, legal penalties prescribed by law are discussed in Chapter Three. The SOA announced itself as a 'comprehensive review of sexual offences', with three aims: (1) to modernise the catalogue of sexual offences; (2) to render them appropriate for the 20th century; and (3) to protect individuals from sexual crime. The focus of the Act is very clearly on behaviours, offenders and victims. Offences are not described in terms of breaches of moral codes or of decency (with the exception of ss 45–46); consideration is given to the relationship between the victim and the offender (eg familial, breach of trust), and there is a greater awareness of how trafficking links to prostitution, and how both are serious offences against vulnerable victims. The range and nature of crimes identified by the SOA are listed in Table 2.1.

In highlighting the SOA, we draw attention to the current focus on offences and offending behaviours, rather than 'decency'. Sex offence

Table 2.1: Sexual Offences Act 2003 (England and Wales), offences listed by section

Section	Offence
1.	Rape
2–3.	Assault by penetration and sexual assault
4.	Causing sexual activity without consent
5–8.	Rape and other offences against under 13s
9–15.	Child sex offences
16–24.	Abuse of a position of trust
25–29.	Familial child sex offences
30–33.	Offences against persons with a mental disorder impeding choice
34–37.	Inducements to persons with a mental disorder
38–44.	Care workers for persons with a mental disorder
45–46.	Indecent photographs of children
47–56.	Prostitution and child pornography
57–60.	Trafficking for sexual exploitation
61–63.	Preparatory offences (eg drugging, trespass)
64–65.	Sex with and adult relative
66–71.	Other offences (eg exposure, voyeurism, animals, corpses, sex in public lavatories)
72.	Offences outside the UK
73–79.	Supplementary and general (definitions and explanations of terminology in relation to 'consent', 'sexual', 'mental disorder')

law differs across national jurisdictions; however, one issue central to the operation of sex offence law that is internationally common is 'attrition'. Jehle (2012, p 151), in his study of attrition in relation to sex offences in Europe, defines attrition as 'the loss of cases from the level of police to the level of conviction'. We suggest that the 'loss of cases' starts before crimes are reported to the police, in that many harmful sexual acts are never reported to authorities. Thereafter, 'cases' are lost during investigation, at the decision to prosecute and at court. These processes differ across countries, but attrition is an international phenomenon (Kelly and Lovett, 2009; Jehle, 2012). Approximately, only 10% of cases reported to the police result in a criminal conviction (Kelly et al, 2005; Kelly and Lovett, 2009; Jehle, 2012). Figure 2.2 illustrates the process of attrition in relation to sex offences.

The flow chart in Figure 2.2 outlines key issues in the prevalence, identification and processing of sexual crime. It indicates the numbers involved and how attrition works, and illustrates the limitations of relying on actual criminal convictions as an indicator of prevalence.

Biomedical understandings

Medical understandings of sex crimes are rooted in a socio-biological understanding of human behaviour. This generally assumes an evolutionary perspective that locates sex crimes within a context of the survival of the species. Notions of 'natural selection' predominate (see Thornhill and Palmer, 2001), and aggressive sexual conduct is seen as an evolutionary adaptation to ensure the continuation of the species (for a fuller exploration of this perspective, see Thornhill and Palmer, 2000; for feminist critiques of the evolutionary perspective, see Travis, 2003).

The medical perspectives of the 19th and 20th centuries were initially informed by the work of Freud, and the sexologists Krafft-Ebing and Havelock-Ellis (but also later by the work of Kinsey, Masters and Johnson). The sexologists adopted an evolutionary perspective of human sexual behaviour. Krafft-Ebing's work *Psychopathia Sexualis* (2011/1886) was first published in 1886 and the 12th and final edition (written by Krafft-Ebing) was published in 1903. The book was influential in both the legal and medical professions, and it established the framework through which sexual behaviours (and sex crimes) were interpreted (for bibliographic information, see Ooesterhuis, 2012). Ooesterhuis (2012, p 134) describes the changing focus of European psychiatry at the end of the 19th century:

Figure 2.2: Flow of sexual offence cases from victimisation to conviction

Not presented to scale. Victims and offenders may not relate to the same cases.

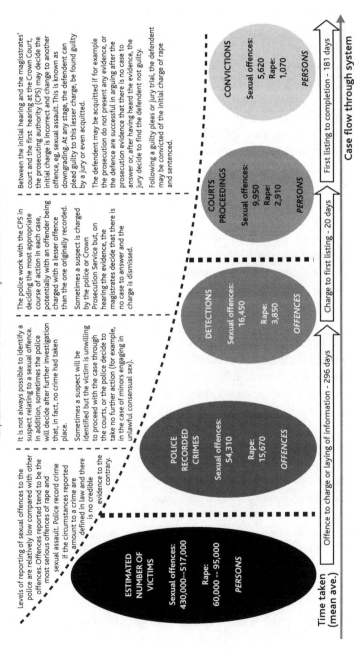

ESTIMATED NUMBER OF VICTIMS

Sexual offences: 430,000–517,000

Rape: 60,000 – 95,000

PERSONS

POLICE RECORDED CRIMES

Sexual offences: 54,310

Rape: 15,670

OFFENCES

DETECTIONS

Sexual offences: 16,450

Rape: 3,850

OFFENCES

COURTS PROCEEDINGS

Sexual offences: 9,950

Rape: 2,910

PERSONS

CONVICTIONS

Sexual offences: 5,620

Rape: 1,070

PERSONS

Levels of reporting of sexual offences to the police are relatively low compared with other offences. Offences reported tend to be the most serious offences of rape and sexual assault. Police record crime if the circumstances reported amount to a crime are defined in law and there is no credible evidence to the contrary.

It is not always possible to identify a suspect relating to a sexual offence. In addition, sometimes the police will decide after further investigation that, in fact, no crime had taken place.

Sometimes a suspect will be identified but the victim is unwilling to proceed with the case through the courts, or the police decide to take no further action (for example, in the case of minors engaging in unlawful consensual sex).

The police work with the CPS in deciding the most appropriate course of action in each case, potentially with an offender being charged with a lesser offence than the one originally recorded.

Sometimes a suspect is charged by the police or Crown Prosecution Service but, on hearing the evidence, the magistrates decide that there is no case to answer and the charge is dismissed.

Between the initial hearing and the magistrates' court and the first hearing at the Crown Court, the prosecuting authority (CPS) may decide the initial charge is incorrect and change to another offence, eg. sexual assault. This is known as downgrading. At any stage, the defendant can plead guilty to this lesser charge, be found guilty by a jury or even acquitted.

The defendant may be acquitted if for example the prosecution do not present any evidence, or the defence are successful in arguing after the prosecution evidence that there is no case to answer or, after having heard the evidence, the jury decide to find the defendant not guilty.

Following a guilty pleas or jury trial, the defendant may be convicted of the initial charge of rape and sentenced.

Time taken (mean ave.)

Offence to charge or laying of information – 296 days

Charge to first listing – 20 days

First listing to completion – 181 days

Case flow through system

Note: Figures displayed are three-year averages.

Source: Ministry of Justice, Home Office and Office of National Statistics (2013, p 7).

[the] main thrust was that in many cases, irregular sexual behaviour should not be regarded as sin and crime but as symptoms of pathology. Since mental and nervous disorders often diminished responsibility, most sex offenders should not be punished but treated as patients.

With this shift, Oosterhuis (2012, p 134) notes the growth of diagnostic terminology: 'homosexual' and 'heterosexual' preceded more specialist terms such as 'exhibitionism', 'voyeurism', 'fetishism', 'paedophilia', 'bestiality', 'sadism' and 'masochism'; however, 'paraphilia' is a key catch-all term. The *Oxford English Dictionary* (OED, 2015) defines 'paraphilia' as 'Sexual desires regarded as perverted or irregular; *spec.* attraction to unusual or abnormal sexual objects or practices; an instance of this'. The words 'perverted', 'irregular', 'unusual' and 'abnormal' clearly establish the nature of paraphilia against an implied (heterosexual) norm; moreover, this exceptional character is compounded by the word 'disorder'. The naming of 'paraphilic disorders' is, however, in some cases, a controversial process.

The *Diagnostic and Statistical Manual of Mental Disorders* (DSM) was first published in 1952. Now in its fifth iteration (APA, 2013), it is the diagnostic 'manual' for psychiatry in North America, and is influential across the 'Western' world. DSM 5 identifies eight paraphilic disorders: exhibitionistic disorder; fetishistic disorder; frotteuristic disorder; paedophilic disorder; sexual masochism disorder; sexual sadism disorder; transvestic disorder; and voyeuristic disorder. Tosh (2011) outlines the debates about whether to include acts of sexual coercion in the DSM. She notes that rape as a symptom of psychiatric illness has a long history dating back to the early 20th century. Rape and sexual assault were included in the first DSM in 1952 under the 'vague' diagnosis of 'sexual deviance', which included the subcategory of 'sexual sadism', which seems to be a 'catch-all' for rape and many other sex offences (Tosh, 2011, p 2). Tosh (2011, pp 3–4) raises concerns about the 'medicalisation' of rape. Frances and First (2011, pp 558–9) similarly express concerns about the attempts of the US legal system to use the medicalisation of rape as a justification for the extended incarceration of rapists; they note that 'the act of being a rapist is almost always an aspect of simple criminality, and that rapists need to receive longer prison sentences not psychiatric hospitalizations'.

Medical treatments are available for sex offenders – primarily in the form of anti-libidinal medication – which are usually combined with some form of 'talking' therapy. The evidence for the effectiveness of this treatment is inconclusive, although there are concerns about the long-term side effects of medication (Basdekis-Jozsa et al, 2013). However, medical understandings and responses to sex offending highlight a central issue for (medical) practitioners: 'as long as paraphilias are regarded as a disorder, sexual offenders with paraphilias have to be seen as patients first and not (only) as perpetrators' (Basdekis-Jozsa et al, 2013, p 314). The majority of medical theorising and treatments are focused on male offenders; there does not appear to be a significant body of literature that addresses biological perspectives directly relating to female offenders.

Understanding sex offenders

This section concerns how responses to sex offenders are shaped within some academic disciplines. Some approaches consider both the offender and the crime/offending. Theological and biomedical perspectives contain an overview of the nature of the offences and a response to the individual offender, which was briefly explored in the previous section. Sociological theory does not propose responses to the individual offender, but locates individual offenders, inextricably, within their social context (Messerschmidt, 1993, 2012). This section is primarily concerned with psychological understandings of individual sex offenders; while the bulk of the literature considers adult male sex offenders, we also consider female and young sex offenders.

Psychologically informed understandings of sex offenders

Approaches to *convicted* sex offenders are primarily rooted in the discipline of psychology and are accessed through criminal justice systems. An aspect of early psychological theorising was the development of classification systems for both (convicted) rapists (eg Groth et al, 1977) and men who had sexually harmed children ('child molesters') (eg Knight et al, 1989). These systems were based on the study of convicted populations; they focused on offending behaviour and apparent motivations. Initial systems were strongly influenced by psychiatric perspectives. In 1998, Fisher and Mair (1998, abstract) undertook a comprehensive review of these systems and noted: 'none of the existing classification systems reviewed complied with the requirements of being reliable, efficient, pertinent to a large number of offenders, and simple to administer'. Bickley and Beech (2001, p 65) raise similar concerns about these systems, particularly their inability to discriminate suitable treatments for different groups. They suggested that a way forward would be to develop a wider 'conceptual model' for understanding the process of offending. However, interest in developing classification systems continues (Marshall et al, 2015); the main objective appears to be greater precision in identifying offender type and effectively targeting appropriate treatment. Recently, Ward and Beech (2015) have suggested that classification systems need to be much more rigorous in accounting for their intellectual foundations. They suggest using 'exemplars' as a way to avoid conflating description (of offenders) and explanation (the development of theory in relation to offending).

Critically examining professional knowledge is of central importance to developing robust theory. Beech and Ward (2004) suggest that risk assessment be rooted in a clear aetiological theory of offending. Aetiological theory is important in accounting for the onset and continuance of sexual offending (Ward and Hudson, 1998). Three types of theory are identified (Ward and Hudson, 1998): single-factor theories focus on one issue to account for the aetiology and continuance of sex offending; multi-factorial theories offer a complex account of the aetiology and continuance of sex offending; and micro-level or offence process theories give particular attention to an aspect of offending behaviour. In the mid-20th century, single-factor theories were common and often in conflict with one another (eg feminist theory and evolutionary perspectives).

A key aspect of multi-factorial theories is that they have been developed from analyses of empirical studies of sex offenders, their personal histories and their offence patterns. Multi-factorial explanations incorporate physiological, psychological and emotional dimensions relating to the offender, along with situational and historical (fixed) matters. Apart from these issues, the models are also mindful of time and change; thus, *change* in physiological, psychological and emotional states is important. Key contributions to this area of theory include: the confluence model of sexual aggression (Malamuth et al, 1996); integrated theory (Marshall and Barbaree, 1990); the quadripartite model of sexual aggression (Hall and Hirschman, 1991); the four preconditions model (Finkelhor, 1984); the pathways model (Ward and Siegert, 2002); the integrated theory of sexual offending (Ward and Beech, 2006), and a 'new integrated theory' of 'child sexual abuse' (Smallbone et al, 2008). Summarising the content of (multi-factorial) theories, Hanson and Morton-Bourgon (2005, pp 1154–5) comment:

> Contemporary theories posit … that, apart from sexual deviancy and lifestyle instability, there may be three additional characteristics of persistent sexual offenders: (a) negative family background, (b) problems forming affectionate bonds with friends and lovers, and (c) attitudes tolerant of sexual assault.

However, while Hanson and Morton-Bourgon (2005) acknowledge the value of multi-factorial explanations of sex offending, they note that the evidence behind the identification of the factors and how they interrelate with reoffending is weak. They suggest that if the primary therapeutic objective of correctional work with sex offenders is to reduce recidivism (reconviction), then detailed attention must focus on what, statistically, can be shown to be directly related to reoffending. A statistical means of analysing large amounts of quantitative data from many studies is *meta-analysis*, and it is by using meta-analysis that issues directly related to sex offending have been identified. Table 2.2 outlines the key features of meta-analysis.

Table 2.2: What is meta-analysis?

Meta-analysis is a statistical technique for combining the findings from independent studies.
Meta-analysis is most often used to assess the *clinical effectiveness of health-care interventions*; it does this by combining data from two or more randomised control trials.
Meta-analysis of trials provides a *precise estimate of treatment effect*, giving due weight to the size of the different studies included.
The validity of the meta-analysis depends on the *quality of the systematic review* on which it is based.
Good meta-analyses aim for *complete coverage of all relevant studies*, look for the *presence of heterogeneity* and explore the robustness of the main findings using *sensitivity analysis*.

Source: Crombie and Davies (2009).

Although meta-analysis is an efficient and effective way of collating and analysing large amounts of data, and it is clearly very influential, the analysis is susceptible to bias. A good meta-analysis carefully outlines the detail of the data included and excluded, and highlights the limitations of the study.

Karl Hanson and colleagues (eg Hanson and Bussiere, 1998; Harris and Hanson, 2004; Hanson and Morton–Bourgon, 2005) conducted a series of meta-analyses relating to sex offender recidivism. The early study (Hanson and Bussiere, 1998) was of major significance in highlighting the low recidivism rate of sex offenders. Moreover, meta-analyses raise questions about some elements common in treatment programmes that appeared to be unrelated to reoffending (the index offence, the nature of that offence, the denial of responsibility and the motivation for treatment). Hanson and Morton–Bourgon (2005, p 1154) suggest that the key factors linked to recidivism are 'deviant sexual preferences and anti-social orientation', while many well-established treatment targets – such as 'psychological distress, denial of sex crime, victim empathy, stated motivation for treatment' – 'had little or no relationship with sexual or violent recidivism'.

The importance of developing a subtle (multi-factorial) understanding of sex offenders is not only to develop treatment programmes, but also to more accurately assess risk. There is an immense psychological literature on risk assessment and risk management in relation to sex offenders (for reviews of this literature, see Beech and Ward, 2004; Bengtson and Långström, 2007;

see also Chapter Five). The literature distinguishes between actuarial and clinical approaches to assessing risk (Grubin, 1999). *Actuarial* approaches use risk factors that have been consistently identified in a wide range of research studies of convicted sex offenders. Typically, these factors are previous offences, relationship history and criminality (Beech and Ward, 2004, p 32), and are described as being *static* (ie they are not amenable to change). *Clinical* approaches rely on the judgement of the clinician dealing with the individual person who may pose a risk to others. The clinician's assessment may or may not be based on research literature, but generally includes consideration of the *dynamic* factors (eg mood, attitudes, physical circumstances – including the availability of victims) affecting the individual under assessment. The actuarial tendency in assessing sex offender risk is strong (Beech and Ward, 2004, p 33) and the research literature continues to indicate that a pure actuarial approach is more accurate in predicting reoffending (Bengtson and Långström, 2007). However, Beech and Ward (2004, p 32) summarise a range of weaknesses with a pure actuarial approach (including its inability to deal with the unusual and contingent dynamic factors, and its dependence on official recidivism data that may underestimate recidivism rates and therefore levels of risk). Recently, Ward and Beech (2015) have critiqued the concept of 'dynamic risk factors' as being inadequately theorised and potentially leading clinical practice and research into a cul-de-sac. They argue that the concept needs clearer definition, and that descriptive and explanatory components need to be clearly distinguished. They propose a way forward of developing 'exemplars' of sex offending that first describe the phenomenon, and then seek to explain it. This work is in the early stage of development but looks promising as a way of further clarifying psychological approaches to assessing risk.

The third area of theory highlighted by Ward and Hudson (1998) concerns 'micro-' issues. Two particular areas are given as examples of micro-issues: relapse prevention (RP) and 'grooming'. Much has been written over many years about relapse prevention (eg Pithers, 1990; Ward, 2000; see also p 131 below). The notion of 'relapse' was derived and developed from addiction theory (Marlatt, 1985), which identified and named the stages of 'relapse'. In relation to sex offending, the model was slightly adapted, but it was very popular from the mid-1980s through to the mid-2000s. RP modules featured in both community and prison programmes. The model has come in for serious criticism from Ward (2000), who proposed an alternative 'self-regulation' model of relapse. Understanding the minutiae of reoffending remains an important research target and treatment component, although the pure RP model is increasingly considered to be unsuitable for use with sex offenders (Laws, 2003; Yates et al, 2010). More recently, consideration of the 'pathways' to offending model has led to the development of more sophisticated conceptualising of the processes leading to offending behaviour (see pp 132–3 below). Kingston and Yates (2012) and Ward and colleagues (2006), among others, have developed the 'self-regulation' model of sexual offending, within which are identified four offence pathways, all of which have implications for intervention(s). The model is conceptually linked with the Good Lives therapeutic model, which is discussed later in the book.

The word 'grooming', referring to how a sex offender prepares both potential victims and the environment where s/he intends to offend, has entered the popular vocabulary through media reportage, and (in the UK) through the Sex Offenders Act 2003, which created a specific offence of 'Grooming'. Olson et al (2007, p 241) describe grooming as 'the subtle communication strategies that child sexual abusers use to prepare their potential victims to accept sexual contact'. This involves both controlling the victim by concealing the threat posed, and manipulating the environment to ensure that the offence will occur without disturbance. Campbell (2009) presents a clear account of the processes of grooming. She highlights that grooming involves 'strategies to present a specific image in an interpersonal relationship through the use of language that indicates the sender's "persona" to the receiver' (Campbell, 2009, p 432). Campbell (2009, p 434) identifies five particular grooming strategies employed by offenders: supplication (presenting a helpless public persona): intimidation (presenting a powerful or harmful persona): self-promotion (presenting as competent): ingratiation (presenting likeable or affiliative behaviours); and exemplification (presenting a self that is worthy – demonstrating high moral values). Research focusing on the minutiae of the process of offending or grooming strategies enables practitioners to be more aware of the complexities of offending behaviour and more able to interpret seemingly 'innocent' behaviours in the context of sexual offending.

The female sex offender

The preceding psychological understandings of sex offenders do not explicitly include female sex offenders. As mentioned earlier, until recently, the female sex offender was not considered in accounts of sex offending. However, Williams and Bierie (2015, p 236), using 2011 national US data, identify that women accounted for '1.2% of forcible rape arrests and 8.1% of forcible sex offense arrests', arguing that this was likely to be an underestimate. They quote Lawson (1993, p 264), who states that 'the taboo against disclosure [of female sexual abuse is] stronger than the taboo against the behavior itself', a situation that seems to be consistent across much research. Cortoni, Hanson and Coache (2010) studied victimisation surveys, and suggested that 5% of sexual offenders were women.

Williams and Bierie (2015) analysed 802,150 sexual offences committed in the US between 1992 and 2011. Women were involved in 43,018 offences, and of these, women were the sole perpetrator in 26,630 cases (61.9%), with 13,986 (32.5%) co-offending with a man. This is different from the men in the study, who had a higher incidence of solo offending (88.2%), but it still seems that the largest number of women offenders do so alone, and without any evidence of male coercion or involvement. The women had a higher incidence of offending against same-sex victims (50%) than men (10%), and there were differences in the type of sexual assaults, although this may partly be a product of definitional issues (eg the definition of rape changed from the gender-specific 'penetration of vagina by the penis' to a broader construction, enabling other forms of penetrative abuse to be included).

There have been various attempts to classify female sexual offenders, although it is too soon to do so with any confidence. Cortoni, Sandler and Freeman (2015) identify three broad categories based on victim characteristics: those who offend against children; those who offend against adolescents; and those who offend against adults. There are further categorisations based on the psychological type of offending process. *Directed-Avoidant* are those women who offend with a man, sometimes coerced, and this process is specific to women (rather than men) where passivity, dependency and subjugation to male authority are present. *Implicit-Disorganised* offenders are impulsive, and *Explicit-Approach* offenders plan their offences for sexual or other gain (Gannon et al, 2013). The evidence indicates that women offenders should not be assumed to have a male accomplice coercing them (physically, financially, socially or emotionally) into their behaviour; some women are quite capable of making decisions to offend on their own.

Drawing on the work of Schippers (2007), Hayes and Baker (2014) argue that the female sexual offender is better understood as someone who transgresses established gender roles of both hegemonic masculinity and femininity, and as a woman who fails to conform to the expected gender stereotypes of hegemonic femininity. Schippers describes women who do not meet these expectations as having 'pariah femininity' as they challenge heteronormativity, are often ostracised and are viewed as being socially dangerous. They are defined as deviant and/or maladjusted and need to be disciplined back into a conformist gender role. Hegemonic femininity idealises women as sexually passive, nurturing and caring, naturalising this through stories of biology and psychology (and increasingly neuroscience). This can lead to under-reporting, minimisation (Denov, 2004) and denial by professionals and laypeople alike.

Reflective exercise

- Make a list of all the social expectations of being a woman.
- Discuss how each of these might affect our understanding and response to sexual abuse by women.
- How is this different from understandings and responses to abuse by men?

The 'juvenile' sex offender

Terminology identifying this group of sex offenders varies considerably, dependent on which academic discipline is defining the behaviour. Criminal justice-oriented definitions use the language of law; more therapeutically inclined disciplines consider developmental issues beyond the letter of the law. Socio-legal scholarship highlights significant issues in relation to defining the sexually harmful actions of young people as *crime*, in particular, the age at which children can be considered to understand their actions, and the consequences of these actions, both for themselves and for their victims (see Cipriani, 2009), and the age of consent (Waites, 2009). In relation to therapeutic understandings, Araji (1997, p 195) notes:

> I believe the concept 'sexually aggressive' is the one that best describes abusive behaviors by children that have a sexual and an aggressive component. It clearly describes the behavior, and both components are measurable. This term can also be used to differentiate children who are engaged in these types of behavior from those engaged in other normal and sexual misbehaviors that do not include aggressive or violent components.

The Association for the Treatment of Sexual Abusers (ATSA, 2012) discriminates between 'adolescents' and 'young children'. For this international organisation, 'the term "adolescents" indicates youth aged 13 to 18 years'. The term 'adolescent' is chosen 'to emphasize that these youth are teenagers who are developing and maturing and should not be defined by their abusive behavior' (ATSA, 2012, p 1). Ryan et al (2010) note that young people from the age of three to 18 have been identified as behaving in sexually coercive and harmful ways to others. Moreover, they note that this young population comprises 'all racial, ethnic, religious, geographic and socioeconomic groups in approximate proportion to these characteristics in the general population' (Ryan et al, 2010, p 6). ATSA (no date) asserts that 'Children with sexual behavior problems should not be considered "sex offenders" similar to adolescents and adults who engage in some of the same victimizing behaviors'. They highlight seven developmental ways in which this group is different, and consider the treatment implications of these differences.

Research on adolescent females who commit sexual offences is limited as compared to research on males who commit sexual offences. Most studies are descriptive and characterised by small sample sizes. However, they point to high prevalence of sexual victimisation, non-sexual child maltreatment (including physical and emotional abuse), and co-occurring mental health problems. These young women are more likely to engage in sexually abusive behaviour towards young children within the family or with whom they are familiar, more likely to target victims of either gender, and to act alone, often within the context of care-giving activities such as babysitting. Wijkman et al (2015) studied groups of adolescent girls who had sexually assaulted others, and found that their motivations were to harass the victim, gain sexual gratification and take revenge. These motivations were similar to groups of young males except in 'taking revenge', which figured less with the boys, and indicates that there are group and other dynamics at work that are broader than just sexual intention. Wijkman et al raise questions about whether group offences of this kind should more properly be seen as violent offences, with an added sexual element to increase the humiliation of the victim; thereby decentring the sexual aspects of the behaviour.

Psychological theory is a major contributor to knowledge of sex offenders and sex offending. However, recently, there has been recognition that it cannot, on its own, provide a full account of sex crimes. Ward and Beech (2015) sketch out what may be a way forward in developing understanding, proposing the concept of 'Integrative Pluralism', which involves wider perspectives more fully in order to understand the sex offender and sex crimes. We return to this issue in the final chapter of the book.

Summary

- There are a variety of different academic disciplines that contribute to knowledge about sex offenders and sex crimes.
- It is important for social workers to develop a critical understanding of this range of knowledge that goes beyond merely focusing on clinical utility.
- To have a wide understanding of sex offenders and sex crimes facilitates creative thinking and imaginative practice.

Notes
[1] See: http://itsonus.org/#landing
[2] See: http://www.whiteribboncampaign.co.uk

Penal responses to the sex offender

Introduction

This chapter provides an account of penal responses to the sex offender. We begin by outlining justifications for punishment, and then look more closely at official sentencing guidelines in relation to sex offences. Thereafter, penal responses to sex offenders are presented within a framework of the justifications for punishment. Although we are concentrating on how the criminal justice system of England and Wales deals with sex offenders, there will be some similarities, and, of course, differences, across the globe. The underlying justifications for punishment, however, remain the same. The main part of the chapter is divided into three sections, considering, in turn, retributive, consequentialist and communicative ways in which penal policy is shaped and implemented. However, a word of warning is appropriate here. Most sentences do not exclusively fit into one type of justification for punishment; we will highlight ambiguities as they occur. Criminal law is not the only framework that deals with sex offenders and sex crimes; in the final section of the chapter, we briefly outline the areas of contribution made by civil law.

Understanding punishment

Sentencing sex offenders marks public recognition of the 'wrong' of sexual offences. The 'expressive function of punishment' (Feinberg, 1965, p 400) denounces the offence and the offender to wider society:

> punishment is a conventional device for the expression of attitudes of resentment and indignation, and of judgements of disapproval and reprobation, on the part either of the punishing authority ... or of those 'in whose name' the punishment is inflicted. Punishment, in short, has a symbolic significance largely missing from other penalties.

Ward and Rose (2013, p 274) identify 'six essential elements' of punishment:

1. It follows on from an offence against legal rules.
2. It is imposed and implemented by individuals authorised by the state.
3. It is intentional (directed towards a particular outcome).
4. It expresses disapproval or censure.
5. It is retributive – it follows a wrongful act committed by an offender.
6. It is harmful, inflicting suffering, a burden or deprivation on the offender.

There are three dominant 'justifications' for punishment: retributive, consequentialist and communicative (Duff and Garland, 1998). Retributive justifications look back to the offence and justify punishment in terms of a response to the offence. The response seeks both to hold the offender to account for his/her actions and to inflict a punishment that is commensurate with the offence. Ward and Rose (2013, p 275) note that 'retributive justifications typically utilize the notion of just deserts: offenders deserve to suffer for the wrongful acts that they have committed'. Underpinning retributive approaches is the assumption that the offender knowingly/ intentionally committed the offence and therefore bears responsibility for it. Punishment is predicated on the offender's responsibility and *moral accountability* for the offences. A retributive perspective 'encourages offenders to face up to the nature of the harm inflicted and to make amends through accepting the burdens associated with hard treatment' and also 'allows victims to express their anger and have their experiences taken into account in the sentencing process' (Ward and Rose, 2013, p 280).

Consequentialist justifications of punishment look forward from the offence and are concerned with reducing individual and overall rates of reoffending. They are concerned with deterrence, incapacitation and reform. Central to these concerns is the assessment and management of *risk* (Ward and Rose, 2013, p 281). As such, the concern of the practitioner is not with the well-being of the sex offender, but rather with community safety: the justification for a consequentialist approach to punishing sex offenders is utilitarian, focusing on the future 'good' of the wider community.

Communicative justifications do not objectify the offender, as do the other two approaches; instead, s/he is viewed as someone who must be held to account for the wrong that they have done and then positively reintegrated into their community. This requires a different orientation to the offender, one that sees her/him as a 'fellow traveller' (Ward and Rose, 2013, p 282) rather than an alien to be punished or assessed. Communicative justifications underpin restorative justice approaches to sex offenders (eg family group conferences, mediatory approaches and 'circles') (see Daly, 2002; McAlinden, 2013; Cowburn et al, 2015). A key element of seeing the sex offender as a morally equal member of society is to recognise her/ his human rights (Connolly and Ward, 2008). We explore this further in the final chapter.

Sentencing the sex offender

Until 2014, in England and Wales, sentencing guidance in relation to sex offences was piecemeal and partial. In 2011, Thomas (2011, p 91) noted:

> The principles of sentencing that we do have are based on the precedent of previous court judgements and especially those of the Court of Appeal. Since 1980, the Court of Appeal has periodically produced what are called 'guideline' judgements, which go beyond the confines of the immediate case to guide other courts coming across similar cases.

In 1986, the case of *Billam* (*R v Billam* (1986) 82 Cr App R. 347; cited in Thomas, 2011, p 91) produced a guideline judgement in relation to rape. Focusing on the details of the offence(s), it established five incremental tiers of seriousness that attracted a correspondingly punitive sentence. Issues associated with the offence that could affect the final judgement were known as 'aggravating' or 'mitigating' factors. Aggravating factors related to how the offence was carried out (eg planning, use of weapons, gratuitous violence) and the victim (eg the age of the victim and the impact of the offences). Mitigating factors could include an early plea of guilty. Following this guideline judgement, there were successive attempts to refine and develop them (see Thomas, 2011, pp 92–4). In 2010, the Sentencing Council was established in England and Wales with the specific remit of developing greater consistency in sentencing, and a major means of achieving this was through issuing sentencing guidelines.[1] In April 2014, the 'Sexual Offences: Definitive Guideline' (Sentencing Council, 2013a) and 'Sexual Offences: Note of Approach when Sentencing Offenders under 18' (Sentencing Council, 2013b) became effective. The latter document is strongly linked to the 'Definitive Guideline' and also to the 'Overarching Principles: Sentencing Youths: Definitive Guideline' (Sentencing Guidelines Council, 2009). Within the scope of this chapter, it is not possible to outline details in relation to every offence; we strongly advise readers to refer to the appropriate sentencing guidelines.

The 'Definitive Guideline' refers to all of the offences in the Sex Offences Act 2003, plus a few identified in other Acts of Parliament. Additionally, the 'Guideline' provides advice in relation to offences committed by offenders under 18 (this is advice rather than a guideline), as well as ancillary orders, automatic orders on conviction, historic offences, fine bands and community orders. The 'Guideline' offers a systematic, nine-step process whereby all sexual offences can be considered for sentencing (see Table 3.1).

Table 3.1: Nine-step process for sentencing sex offenders

Step One: Determining the offence category
Step Two: Starting point and category range
Aggravating Factors
Mitigating Factors
Step Three: Considering sentence reduction
Step Four: Guilty pleas
Step Five: Dangerousness
Step Six: Totality principle
Step Seven: Ancillary orders
Step Eight: Explaining the sentence
Step Nine: Time spent on bail

It is not appropriate here to explore the sentencing process in depth. We refer readers to Sentencing Council (2013, pp 37–40), where detailed guidance is available. However, we briefly summarise the main points in relation to each of these steps. It is important to note that the first two steps in the sentencing process significantly shape the direction in which sentencing will progress. *Determining the offence category* is concerned with the harm caused by the offence and is predicated primarily upon factors directly relating to the commission of the offence; three categories are identified and category 1 offences are viewed most seriously. The key issue in the second step is *culpability*. The following factors are taken into account:

- significant degree of planning;
- offender acts together with others to commit an offence;
- use of alcohol/drugs on victim to facilitate the offence;
- grooming behaviour used against victim;
- abuse of trust;
- previous violence against victim;
- offence committed in the course of a burglary;
- sexual images of victim recorded, retained, solicited or shared;
- deliberate isolation of victim;
- commercial exploitation and/or motivation;
- offence racially or religiously motivated;

- offence motivated by, or demonstrating, hostility to the victim based on his or her sexual orientation (or presumed sexual orientation) or transgender identity (or presumed transgender identity); and
- offence motivated by, or demonstrating, hostility to the victim based on his or her disability (or presumed disability).

Two categories of culpability are identified (A and B, with category A being considered the most serious). If any of the aforementioned factors are involved in the offending, then the offence is categorised A for culpability. The two elements of harm and culpability then shape the next step in the process, which is concerned with identifying the appropriate range of sentencing. The starting point for coming to a suitable sentence is achieved by relating the details of the offending to the culpability factors. However, this process merely identifies a starting point. In this step, consideration is also given to aggravating and mitigating factors that could lead to an increase or decrease from the starting point.

Some aggravating factors have a statutory basis and must be taken into account. These are if the offender has previous convictions (having regard to the nature of the offence to which the conviction relates and its relevance to the current offence, as well as the time that has elapsed since the conviction), and if the offence was committed while on bail. The presence of these factors immediately propels the offence into a more serious category. Other aggravating factors include: specific targeting of a particularly vulnerable child; blackmail or other threats made (where not taken into account at step one); location of offence; timing of offence; use of weapon or other item to frighten or injure; victim compelled to leave their home, school and so on; failure to comply with current court orders; offence committed while on licence; exploiting contact arrangements with a child to commit an offence; presence of others, especially other children; any steps taken to prevent the victim from reporting the incident, obtaining assistance and/or assisting or supporting the prosecution; attempts to dispose of or conceal evidence; commission of offence while under the influence of alcohol or drugs; and victim encouraged to recruit others.

Mitigating factors include: the offender having no previous convictions or no relevant/recent convictions; if the offender has shown remorse for their actions; their age and/or lack of maturity where it affects the responsibility of the offender; any mental disorder or learning disability, particularly where linked to the commission of the offence; and their previous good character and/or exemplary conduct. However, previous good character/exemplary conduct is different from having no previous convictions, but the more serious the offence, the less the weight is attributed to this factor. Where previous good character/exemplary conduct has been used to facilitate the offence, this mitigation should not normally be allowed and may, in fact, constitute an aggravating factor. In the context of a sexual offence against a child, previous good character/exemplary conduct should not normally be given any significant weight and will not normally justify a reduction in what would otherwise be the appropriate sentence.

Steps three and four address issues that may reduce the sentence identified at the end of step two. These factors include whether the guilty party has assisted the prosecution or pleaded guilty to the offences (which would reduce the necessity of the victim attending court and giving evidence).

Step five requires the court to consider whether an exceptional sentence is required because of the danger posed by the offender (in terms of section 226A [extended sentence for certain violent or sexual offences] of the Criminal Justice Act 2003). Step six (the totality principle) requires the court to take account of other sentences that the offenders may be serving and ensure that 'the total sentence is just and proportionate to the offending behaviour' (Sentencing Council, 2013, p 40).

The seventh step requires the court to consider whether any ancillary orders (such as compensation, confiscation, deprivation of property, disqualification from working with children, restraining order, serious crime prevention order and sexual offences prevention order) may be appropriate. The final two steps of the guideline are procedural – step eight ensures that the reasons for the specific sentence are explained to the offender, and the final step ensures that any time spent on bail is taken into consideration.

The practice-based learning exercise that follows allows you to reflect on this somewhat lengthy process in the light of a case study.

Reflective exercise: Reflection on the process of sentencing – a case study

Steven, a white 45-year-old man, has been found guilty after a four-day trial of 'sexual assault of a child under 13'. His victim was Kayley, the daughter of his partner (Jemma), with whom he lived. She gave evidence in court. At the time of the offences, Kayley was 11 years old. The offences occurred over a six-month period, on Thursday evenings. Steven gave his partner some money to spend at Bingo, he said that she needed some leisure time free from childcare responsibilities and he offered to take care of Kayley and her two younger sisters (Rhiannon, aged seven, and Lauren, aged five).

When Jemma left the house at 6.30pm to go to Bingo, Steven would advance the clocks in the house by 90 minutes. He would then urge the younger children to get ready for bed. When Rhiannon and Lauren were in bed and quiet, Steven would close the bedroom doors and watch television with Kayley. He would drink lager and also gave her alcohol mixed into fizzy drinks. He would sexualise the conversation pointing out how much older than 11 she looked. He then kissed her and touched both outside and inside her clothing on her breast area and between her legs. He stopped the offending 30 minutes before Jemma was due to return home. He warned Kayley that she must not tell her mother anything about what had happened because if she did, it would distress her mother and break up the family. He emphasised that such consequences would be totally due to her speaking out.

Task
Work through the steps of the sentencing guidelines to arrive at a sentence for Steven. Identify mitigating and aggravating factors.

The 'Sentencing Guidelines' provide specific advice for each sex offence. While most offences attract custodial sentences, the 'Guidelines' also point to the possibility of offenders being offered community sentences in some circumstances. The primary concern of these 'Guidelines' is to match the sentence with the harm caused to the victim and the culpability of the offender; generally, this means that many people convicted of a sexual offence will receive a custodial sentence. This does not mean, however, that all sentences are solely retributive in nature – what happens to a sex offender after s/he has been sentenced is complex and often comprises a mixture of measures across the punitive spectrum, which we now review in more detail.

Retributive responses

Punishment, as we noted earlier, is a means whereby the state expresses disapproval of the offence(s) and the offender. Retributive responses look back to the offence, and the severity of punishment is linked to the harm caused by the offending. Across the world, in various jurisdictions, capital punishment is available for some sex offenders (eg Iran [see International Federation for Human Rights, 2009] and India [see BBC News India, 2014]). In the US, various states have unsuccessfully attempted to implement the death sentence for various types of sex offender (Death Penalty Information Center, 2014). However, in England and Wales, the principal retributive sentence is imprisonment, which may also entail further restrictions on liberty after the offender is released from prison. It could also be argued that putting sex offenders' names on a register that is available for public inspection also carries with it some retributive component. However, we will review this more fully when considering consequentialist responses.

Between 2005 and 2011 in England and Wales, the most common sentence at Crown Court for convicted sex offenders was immediate custody, with 60% being so sentenced (Ministry of Justice, Home Office and Office for National Statistics, 2013, p 9). This pattern has not changed significantly; in 1995, 55% of convicted sex offenders received a custodial sentence, and in 2005, 60% received a prison sentence (Davidson, 2008, p 109). In very serious cases, offenders may be detained indefinitely (section 226A [extended sentence for certain violent or sexual offences] of the Criminal Justice Act 2003). While deprivation of liberty is intended to be the essence of punishment, there are often added hardships for the sex offender in prison. Craig Topping (2009), a prisoner writing in a UK prisoners' newspaper, describes what may lie in store for some sex offenders who are not located in protected settings:

> cells being ransacked; property being stolen or destroyed; police depositions being stapled to the walls of the wing; staff and prisoner bullying of the individual; urine being deposited in their bedding and hot-water flasks; and the worst incident yet – faeces being smeared in the suspect individual's face and mouth during an association period. So having witnessed all of this happening with my own eyes, I realise that to be a sex offender is not the easiest or happiest of situations.

However, many sex offenders are now accommodated in various protected settings within prison (eg Vulnerable Prisoner Units, or specific accommodation for Rule 45 prisoners). Prison Rule 45 allows prisoners to be segregated from other prisoners for their own safety. Within some prisons, Sex Offender Treatment Programmes (SOTPs) are available. We discuss these programmes more fully later in this chapter, but for present purposes, we note that although these programmes are available for male offenders, there is a long waiting list for a place on a programme, most sex offenders are not able to complete a programme and the number of programmes is reducing (Comptroller and Auditor General, 2013), and there are currently no groupwork programmes for women.

Consequentialist responses

While retributive approaches to sentencing look back to the offence, consequentialist approaches look to the future with a view to preventing further offending. This is done through: (1) therapeutic correctional programmes in prison and in the community; (2) statutory (licence) supervision; (3) surveillance and public notification; and (4) Multi-Agency

Public Protection Arrangements (MAPPA). In each case, the initiatives are motivated by a desire to anticipate future risks and change behaviour, thereby reducing risk and helping to make communities safer. We review each approach in turn but recognise that these approaches are not delivered in isolation, but often coincide and complement each other.

Therapeutic correctional programmes in prison and in the community

Therapeutic programmes for sex offenders in the community and in prisons have been delivered in the UK since the late 1970s, although it was not until the 1990s that programmes became standardised. The programmes are predominantly cognitive-behavioural and delivered through groupwork. They are almost exclusively delivered to adult male offenders; however, programmes delivered to young male offenders address more developmental issues than the adult programmes. In England and Wales during the mid-1990s, two small 'expert' panels were established within the Prison Service to 'accredit' the content and means of delivery of groupwork programmes for prisoners. In 1999, these panels became the Joint Prison/ Probation Services Accreditation Panel (later known as the Correctional Services Accreditation Panel [CSAP] within the Ministry of Justice). For many years, accredited programmes for sex offenders in prisons and in the community shared similar aims and a very similar curriculum, focusing on offender responsibility, victim empathy and relapse prevention (Beech and Fisher, 2004). The programmes were underpinned by the 'risk, need, responsivity' (RNR) model developed by Bonta, Andrews and colleagues (eg Andrews et al, 1990a, 1990b, 2011; see also Chapter Six). The approach is based on addressing factors associated with reoffending identified through using statistical analytical techniques. Both personal history and current circumstances were considered relevant to reoffending. The main focus of these programmes was to help offenders recognise the risks that they posed and to find ways of reducing these risks. Evaluations of these programmes indicated that they were, to some extent, effective (Ministry of Justice: National Offender Management Service, 2010).

However, the RNR approach has come under criticism for its preoccupation with risk and risk management as a vehicle for offender rehabilitation (Ward et al, 2012). Attention has shifted to considering what an offender needs to live a 'good life'; central to this consideration is the notion of *desistance*, which was discussed in Chapter Two. From an interest in desistance, the 'Good Lives Model' (GLM) has developed, a positively focused therapeutic programme that is used with many groups of offenders, including sex offenders (see Chapter Six). The model includes risk assessment and risk management but seeks to provide a wider, more holistic, therapeutic response to the sex offender informed by prudential values that have at their heart recognition that people have an intrinsic equality and that social relations are fundamentally important to developing a positive way of life (Connolly and Ward, 2008; see also pp 111–12 below).

These two dominant psychological approaches to working with sex offenders in the West (for RNR, see Andrews et al, 2011; for GLM, see Ward et al, 2012) are both underpinned by a multi-factorial theory of sexual offending and offer evidence in relation to the effectiveness of their interventions. Both models recognise the importance of assessing risk, and link therapeutic programmes to identified areas of risk. The two approaches, however, are not irreconcilable; the recent revision in the provision of accredited groupwork for sex offenders clearly shows the influence of both approaches. Moreover, these revisions also show an awareness that one therapeutic programme does not 'fit' all types of offenders. Table 3.2 summarises the groupwork programmes currently available for sex offenders in England and Wales. Such innovative developments, taking into account recent research, are to be applauded.

However, in concluding this section, it is important to note the issue that we raised in the introduction to this book: black and minority ethnic (BME) sex offenders are under-represented in these groupwork programmes (Cowburn et al, 2008). The reasons for this non-involvement are complex and may involve programme content, programme process and community and cultural issues (see Cowburn et al, 2015).

Statutory (licence) supervision

Statutory supervision of sex offenders in the community can occur either as part of a community sentence or on a supervision licence following a prison sentence. Both forms reflect a hybrid punitive orientation. Both forms of supervision are subject to frequent amendment and change; we are therefore not providing a detailed account of how these operate at the moment.

Originally, the community-based order, in its form as the 'probation order', required probation officers 'to advise, assist and befriend' offenders placed on probation – there was clearly little or no retributive element in this order. However, the later 20th and early 21st centuries saw a radical transformation in the community-based order (Mair, 2011). The community order (and the suspended sentence order) introduced in the Criminal Justice Act 2003 and implemented in 2005 were both 'intended to provide a more punitive sentence' and were seen as direct alternatives to a custodial sentence (Mair, 2011, p 228); both orders could contain 12 possible requirements,

Table 3.2: Ministry of Justice groupwork programmes currently available for sex offenders in England and Wales

SOTPs (Sex Offender Treatment Programmes) – A range of programmes are available for sexual offenders, providing a menu that is offered according to the level of risk and need of the offender.

C-SOGP (Community Sex Offenders Group Programme) – Helps offenders develop understanding of how and why they have committed sexual offences. The programme also increases awareness of victim harm. The main focus is to help the offender develop meaningful life goals and practice new thinking and behavioural skills that will lead him away from offending.

NSOGP (Northumbria Sex Offenders Group Programme) – Helps offenders develop understanding of how and why they have committed sexual offences. The programme also increases awareness of victim harm. The main focus is to help the offender develop meaningful life goals and practice new thinking and behavioural skills that will lead him away from offending.

NSOGP Community Better Lives (RP) BL and RP (Community) – A sex offender treatment programme that follows on from 'core' programmes such as NSOGP or SOTP. Its aim is to reinforce and consolidate core learning and to develop and practice skills essential in assisting men to formulate appropriate relapse prevention strategies.

TVSOGP (Thames Valley Sex Offenders Group Programme) – Helps offenders develop understanding of how and why they have committed sexual offences. The programme also increases awareness of victim harm. The main focus is to help the offender develop meaningful life goals and practice new thinking and behavioural skills that will lead him away from offending.

I-SOTP (Internet Sex Offender Treatment Programme) – A programme designed to explore and address the thoughts, feelings and beliefs underpinning the group members' internet sex offending. The aim is to reduce the risk of further similar offending and, like other sex offender programmes, increase the offenders' understanding of the impact of their offending on others, including their victims.

ASOTP-CV (Adapted Sex Offender Treatment Programme – Community Version) – Adapted community sex offender programme similar to SOTP but adapted for those who have social or learning difficulties. It is designed to increase sexual knowledge, modify offence-justifying thinking, develop the ability to recognise feelings in themselves and others, gain an understanding of victim harm, and develop relapse prevention skills.

SOTP Core (Sex Offenders Treatment Programme) – Core helps offenders develop understanding of how and why they have committed sexual offences. The programme also increases awareness of victim harm. The main focus is to help the offender develop meaningful life goals and practice new thinking and behavioural skills that will lead him away from offending.

SOTP BNM (Sex Offenders Treatment Programme Becoming New Me) – Covers similar areas to SOTP Core but adapted for those who have social or learning difficulties. It is designed to increase sexual knowledge, modify offence-justifying thinking, develop the ability to recognise feelings in themselves and others, gain an understanding of victim harm, and develop relapse prevention skills.

SOTP BLB (Sex Offenders Treatment Programme Better Lives Booster) – Designed to boost sexual offenders' learning from other SOTPs and provide additional opportunities to practice personally relevant skills. It can be run in two forms: a low-intensity (one session a week) programme helps to maintain change in long-term prisoners; and the high intensity, pre-release programme is particularly focused on preparation for transition into the community.

SOTP ABLB (Sex Offenders Treatment Programme Adapted Better Lives Booster) – Aimed at those who have completed the Adapted SOTP. Shares the same aims as the Core version but the treatment delivery methods are different to accommodate different learning styles and abilities. A low-intensity version is for long-term prisoners and a high-intensity version is for those who are in the last year of their sentence, preparing them for release.

SOTP Extended (Sex Offenders Treatment Programme Extended) – Extended is targeted at high- and very high-risk men who have successfully met the treatment targets of the Core programme. The programme covers four areas: recognising and modifying patterns of dysfunctional thinking; emotional regulation; intimacy skills; and relapse prevention.

SOTP HSF (Sex Offenders Treatment Programme Healthy Sexual Functioning) – Aims to promote healthy sexual functioning, mainly in high-risk sexual offenders who acknowledge current or very recent offence-related sexual interests. Modules include developing a more healthy sexuality, patterns in sexual arousal, behavioural strategies for promoting healthy sexual interest and relapse prevention.

SOTP Rolling (Sex Offenders Treatment Programme Rolling) – Rolling provides a less intensive level of treatment, with more emphasis on relationships skills and attachment style deficits. The group rolls continuously with members joining and leaving as it rolls along, so members will therefore be at different stages of treatment depending on when they joined the group.

Source: https://www.justice.gov.uk/offenders/before-after-release/obp

including supervision (up to 36 months), attendance at an accredited programme and curfews (for a full account, see Mair, 2011). Failure to comply with the requirements of either order could result in the offender being imprisoned. These orders are supervised by probation officers.

Post-custodial licences are statutory supervision also by probation officers, following a period of imprisonment. They have both a punitive element – the ex-prisoner is required to continue to report to a probation officer at regular intervals, informing her/him of any changes (eg address and employment) in their circumstances – and a rehabilitative/consequentialist element. The recent National Offender Management Service (NOMS) instruction indicates that the licence clearly has consequentialist objectives:

> The aims of the licence period are to protect the public, to prevent re-offending and to secure the successful re-integration of the offender into the community. *Licence conditions must be preventative as opposed to punitive and must be proportionate, reasonable and necessary.* (NOMS, 2014, para 1.3, emphasis in original)

The Prison Reform Trust (2013) has produced generic information 'for people on licence for a sex offence' that provides clear information on various post-custodial licences. Licences require offenders: to keep in touch with their supervising officer; to receive home visits from their supervising officer; to live permanently at an address approved by their supervising officer; to only work as approved by their supervising officer; to not travel outside the UK; and to be of good behaviour. Additionally, licences may contain extra conditions: specific restrictions on activities; restrictions on using the internet; restrictions on using mobile phones and cameras; requirements to take part in a sex offender programme; not to contact their victim, or anyone under 18; not be permitted to stay in a house with anyone under 18; not to enter or be within sight of places where there are children, such as schools or children's play areas; to inform their supervisor if they start a new relationship with a person who lives with someone under 18; not to associate with known sex offenders (except if they are resident at the same hostel); to stay at home within certain hours (curfew); to report to a police station as directed; not to go to a certain place or enter a certain area (an 'exclusion zone'); to give details of any car they use to the police; and to attend appointments with a psychiatrist or mental health worker (this can only be used with the offender's and service's consent and agreement) (Prison Reform Trust, 2013).

In January 2014, a condition of 'polygraph testing' was added to the list of possible licence conditions (Prison Reform Trust, 2013; NOMS, 2014). It became operational in October 2014 and will only be used with approximately 1,000 of the 'most serious' sex offenders (Ministry of Justice,

2014). The justification for introducing this addition to licence conditions is twofold. The Attorney General, the Right Honourable Jeremy Wright MP, states in the Ministry of Justice (2014) press release: 'We are determined that the UK has one of the toughest regimes in the world for managing sex offenders, to stop reoffending and to protect victims'.

Here, the emphasis is on 'toughness'. The evidence, however, in relation to the accuracy of polygraph testing is, at best, ambivalent (Wilcox, 2013). A Ministry of Justice-commissioned study (Gannon et al, 2012, p ii) found that offenders who were subject to polygraph testing 'made more CSDs [clinically significant disclosures] than those in the comparison group. The majority of these CSDs were made within a polygraph session and related to "changes in circumstance or risk".' It would therefore appear that the accuracy of the technology becomes less relevant if people admit more CSDs through the use of this procedure.

Statutory licence supervision is primarily a means of monitoring sex offenders in the community. It requires offenders to provide detailed information about where they live, socialise and work. More serious offenders may also be required to undergo regular polygraph testing. Licences also contain conditions that require offenders to attend therapeutic programmes to change their behaviour. Such severe constraints on a person's liberty raise questions about human rights – do these constraints contravene an individual's right to a private and family life? We return to this issue in the final chapter of the book; at this point, it is noteworthy that although these requirements are clearly consequentialist in their focus, the constraints that they can potentially impose on an individual may also be understood as retributive. This perspective is supported when consideration is given to surveillance of the sex offender following the conclusion of statutory supervision. For most sex offenders, surveillance in the community does not finish when their statutory licences come to an end. The 'sex offender register' and public notification schemes continue to monitor most sex offenders beyond the termination of statutory supervision.

Surveillance and public notification

'Sex offender registers' are, in policy terms, construed as a key part of an ongoing community safety strategy (Thomas, 2004). Yet, as Thomas (2008) indicates, legally, there is no such thing as the 'register', although it has entered common parlance as a key feature of governmental community safety strategy. The Sex Offenders Act 1997 and the Sexual Offences Act 2003 in England and Wales, which introduced and developed the relevant legislation, refer to the requirements for those convicted of sexual offences to notify the police of their address and place of employment. Two elements are relevant to the present discussion: (1) the registration process; and (2) public notification of registered sex offenders.

The registration process

The Sex Offences Act specifies specific periods of 'registration' according to the sentence given to the offender; Table 3.3 identifies the registration periods according to sentence.

The sex offender, following sentence (and, where appropriate, release from prison) is required to 'notify' the police of details of their domestic and employment situation (see Table 3.4).

Additionally, offenders are required to notify the police in person of any subsequent changes in their circumstances within three days (including any fresh offence). Offenders also have to report annually to a police station to review their circumstances, and to receive (notified and unannounced) visits from the police at their accommodation. Offenders without fixed accommodation are required to report to the police weekly. Should a registered sex offender wish to travel abroad, the full details must also be notified to the police three days before travel. Failure to comply with the

Table 3.3: Period of notification orders (sex offender register)

Description of relevant court disposal	Notification period
Person sentenced for a term of more than 30 months' imprisonment (including life imprisonment)	An indefinite period beginning with the relevant date (subject to review after 15 years)[a]
Person detained under Mental Health Act restriction orders	An indefinite period beginning with that date
Person sentenced to more than six months but less than 30 months	10 years beginning with that date
Person sentenced to imprisonment of six months or less	Seven years beginning with that date
Person admitted to hospital but no restriction order	Seven years beginning with that date
Person subject to a caution	Two years beginning with that dates
Person subject to conditional discharge	Period of the discharge
Person of any other description	Five years beginning with the relevant date

Note: [a] This period was originally intended to be indefinite but following a European Court ruling that considered the incompatibility of this requirement with article 8 of the Human Rights Act 1988, the review process was instituted: *R (on the application of F) v Secretary of State for Justice* [2010] UKSC 17). See: http://www.justice.gov.uk/downloads/publications/policy/moj/responding-human-rights-judgments.pdf

Table 3.4: Sex offender notification requirements

Notify police within 48 hours of the relevant date of discharge from custody/court:
Date of birth
National insurance number
Name on relevant date (other names if used)
Home address on relevant date
Name on the date on which notification is given (other names if used)
Home address on the date on which notification is given
The address of other premises in UK in which he regularly resides
If they are living at an address where a child (under 18) resides
Passport details
Bank account details
Credit card details
Additionally, offenders will be photographed and fingerprinted

notification requirements is a criminal offence and can result in up to five years' imprisonment (also see Lines, 2013). Young offenders have shorter periods of notification.

The evidence in relation to the effectiveness of 'registers' as a part of a community safety strategy is not strong. In the UK, there is evidence of a high rate of compliance (from convicted sex offenders) with the terms of notification (of address and employment), but in relation to their part in making the community safer, Thomas (2008, p 229) quotes a Home Office study (Plotnikoff and Woolfson, 2000) which notes that there is no simple way of evaluating this. In a review of the operation of 'registers' in the US, Meloy, Saleh and Wolff (2007, p 438) more openly question the value of these strategies, noting that they misrepresent risk because most sex offences are never reported to law enforcement agencies. Thus, while sex offender registration may be popular with politicians (Thomas, 2008, p 229), it is very doubtful if it contributes anything towards a wider strategy addressing community safety in relation to sexual harm.

Public notification of registered sex offenders

While the registration of sex offenders in the UK began in 1997, it was only in the mid-2000s that public notification of registered sex offenders' whereabouts became a possibility. Campaigns in the US and in the UK following the rape and murder of children by previously convicted sex offenders preceded the introduction of 'disclosure' schemes in both countries (for a full account and analysis, see Blacker and Griffin, 2010) – 'Megan's

Law' in the US and 'Sarah's Law' in England, Wales and Scotland were the popular names for the respective notification schemes. The scheme in the US is far more extensive than in England, Wales and Scotland, and in some states, it allows for the publication of the names, addresses and photographs of offenders. In England, Wales and Scotland, the scheme for allowing members of the public to inquire about the possible presence of convicted sex offenders in their locality was piloted in four areas in 2008. The results indicated that: fewer inquiries than expected were made; applicants were generally satisfied with the scheme, although it did leave some unresolved anxieties; professionals involved in managing sex offenders pointed to possible areas of duplication; and registered sex offenders expressed anxieties about the possibilities of vigilante action, although these lessened as the scheme continued (Kemshall et al, 2010). In October 2010, the scheme was introduced in all of the 43 police areas in England and Wales. In relation to how much use is made of it, BBC News UK (2013) notes:

> Some 4,754 applications [through the notification scheme] have been made since the system was introduced two-and-a-half years ago but the number is falling. There were 1,944 in 2011–12 and 1,106 so far in 2013–14, while disclosures were 281 in the first year and 122 in current year to April.

Generally, the fears that the scheme would precipitate violent reactions against people convicted of sexual assaults have not been substantiated. Yet, the potential for violence remains; Richard Garside (2013) of the Centre for Crime and Justice Studies has pointed to:

> The appalling case of Bijam Ebrahimi, a disabled Iranian national subjected to a sustained campaign of victimisation and attacks by his neighbours, [as] a salutary lesson in what can happen when fear and loathing is stirred up. Wrongly branded a paedophile, Bijam Ebrahimi was killed earlier this year.

The notification scheme is available, but whether it is merely a facet of populist penal policies or an effective element in public protection remains to be seen. Richard Garside (2013) is clear in his criticism of the scheme and why relatively few have used it:

> worried parents, alongside individuals with possibly more base motives, are offered the chance to get the lowdown on a disliked neighbour, a weird relative, a new partner of an ex-partner or just someone who seems a bit odd. That so few have taken up this opportunity suggests that the British public are more thoughtful

and intelligent than policy makers and tabloid newspapers often tend to treat them.

Multi-Agency Public Protection Arrangements

Although the Sex Offenders Act 1997 required police and probation to work together in assessing the risk posed by registered sex offenders, it did not specify how this collaboration was to occur. Thus, prior to 2001, there was great variety in how local areas structured the inter-agency work, as well as in the quality of that work (Maguire and Kemshall, 2004). Under the terms of the Criminal Justice and Courts Services Act 2000, the Home Office was given power to standardise local arrangements and to improve the quality of the work. In March 2001, it produced clear guidance for the local police and probation areas in relation to MAPPA (Home Office, 2001).

MAPPA are concerned with identifying and managing the risk possibly posed by convicted sex offenders. It is concerned with looking to the future and managing known offenders. MAPPA meetings are likely to involve social workers and are one example of interdisciplinary practice, which will be explored further in Chapter Four.

This concludes our consideration of penal responses influenced by a consequentialist punitive perspective. We now turn attention to an approach that, in many ways, blends both consequentialist and retributivist approaches.

Communicative responses: the challenge of restorative justice

Retributive and consequentialist approaches to punishing sex offenders underpin the majority of penal responses to sex offenders. A characteristic of both approaches is that there is little active involvement of the victim in the processes of justice. Communicative responses, as the name suggests, encourage communication, particularly between victims and offenders. As we have seen, victim harm is a factor in determining the sentence that the offender is given. In the UK, since 10 December 2013, victims have been able to make a statement, which can be read aloud, to the court concerning how the offence has affected them. The 'Victim Personal Statement' can be part of a witness statement or a stand-alone document. This procedure begins to assert a victim presence in the court proceedings. Restorative justice approaches take this further. The UK Ministry of Justice (2012, p 3) has noted:

Restorative justice (RJ) provides opportunities for victims to be heard and to have a say in the resolution of offences. It has the potential to transform the way in which the needs of the victim are met. Importantly, restorative justice also enables offenders to face the consequences of their actions and the impact that it has had upon others. This has been shown to be effective in motivating offenders to change, make use of support being offered, and stop offending.

Restorative justice is used in addition to a criminal justice system penalty or sentence. It can involve victims:

- explaining to an offender the impact of the crime on them;
- seeking an explanation and apology from the offender; and
- playing a part in agreeing restorative or reparative activity for the offender, for example, working for free for a charity, paying to repair any material damage or keeping the victim informed of their progress in getting off drugs or finding a job.

The matter of victims of sex offences meeting with the person who has harmed them is a very sensitive issue. Throughout any restorative process, it is the victim's wishes that are the guiding force. Thus, if the victim does not wish to have any contact with the person who hurt them, then restorative approaches are not considered. However, restorative approaches currently used with sex offenders include family conferences (these are regularly used in Australia and New Zealand with young sex offenders), mediation and 'circles' (McAlinden, 2013, p 117). Mediation is less commonly used with sex offenders, largely because of concerns that mediators unaware of the power dynamics involved in sex offending may unwittingly support the same dynamics during mediation, and leave the power of male abusers unchallenged (McGlynn et al, 2012). In relation to family group conferences, Daly (2002) describes how the intervention moves through a retributive phase, where offenders are held to account for what they have done and their crimes are identified as morally wrong, to a restorative/reparative phase that requires the offender to make amends for what they have done to their victim(s); the final phase of the programme focuses on rehabilitation (Daly 2002, pp 69–70). Case-study research points to the benefits for victims of well-managed conferences; one rape survivor in the McGlynn study (McGlynn et al, 2012, p 228) outlined the positive aspects of the process as follows:

it's made me understand my position as a victim and see him as the offender, which has enabled me to resolve a lot of conflict … in retrospect ... it was more important to have my say and have him listen than for him to go to prison.

The authors conclude (McGlynn et al, 2012, p 240) that:

Restorative justice in cases of sexual violence does demand greater scrutiny and expertise, greater preparation and risk assessment, and therefore greater resources. But excluding victim-survivors of sexual violence from the opportunity to address their offender, tell of their harm and see some form of justice, for those who request it, cannot be justified.

Circles of Support and Accountability (CoSA) are the principal restorative justice response to sex offenders in the UK. CoSA originate in Canada, when a pastor from a Mennonite church set up a community-based circle of church members to support and monitor a serious sex offender who was to be discharged from prison after serving a long sentence. The church group remained in contact with the ex-offender for many years and he did not reoffend. This initiative spread across Canada, and in 2000, it crossed the Atlantic and became established in the UK. The key difference in the UK scheme was that criminal justice agencies were statutorily involved with the circle – this was not the case in the Canadian model. We discuss this approach more fully in Chapter Six.

Restorative justice responses to sex offenders do not pathologise the offender, but seek to find ways of reintegrating him/her into the wider community. Key to this reintegration is the offender accepting responsibility for his/her offences and recognising the harm that has been done to the victim. While the relevance of these elements is being questioned in relation to offending behaviour programmes, they remain of central importance in wider responses to the sex offender's reintegration into the community.

Civil law

The focus of the discussion so far has been on criminal law responses to sex crimes. Civil court responses to sex crimes are generally used to: (1) prevent the possibilities of an offence occurring, where there is insufficient evidence to secure a criminal conviction; and (2) offer reparation to victims, again where there is insufficient evidence to secure a criminal conviction, but where the balance of probabilities points to the likelihood of both an identified perpetrator, named victims and evidenced harm. These are both very complex areas and we only outline key issues here (for further information, see the sources that we cite).

Civil orders to prevent offending

In the UK, the following legislation offers possible ways to prevent future offences from occurring where there is an identified potential perpetrator:

- Notification order (Sexual Offences Act 2003, ss 97–101).
- Risk of sexual harm order (Sexual Offences Act 2003, ss 123–129).
- Sexual offences prevention order (Sexual Offences Act 2003, ss 104, 106, 107, 108, 110 and 113).
- Foreign travel order (Sexual Offences Act 2003, ss 114–122).
- Violent offender order (Criminal Justice and Immigration Act 2008, ch 4, part 8).

However, these orders have been criticised in relation to how they may affect an individual's civil liberties and human rights. Thomas and Thompson (2013) comment:

> The criticism of these orders is that the police are just being given an easy way of dealing with people in the civil courts that avoids the extra work of having to bring them to a criminal court. These people will go on the sex offender register without having committed a crime. If they breach the order we will have people being punished for that rather than for committing any substantive crime.

Additionally, in the UK, the city of Birmingham has also used court injunctions to deter named individuals from contacting named and unnamed girls (Rozenberg, 2014).

Where there are specific medical (psychiatric) indications, a person may be detained under mental health legislation. Jackson and Covell (2013) note that such legislation 'place[s] two fundamental values in opposition (personal liberty versus public safety)'. The use of medical diagnostic criteria, originally and primarily designed to improve individual health, as decision-making factors focused on 'public safety' is, it is argued by some, a misuse of medical science and, as such, unethical (for a fuller discussion of these issues, see Jackson and Covell, 2013; see also p 38 above).

Civil court action to offer reparation to victims

This is an area that is growing rapidly, largely in response to cases of historical abuse by members of the clergy and other people employed in positions of trust (eg school teachers). It is a complex area of law (for a recent review, see Chamallas, 2013) that we are not competent to discuss; however, an important issue is that victim–survivors are finding other powerful ways of having their experiences recognised and perpetrators (in some cases, vicariously) punished.

Summary

- This chapter considered penal responses to sex crimes and sex offenders.
- It has used reviewed and used theoretical justifications for punishment as a way to structure and understand the various penal responses.
- The three justifications that we have used are retributivism, consequentialism and communicative-based responses.
- Penal responses inevitably both look back to the offence and look forward to trying to reduce the risk that known offenders will cause further harms. While retributivism and consequentialism are very important elements in responding to sex offenders, as concepts, they do not consider in any detail how and where the offender will live after the custodial part of the sentence is completed.
- Communicative-based approaches (restorative justice) directly address this problem.
- Civil law responses to sex offenders offer a different avenue to deal with some sex crimes.

Note

[1] See: http://sentencingcouncil.judiciary.gov.uk/sentencing-guidelines.htm

4

Working together: policy into practice

Introduction

In this chapter, we look at systems and processes designed to manage sexual offenders and sexual offending, with a particular focus on interprofessional working, drawing on research and investigations into sexual abuse. The organisational context of safeguarding people from sexual abuse is important in providing the framework within which various agencies can make sound, informed decisions and take appropriate actions. Social workers are located within these systems and practise in spaces where the criminal law may not be adequate to protect people. We look at current structures and how these function, including the Multi-Agency Public Protection Arrangements (MAPPA), and consider what recent reports into child sexual exploitation (CSE) tell us about what needs to be done differently to avoid failing the victims of sexual abuse. Although we specifically address issues relating to England and Wales, the nature of interprofessional collaboration in this area is an international problem and we hope that our perspectives will contribute to international debate and policy development.

Safeguarding

The term 'safeguarding' has become commonplace in the UK to describe the ways in which we protect people from abuse, harm and neglect, including sexual harm. It is usually focused on those groups that are deemed vulnerable, such as children, young people and those adults who are perhaps more open to discrimination and exploitation through their physical, mental or intellectual impairments. Individual and structural prejudices based on age, disability and health underpin the construction of such vulnerability, and these are complicated by other factors such as gender, race/ethnicity, sexuality and class. Social work has played a significant role in developing and implementing safeguarding policies and practices to protect people from sexual abuse.

Safeguarding adults

The Care Act 2014 (CA 2014) (ss 42–46) replaces previous legislation and guidance and creates a framework for the safeguarding of adults in England, coming into effect in April 2015.[1] It applies to any adult who has need for care and support, is experiencing (or at risk of) abuse or neglect, and as a result of their care and support needs, is unable to protect themselves (Department of Health, 2014). This has clear implications for responding to sexual offending. The prime agency with responsibility for implementation is the local authority and it must cooperate with other relevant partners (CA 2014, s 6(7)), such as NHS England, Clinical Commissioning Groups (CCGs), NHS Trusts and NHS Foundation Trusts, the Department for Work and Pensions, and the police, prisons and probation services, and these other agencies have a duty to reciprocate. In addition to these, any other health or social care organisations can be requested to cooperate where appropriate with the aim of creating a multi-agency partnership that leads adult safeguarding. Services are coordinated through a Safeguarding Adults Board (SAB), which has to be established in every local authority area, and the SAB has responsibility for developing and reviewing policies and procedures, although accountability for the creation and maintenance of the partnership lies with the local authority, usually designated to the Director of Adult Services. Social workers have a key role in these processes, which is acknowledged by the Department of Health (2014, p 246) guidance:

> It is likely that many enquiries will require the input and supervision of a social worker, particularly the more complex situations and to support the adult to realise the outcomes they want and to reach a resolution or recovery. For example, where abuse or neglect is suspected within a family or informal relationship it is likely that a social worker will be the most appropriate lead.

The following principles underpin adult safeguarding work and will be recognisable to social workers through their value base (Department of Health, 2014, p 232):

- Empowerment: People being supported and encouraged to make their own decisions and informed consent.
- Prevention: It is better to take action before harm occurs.
- Proportionality: The least intrusive response appropriate to the risk presented.
- Protection: Support and representation for those in greatest need.

■ Partnership: Local solutions through services working with their communities. Communities have a part to play in preventing, detecting and reporting neglect and abuse.

■ Accountability: Accountability and transparency in delivering safeguarding.

Local authorities must investigate where there is reason to suspect that an individual is being abused or neglected, or is at risk of this (CA 2014, s 42), and although the local authority takes the lead in this, it may be useful to involve the police where criminal activity is suspected. There are difficulties with the criminal law where victims are vulnerable due to their mental capacity as they may not be deemed competent or reliable witnesses. Recognising this, there are safeguards to support people in this situation through the Vulnerable Adult and Intimidated Witness provisions in sections 16 and 17 of the Youth Justice and Criminal Evidence Act 1999 (YJCEA 1999). Victims who have a mental disorder or a learning or physical disability can be supported to give evidence in court through, for example, video links and the use of a trained and accredited intermediary to assist in understanding questions. The CA 2014 also states that the local authority must provide an independent advocate to assist the victim if they have substantial difficulty in understanding the process and if it would help them. However, this support may not be adequate for the Crown Prosecution Service to believe that someone with learning difficulties who has been subjected to a sexual offence can make a credible witness in any trial. Each case is assessed and if it is felt that the victim is unlikely to withstand examination, then a prosecution may not be taken forward. This places victims in an extremely vulnerable position and demonstrates some of the limitations of the criminal justice process.

Similarly, people with learning disabilities accused of sex offences are also vulnerable in the criminal justice system. This has been recognised in reports such as Bradley (2009) and Criminal Justice Joint Inspection (CJJI) (CJJI, 2014), where the need for specialist support was highlighted. The Police and Criminal Evidence Act 1984 (PACE 1984) created the supporting role of Appropriate Adult (AA) for vulnerable people in police custody, recognising that some people (including those with learning disabilities) may be frightened, confused or unclear about the process, leading to possible miscarriages of justice. The CJJI found that an AA was not being routinely called for adults with learning disabilities even when they had been identified as being vulnerable, and also that AA understanding of learning disabilities needed to be improved. Provision for trained and accredited intermediaries for defendants was introduced in section 104 of the Coroners and Justice Act 2009, but this has not been implemented and such support is not routinely available. The CJJI (2014) was concerned that the lack of this provision could create unnecessary delays and increase the chances of a Mental Health Act finding of unfit to plead, which could have serious consequences for the liberty of the offender. Social workers often take on the AA role and work in court liaison, diversion and support services, and so need to be clear about criminal justice structures and the needs of people with learning disabilities.

Making a safeguarding enquiry

Concerns about the safety of people can come from a variety of sources – the general public, family members or concerned professionals – and can be raised with any agency that has social responsibilities. All such agencies have safeguarding protocols that require concerns to be shared. Social workers are likely to lead safeguarding enquiries into sexual abuse and need to be clear about the purpose and scope of this activity. The enquiry is to: establish facts; ascertain the adult's views and wishes; assess the needs of the adult for protection, support and redress and how they might be met; protect the adult from the abuse and neglect, in accordance with their wishes; make decisions as to what follow-up action should be taken with regard to the person or organisation responsible for the abuse or neglect; and enable the adult to achieve resolution and recovery (Department of Health, 2014, p 253). Each SAB agency has a Designated Adult Safeguarding Manager (DASM), who can provide advice and guidance, as well as take responsibility for more complex cases. DASMs also ensure that recording systems are in place so that decision-making is clear and understood by all relevant parties.

The legal framework for protecting people is complicated, and SABs have a role in clarifying the national context and how this may apply locally, including distributing clear guidance. For example, the Mental Capacity Act 2005 (MCA 2005) presumes that people have the capacity to make decisions even when these may place them at risk, perhaps of sexual abuse, and great caution needs to be taken when deciding if it is in someone's best interests to deny them this choice. Assisting people to recognise and manage risk should be part of the social work task, and this may be a process rather than an event. It may take some time to discuss with people the issues involved and for them to make a more fully informed decision; until then, they may need to be safeguarded from serious harm through an approach of harm reduction. These judgements are very complex and require skill and support (Fulton and Richardson, 2014), and workers need to be familiar with the Deprivation of Liberty Safeguards within the Mental Health Act 2007.[2]

Reflective exercise: Case from Department for Health (2014, p 241)

Miss Y is a 24-year-old woman with a learning disability and limited support from her family who was not engaged with health and social care services. Miss Y was befriended by an individual who took her to parties where she was given drugs and alcohol and forced to have sex with different men. Sometimes, she would be given money or gifts in return for having sex with the men. Miss Y disclosed this to a social worker and it was discovered that there were a number of young people and vulnerable adults who were being sexually exploited by multiple perpetrators. Miss Y lacked mental capacity in order to be able to consent to having sex, as well as in relation to her accommodation, finances or personal safety. The perpetrators sought out Miss Y and others because of their vulnerability – whether that was because of their age, disability, mental illness or their previous history as a victim of abuse.

- What steps can be taken to protect Miss Y and others from further abuse?
- How would you go about achieving this?
- What legal measures could be taken?
- If Miss Y expressed a wish for the situation to continue, how would this affect your intervention?
- Consider how issues of ethnicity might affect this case scenario: what ethnicity did you assume for Miss Y? What ethnicity did you assume for the perpetrators? How might different ethnic backgrounds impact on understanding and responding to this situation, including those of the social worker?

The local authority retains responsibility for managing the assessment, implementation and review of any plans required to safeguard the person, and it is likely (but not compulsory – it depends on the circumstances as to who is best placed to deliver this) that social workers will be delivering this service. The planning needs to include the person and other concerned agencies and carers (where appropriate) and plans need to be focused on the safety and best interests of the person. Actions need to be clear and measurable, with allocation of responsibility to individuals and agencies. In making recommendations, the social worker needs to consider the range of civil and criminal justice responses relevant to the situation and other interventions that might help to promote the well-being of the person, including therapeutic or family work, mediation, and victim support.

Information sharing is important for an effective multi-agency response, and the adult safeguarding process follows the Caldicott (2013) principles[3] of: justify the purpose(s); do not use personal confidential data unless it is absolutely necessary; use the minimum necessary personal confidential data; access to personal confidential data should be on a strict need-to-know basis; everyone with access to personal confidential data should be aware of their responsibilities; comply with the law; and the duty to share information can be as important as the duty to protect patient confidentiality. Absolute confidentiality cannot be maintained where there is a risk of harm to others, and it may be necessary to go against the wishes of the person to prevent (further) abuse.

Safeguarding children and young people

The notion of 'safeguarding' children and young people (under 18) has developed from the changes brought in by the Children Act 2004 (CA 2004), where it was felt that there was a need to broaden out from a narrow perspective on 'child protection' to enabling children to be supported in their well-being and general personal and social achievement. Safeguarding and promoting the welfare of children is now the preferred phraseology, and this is defined as: 'protecting children from maltreatment; preventing impairment of children's health or development; ensuring that children grow up in circumstances consistent with the provision of safe and effective care; and taking action to enable all children to have the best outcomes' (Department of Education, 2015, p 5). The protection of children is located within this framework.

Local authorities have lead responsibility for safeguarding children, but it is recognised that everyone, professional and public alike, has a part to play in this and that all agencies need to work together to meet the needs and understand the views of children. Enquiries into the deaths of children have consistently raised the need for effective multidisciplinary working, not simply about communicating with each other, but about understanding each other's professional perspective (Featherstone et al, 2014). The CA 2004 (s 13) requires each local authority to establish a Local Children's Safeguarding Board (LCSB), with the objectives of: coordinating what is done by each person or body represented on the LCSB for the purposes of safeguarding and promoting the welfare of children in the area; and ensuring the effectiveness of what is done by each such person or body for those purposes. This includes the development of policies and procedures about: thresholds for intervention; the recruitment, supervision and training of people who work with children; dealing with allegations against staff; and cooperation with other local authorities.

LCSB membership includes the following representatives:

- the chief officer of police;
- the National Probation Service and Community Rehabilitation Companies;
- the Youth Offending Team;
- NHS England and CCGs;
- NHS Trusts and NHS Foundation Trusts, all or most of whose hospitals, establishments and facilities are situated in the local authority area;
- the Child and Family Court Advisory and Support Service (Cafcass); and
- the governor or director of any secure training centre or prison in the area of the authority that ordinarily detains children.

The LCSB has an independent chair who coordinates the activities. As in adult safeguarding, information sharing is heavily emphasised and there is specific and detailed guidance on how this should be managed (HM Government, 2015a). The principles for sharing are that it should be: necessary and proportionate; relevant; adequate; accurate; timely; secure; and recorded. The information-sharing guidance provides a helpful flow chart of how and when this should happen (HM Government, 2015a, p 12).

Social workers have key roles in safeguarding children. Assessment is central to their activities and the purpose of this is to identify what needs to be done to protect and promote the welfare of the child. Just what constitutes enough concern to trigger intervention is assisted by the duty on the LSCB to produce a document about the thresholds required for:

- early help assessment and the type and level of early help services to be provided;
- the criteria, including the level of need, for when a case should be referred to local authority children's social care for assessment and for statutory services under section 17 of the Children Act 1989 (CA 1989) (*children in need*);
- section 47 of the CA 1989 (*reasonable cause to suspect children suffering or likely to suffer significant harm*);
- section 31 of the CA 1989 (*care orders*); and
- section 20 of the CA 1989 (*duty to accommodate a child*).

The 2015 guidance also specified a new requirement of LSCBs to produce 'clear procedures and processes for cases relating to the sexual exploitation of children and young people' (Department of Education, 2015, p 16), following the recognition of CSE as a major problem.

Social workers undertaking an assessment need to ensure that these are: child-centred; rooted in child development and informed by evidence; focused on action and outcomes for children; holistic in approach, addressing the child's needs within their family and wider community;

able to ensure equality of opportunity; able to involve children and their families; built on strengths as well as identifying difficulties; integrated in approach; a continuing process not an event; lead to action, including the provision of services; reviewed on an ongoing basis; and transparent and open to challenge (Department of Education, 2015, p 21). Of course, these assessment principles hold true for children who have committed sexual abuse and for those who have been victims.

Where an assessment is made about an allegation of the sexual abuse of a child, there are legal options to consider for their safety. Where a child requires immediate protection, then an Emergency Protection Order (EPO) can be sought at short notice from a court. The police do have powers to remove a child in an emergency; however, these should be used sparingly. The referral may lead to the categorisation of the child, under section 17 of the CA 1989, as a *Child in Need* of services over and above what is universally available to all children and their families In cases of alleged sexual abuse, it is likely that there will be action taken under section 47 of the CA 1989, which is about the child suffering or being likely to suffer *significant harm*. The assessment process has a statutory time framework with a clear multi-agency approach. Ongoing work with the child and their family may be required and agreed by an Initial Child Protection conference, with a clear plan that: ensures the child is safe from harm and prevents him or her from suffering any further harm; promotes the child's health and development; and supports the family to safeguard and promote the welfare of their child, provided it is in the 'best interests of the child'. A core group of professionals from the most relevant agencies implement the plan, and progress is reviewed at subsequent Child Protection conferences. Any assessment of the perpetrator should be shared with this group as it can provide essential information for the continuing safety of the child.

Deciding just what is in the best interests of the child can be complicated, and each child's situation is very different. There are broad indicators of what this might consist of, including the presumption that having their parents involved in their lives (where safe to do so) is the best option and that their welfare is paramount (CA 1989). The assessments should indicate what the best course of action is for that specific child and this may need to be agreed by the Family Court where appropriate.

Reflective exercise: Differing perspectives

Sharon, a 20-year-old black woman with moderate learning difficulties, is pregnant with the child of James, a 21-year-old white man who has recently been released from prison for a sexual assault on a young girl. Sharon does not believe that James is guilty of the offence and intends to live with him and to bring up their child together.

- What are the concerns (if any) about this situation?
- What steps can be taken to ensure the safety of the child?
- Who would it be useful to discuss this with?
- What legislation may be helpful here?

Multi-Agency Safeguarding Hub

Information sharing is a recurring concern and a model that is being introduced to manage this is the Multi-Agency Safeguarding Hub (MASH), an approach that is gaining wide support (Home Office, 2014). The model is focused on sharing information, but also joint decision-making and coordinated interventions. The key agencies (often children's social care, police, health, education, probation, housing and youth offending) are co-located in the same physical space in order to enable face-to-face contact and discussion. An initial evaluation of MASH (Home Office, 2014) seems to indicate that there is: a more accurate assessment of risk and need; thorough management of cases; better understanding between professions; and greater efficiencies in resources. Intelligence was compiled from a wider range of sources and understood better, cases were managed more closely, the language and terminology used was shared more, and duplication was avoided.

The Home Office (2014, p 10) evaluation identified the following core purposes of MASH: acting as a single point of entry – gathering all notifications related to safeguarding in one place; enabling thorough research of each case to identify potential risk (and therefore the opportunity to address that risk); sharing information between agencies, supported by a joint information-sharing protocol; triaging referrals, exemplified in the use of agreed risk ratings; facilitating early intervention to prevent the need for more intensive interventions at a later stage; and managing cases through coordinated interventions.

Safeguarding children and young people is a key social work task where there are concerns about sexual abuse, and the prevalence of sexual abuse makes it likely that all children's social workers will experience this at some time in their working lives. The guidance for safeguarding children is extensive and has often been driven by public concern. The systems and processes are designed to protect children from harm, including sexual harm, although there have been failures in this that we will explore at the end of this chapter. We now turn in more detail to the specific framework for managing sexual offenders.

Developing public safety

Multi-Agency Public Protection Arrangements

The Criminal Justice Act 2003 (CJA 2003) established MAPPA in each of the 42 criminal justice areas in England and Wales.[4] They are designed to protect the public (including previous victims of crime) from serious harm by both sexual and violent offenders. Local criminal justice agencies and other bodies dealing with offenders are required to work together in partnership to achieve this. MAPPA are not statutory bodies, but mechanisms to enable agencies to better undertake their statutory responsibilities and protect the public in a coordinated manner. Each agency retains its full statutory responsibilities and needs to ensure that these are not compromised by MAPPA.

The Responsible Authority is the police, prison and probation trust in each area and the agencies work together within agreed processes (CJA 2003, ss 325–327B). It has a legal duty to ensure that the risks posed by specified sexual and violent offenders are assessed and managed. Within the local area, other local agencies have a duty to cooperate with the Responsible Authority in this task. These 'duty to cooperate' (DTC) agencies work with the Responsible Authority on particular aspects of an offender's life, recognising that people are potentially engaged with a variety of public bodies. The DTC agencies have a reciprocal duty to cooperate and must do so. Section 325(6) of the CJA 2003 specifies the following as DTC agencies: Youth Offending Teams; employment and welfare benefits agencies (currently Job Centre Plus); the local education authority; the local housing authority; relevant social landlords; social services; relevant health agencies (strategic and primary care); organisations that provide electronic monitoring; and the UK Border Agency. A Strategic Management Board (SMB) established in each area provides local governance, including monitoring performance, ensuring anti-discriminatory practice, measuring compliance with the MAPPA Key Performance Indicators and producing an annual report. It consists of senior staff from the constituent agencies. As part of the assessment and management of risk, the MAPPA need to consider the disclosure of information about convictions in order to protect the public. Offenders are categorised into three levels reflecting their dangerousness: 1 is the lowest category (least dangerous) and 3 the highest (most dangerous).

The police are responsible for managing registered sexual offenders (National Policing Improvement Agency, 2010) and many forces have established specialist Public Protection Units that coordinate community supervision for these Category 1 offenders with probation or Youth Offending Teams. Duties include ensuring that details of offenders are recorded on the Violent and Sex Offender Register (ViSOR) and then enforcing any notification requirements, such as registration, assessment (usually with Risk Matrix 2000; see Thornton, 2010) and regular visits and reviews. The frequency of visits is tailored to the assessed need, and guidance suggests monthly visits for very high-risk, every three months for high-risk, six months for medium-risk and 12 months for low-risk offenders.

The local probation trust manages Category 2 offenders (aged 18+), who received a sentence of 12 months' custody or more and are released for community supervision (licence). Children and young people under 18 are managed by the Youth Offending Team. Mental health and social services manage those offenders who are subject to hospital or guardianship orders. The prison service identifies and monitors all MAPPA offenders in custody through the local Interdepartmental Risk Management Team (IRMT), which is an internal prison service multi-agency meeting. Information should be shared with the relevant Responsible Authority to support safe supervision when they are released into the community, including comprehensive reports and risk assessments that will help to develop management plans.

MAPPA are administrative arrangements that are designed to recognise that proper, effective supervision is necessary to enhance the safety of the public, and that all relevant agencies have a part to play in this. These arrangements are an attempt to avoid any 'collisions' or conflicts between agencies by providing clear forums for discussion and protocols and mechanisms for sharing information. They also provide the opportunity for a more comprehensive support programme for offenders, which will hopefully assist in their rehabilitation. Although the principal criminal justice agencies (police, probation, prison) have and retain key responsibilities, the MAPPA enable a more holistic public health-type approach to be taken.

The voice of victims can be heard in the MAPPA process through the Victim Contact Scheme,[5] which is managed by the Victim Liaison Office (VLO). Where an offender has committed a serious sexual or violent offence and has been sentenced to 12 months' custody or more, then the VLO should establish and maintain contact with the victim(s) and represent their views at the meetings. Victims should also be informed via this service about the release of the offender and any restrictions on their movements or behaviours, or any other strategies to manage risk.

Reflective exercise: Developing public safety (1)

George, aged 64 and of white Irish heritage, is to be released from prison after serving a custodial sentence for sexually abusing the young daughter of a neighbour. He is physically disabled and requires a wheelchair to maximise his mobility. While in prison, he has developed a severe depressive disorder and has made attempts to take his own life. His extended family do not wish to keep contact with him and he cannot return to his previous home due to community anger. He does not have any means of financial support.

- Consider a plan for George's successful return into the community.
- How many different agencies are likely to be involved with George.
- What will they be doing?
- How can they each help to develop safety and prevent George from reoffending?

Multi-Agency Public Protection Arrangement categories and levels of management

Sexual (and violent) offenders are categorised according to their offence, their dangerousness and the legal response to their behaviour. There are three categories and associated levels of management:

- *Category 1*. The offender is a registered sexual offender (RSO), as specified under Part 2 of the Sexual Offences Act 2003.
- *Category 2*. This category contains those convicted of an offence under Schedule 15 of the Criminal Justice Act 2003 and have been sentenced to 12 months or more in custody (including those under 18).[6]
- *Category 3*. Other dangerous offenders: a person who has been cautioned, reprimanded, warned or convicted of an offence which indicates that he or she is capable of causing serious harm and requires multi-agency management at Level 2 or 3. The offence might not be one specified in Schedule 15 of the CJA 2003.[7]

Offenders can only be identified in one of the three categories at a time. Offenders can only be considered for Category 3 if they do not meet the criteria for Category 1 or Category 2. Offenders only fall into Category 2 if they do not meet the criteria for Category 1. However, an offender who ceases to meet the criteria of one category can be identified in a different category if they meet the relevant criteria.

Following categorisation, MAPPA have three levels of management of sexual offenders: Level 1 – ordinary agency management; Level 2 – active multi-agency management; and Level 3 – active enhanced multi-agency management. Level 1 is where the risks can be managed in a fairly straightforward way by the lead agency through their usual supervisory and/or case management arrangements. Practice at Level 2 requires the coordinated intervention of more than one agency to enhance safety due to the assessed high risk of serious harm. Offenders who have previously been managed at Level 3 but no longer need this approach should normally be reassigned to Level 2. Level 3 is for those offenders where there is a high public interest (although not necessarily due to the seriousness of their offending) and they may require significant resource input at short notice, for example, if they need rehousing or returning to custody due to community vigilantism, and decisions may be influenced by considerations of public confidence in the criminal justice system. Cases such as these will be actively overseen by relevant senior management. The minimum appropriate level will be decided upon to achieve a risk management plan (RMP) that is defensible.

Sharing information

The MAPPA recognise the importance of clear information sharing and there are pro-forma referral and assessment documents within the guidance to assist professionals with this. The lead agencies (police, probation trust, prison, Youth Offending Teams, mental health service) have the responsibility for identifying qualifying offenders within three days of sentence and ensuring that they are recorded and processed accordingly. This assessment form includes information about the person and a judgement on their likelihood of reoffending, to whom and how serious and imminent this may be. It also identifies the responsible agency, any assessments or plans for the offender, and which agencies need to be involved. Clearly, some offenders continue to pose a risk to others and steps need to be taken to protect people. If someone has sexually offended against a child, then it would be of concern if they were working or volunteering in an organisation where there are children, or if they began a friendship with an adult who had children. Although there are perhaps more obvious concerns about the protection of children, there can be complications in assessing this, for example, whether an offender poses a danger to other vulnerable groups because of their abusive behaviour.

Sharing information about people in the UK is primarily regulated by the Data Protection Act 1998 and the Human Rights Act 1998, and this is also the case with sexual offenders. Information sharing should be lawful, necessary and proportionate; agencies disclosing details about offenders for the protection of the public must do so within the law, must demonstrate that it is necessary for that protection and must ensure that it is proportionate to the risk posed. These are not always easy judgements to make as the inappropriate disclosure of information could have serious and harmful consequences for the offender, for example, by community reaction. There has to be a balance between the potential harm done and the public benefit, and the MAPPA guidance is clear that all such decisions must be thoroughly considered, including ensuring that all parties to the information are aware of the sensitivities involved and understand the issues of confidentiality. Indeed, such sharing should only be done if there are no other alternatives to managing the case safely, and only the amount of information necessary to reasonably protect the public should be shared. This could include only disclosing situations where risk may be heightened rather than the wholesale detailing of offending history, or being clear about who to contact if people are concerned about behaviours.

Reflective exercise: Developing public safety (2)

Russell, who is white British and has a moderate learning disability, had sexually abused a younger child when he was 18 and had been sentenced to two years in prison. He is due to be released and he would like to work in catering, including taking educational qualifications at the local college.

- Which agencies do you think could be involved with Russell?
- Which agencies do you think need to know about his offence and what is your reasoning for this?
- How do you think any information sharing should be managed to protect possible victims and Russell?

Child sex offender disclosure

As we have seen in earlier chapters, the public outcry about sex offender dangerousness has led to the creation of laws that require offenders to be identified within their communities so that the public can be safeguarded from them. Sex offenders against children who are assessed as being a continuing risk of serious harm can have their details disclosed to people who have responsibility for the protection of individual children where this is necessary. The MAPPA structures are used to manage the processes. Under the relevant section, the Responsible Authority is *required* to consider disclosing details to relevant members of the public and there is a presumption that disclosure *will* be made if necessary for protection. Once this has been done, conditions can be imposed to prevent those who receive the disclosure information from making any further disclosures to any other party.

Wood and Kemshall (2007) found that disclosure was viewed as helpful in promoting safety by professionals and the offender when information was shared with relevant agencies. However, both professionals and the offender thought that broader public disclosure was problematic and that it could lead to vigilante behaviour that would be both difficult and costly to manage, as well as being demotivating for offenders to engage with supervision.

Multi-Agency Public Protection Arrangement risk assessment and planning

A crucial element of the MAPPA process is assessment, and we will look at the various assessment approaches, tools and protocols in Chapter Five. The approved risk assessment tools include: the Offender Assessment System (OASys), Structured Assessment of Risk and Need (SARN) and Spousal Assault Risk Assessment (SARA) used by the National Offender Management Service; the Risk Matrix (RM) 2000 used by the police, probation and prisons; and ASSET, a structured risk assessment used by Youth Offending Teams. An assessment is made about how likely is a risk of serious harm[8] (low, medium, high, very high) and on whom this might be focused (eg specific known individuals, vulnerable groups, children, themselves as a suicide risk), and although it is important that all the agreed processes, protocols and tools are followed and recorded, professional judgement and discretion remain key determinants of the assessment.

An RMP should be generated by the lead agency, and for all Level 2 and Level 3 offenders, there should be an additional, complementary MAPPA plan. Level 3 offenders need to be considered for registration as a Critical Public Protection Case, which would warrant regular senior management review due their high profile. Any RMP will have elements of the following interventions: restrictive, rehabilitative and protective. Restrictive interventions limit the opportunities for further offending, rehabilitative interventions are those that assist the offender to manage their own risk and protective interventions assist the offender to develop an offence-free life.

Multi-Agency Public Protection meetings

The key forum for the discussion and management of sexual offenders are the Multi-Agency Public Protection (MAPP) meetings, where the various agencies are able to make decisions and commit resources to ensure public safety. How these meetings work in terms of individual relationships and group processes is crucial to effective practice, and the guidance also suggests that having a continuity of members assists in maintaining clarity of control and consistency of decision-making. The MAPP meeting identifies risks and supports the MAPPA RMP, and is chaired by a designated 'MAPPA Coordinator' who has responsibility for that area. With echoes of child protection systems, the MAPP meeting can agree a small 'core group' of practitioners who are closely involved with the offender, and the person who made the referral will generally coordinate this group in reviewing progress in between the MAPP meetings. Their responsibilities include taking notes and sending them to the MAPPA. So, for example, a core group may consist of a probation officer, a worker from the offender's supported accommodation, a police representative and a social worker where someone has offended against their own children. This would enable any progress to be shared plus discussion of any changes to the risk assessment, ensuring that known or potential victims are safe. Where the offender is a child, then there should always be a representative from children's services and the meeting should consider the welfare of the child in their discussions and decisions, including the disclosure of information to the public. We have been in situations where we have had to relocate families where their child has committed a sexual offence and the local community has responded violently.

Multi-Agency Risk Assessment Conference

In response to increasing concerns about the impact of domestic violence, Multi-Agency Risk Assessment Conferences have been established over the previous decade. Unlike MAPPA, these do not have a statutory basis, but are comprised of similar agencies to coordinate the professional response to the problem. Domestic violence is defined as 'any incident or pattern of incidents of controlling, coercive or threatening behaviour, violence or abuse between those aged 16 or over who are or have been intimate partners or family members regardless of gender or sexuality' (Home Office, 2013). Domestic violence could and does include sexual violence, and so there can often be overlap between the two systems. To avoid duplication, the MAPPA should take precedence and the systems need to be coordinated.

Impact of Multi-Agency Public Protection Arrangements

Peck (2011) undertook a study on reconviction rates for sexual and violent offenders following the introduction of MAPPA in 2001. Although it is difficult to determine the actual impact of the new arrangements, the study demonstrated a decline in reconviction rates for offenders released between 2001 and 2004 compared to 1998–2000. This seemed to indicate that MAPPA played some role in reducing reoffending, but was far from conclusive. A similar study (Bryant et al, 2015, p 4) concluded that it was likely that 'MAPPA may be making a positive contribution to managing offenders convicted of serious offences', with a claimed 2–4% reduction in proven reoffending. Although modest, it appears that MAPPA are making a difference.

When multi-agency working fails: child sexual exploitation

This chapter has so far outlined the frameworks for protecting the public from sexual offending, describing the principles, policies and practices that any social worker will find themselves working within when facing the issue. One of the key and recurring aspects of this is multi-agency working, where the various concerned organisations come together to provide comprehensive, seamless and safe systems and processes to prevent sexual abuse. However, achieving this is not straightforward and we have chosen to look at how, despite what appear to be thorough and robust organisational arrangements, there can still be significant failures to protect the vulnerable from sexual abuse. We will look at some of the lessons learned from CSE inquiries and how they may improve practice.

The sexual exploitation of children is not a new phenomenon, but it has been highlighted recently in the UK by a series of high-profile cases across the country of groups of men systematically abusing vulnerable children and young people. There have been a series of reports and serious case reviews into this, providing evidence of failings and suggestions for change. Agencies have been severely criticised at all levels and it is worth reading the following reports in detail:

- Jay (2014) *Independent Inquiry into Child Sexual Exploitation in Rotherham 1997–2013.*
- HM Government (2015b) 'Tackling Child Sexual Exploitation'.
- Bedford (2015) *Serious Case Review into Child Sexual Exploitation in Oxfordshire: From the Experiences of Children A, B, C, D, E and F.*

■ OFSTED (2014) 'The Sexual Exploitation of Children: it couldn't happen here could it?'

■ Casey (2015) *Report of Inspection of Rotherham Metropolitan Borough Council.*

These reports provide evidence of the scale and nature of the sexual abuse that children and young people were subjected to, and the responses of those people who were tasked with protecting them. Although there may be criticisms and questions about the ways in which these reports have been used to promote various political agendas, they do give an insight into how values and associated practices can fail to protect children, even when there are systems and processes ostensibly in place to prevent this. We recognise that there are 'moral entrepreneurs' who can use such information in ways that are unhelpful, such as those who accentuate and misrepresent issues of 'race' in the reports, and those who deny and minimise the scale and nature of the problem through problematising the evidence. It is not within the remit of this book to engage in any depth with these issues, but we do maintain a perspective that is focused on the consequences of these discourses for actual and potential victims.

An example of how the ethnicity of offenders can be overemphasised is contained within the following extract from the *Office of the Children's Commissioner's Inquiry into Child Sexual Exploitation in Gangs and Groups* (Berelowitz et al, 2013, p 28):

> During a meeting with two health workers, the Inquiry asked about the profile of perpetrators in the local area. We were told that they were exclusively 'Asian males'. We asked the workers to talk us through one of their live cases. They said the victim had first been exploited in school by her peers, who were all white boys. She was then exploited by an older boyfriend who was an Asian man in his twenties. Following this, she was exploited by an older white man who filmed her having sex with his friends. She was then exploited by a group of older Asian men who sold her at parties. Finally, an older white man, who was addicted to drugs, exploited her. He took her to the homes of much older, disabled men, and sold her to pay for his drug habit. These health workers had mentally screened out the white perpetrators. (Example given at a meeting during Phase 2 of the Inquiry)

The problem with CSE, as with the history of much sexual offending, has been a reluctance to accept that it is a problem at all, and perhaps the more recent focus on it is a welcome development. Stan Cohen, the architect of 'moral panic' theory, accepted that there are beneficial moral panics, something that is often overlooked. Indeed, Cohen used a sexual abuse example to illustrate this in conversation with Le Vrai (2010):

LV: So are moral panics inherently a bad thing?

SC: No. There are good moral panics, and bad. There are moral panics that highlight worthy problems. Society does, at times, deny the presence of certain problems, things are normalised. There was a horrible example recently of an incest case where you had two decades of normalisation, people had covered it up and denied it, what we actually needed there was a good moral panic. Social reaction theory or MP [moral panic] theory is not very significant if it just looks at the over reaction, it has to produce cases of under reaction too.

The National Working Group Network developed the following definition of CSE, which is utilised in UK government guidance and policy (DCSF, 2009):

The sexual exploitation of children and young people under 18 involves exploitative situations, contexts and relationships where young people (or a third person or persons) receive 'something' (e.g. food, accommodation, drugs, alcohol, cigarettes, affection, gifts, money) as a result of performing, and/or others performing on them, sexual activities. Child sexual exploitation can occur through the use of technology without the child's immediate recognition, for example by persuading them to post sexual images on the internet/ mobile phones with no immediate payment or gain. In all cases, those exploiting the child/young person have power over them by virtue of their age, gender, intellect, physical strength and/or economic or other resources. Violence, coercion and intimidation are common, involvement in exploitative relationships being characterised in the main by the child or young person's limited availability of choice resulting from their social/economic and/or emotional vulnerability.

The high profile gained by CSE led the government to respond with a report (HM Government, 2015) that summarised the concerns and made several recommendations for policy and practice. There were key areas where the systems and processes designed to protect children from sexual abuse had failed. The diagram in Figure 4.1 highlights these.

Figure 4.1: System failings

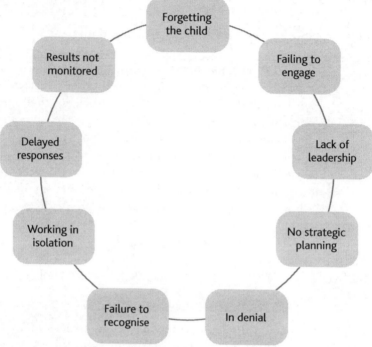

Source: Berelowitz et al (2013, p 22).

CSE was often unrecognised as child abuse and the professional responses reframed it as 'child prostitution' or behaviour that the children had voluntarily become engaged with. These children tended to be very vulnerable and made choices that were not always in their best interests, but they were systematically targeted by men who were manipulative and violent, thus reducing their capacity to choose in any meaningful way. It was noted in Berelowitz et al (2013) that the children were often described as 'putting themselves at risk', which implied playing a part in their abuse, rather than viewing them as being at risk from abusers. There was confusion about the notion of 'consent' to sexual activity, with evidence of misunderstanding of the legal framework. This allowed quite horrific situations to be reframed and reconstructed as not being rape or sexual assault, but as (at least partially) consenting activities.

Children's services were often perceived by the children as being punitive, restrictive and failing to stand by them through difficult experiences. Children were frequently blamed for their circumstances and, indeed, could be very difficult to engage with, but they reported feeling abandoned by services. Police, health and education services all struggled to engage effectively with the children. Families also reported being marginalised by services, as well as being viewed as part of the problem, even when they were actively seeking to work in partnership to safeguard their children. These families often had their own vulnerabilities, which complicated matters and fed into a devaluing of both the family and their children.

Political leaders and senior officials were unable to grasp the complexity and scale of CSE in their areas, leading to a sense of 'denial' that such a problem could exist. This had consequences of reducing resources and commitment to recognising and tackling CSE, which tended to be an issue for older children who were viewed as less of a priority and less vulnerable than younger children. Resources were focused on safeguarding younger children and this was an understandable position given the criticisms in previous high-profile cases of child abuse, where harm towards younger children had been the subject of public concern.

The lack of strategic planning and coordination in local areas compounded difficulties in identification and management, including basic issues such as the incompatibility of information technology systems. Tensions between agencies in how they viewed CSE, the children and each other made a coordinated response problematic and led to failures to follow through with criminal investigations and marginalised important intelligence from some agencies. Some agencies were not open to challenge and acted in defensive and inflexible ways.

Interventions were not systematic and were often ineffective. They were not responsive enough to the particular complexities of CSE and often made the situation worse. Residential care was an unsafe option for many children as these units had been targeted by abusers. Children were frequently 'pushed' away from services by their inappropriateness and 'pulled' into CSE by having limited safe options.

The children, particularly girls, were subjected to sexist values about their behaviour. Rather than being viewed as abused children, they were recast as willing participants choosing to become involved in prostitution. This involved values that linked their gender and class to create stereotypical 'underclass' demonisation. Values around 'race' and ethnicity were also problematic as services were uncomfortable about discussing this, which created the offenders as a racialised 'other', or refused to engage with the issue. There was little evidence that services had a reflective approach to considering ethnicity in their discussions.

Based on the previously recognised barriers to effective practice, the diagram in Figure 4.2 outlines the systemic elements of a safe approach. Key issues include: skills in working with children and their families; the participation of children and their families in initiatives; local leadership and practice arrangements that are strategic, shared, monitored and held to account; and a shared awareness of CSE and how it can be recognised and responded to. For example, Cossar et al (2013) developed a Recognition

Figure 4.2: Good practice in safeguarding children from child sexual exploitation

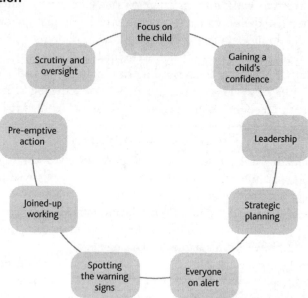

Source: Berelowitz et al (2013, p 33).

and Telling Framework that assists in maintaining a focus on the child and understanding what they may be experiencing, recognising some of the signs of CSE and what approaches help children to engage with services. Berelowitz et al (2013) recommended the following principles in safeguarding children from CSE: the child's best interests must be the top priority; services must include the participation of children and young people and there needs to be enduring relationships and support for them; comprehensive problem profiling should be undertaken, with effective information sharing within and between agencies; staff require quality supervision, support and training; and services should be evaluated and reviewed. Social work values of focusing on the rights of the person, empowering them and protecting them from harm fit well with these principles of good practice.

Summary

- There are detailed policies and systems to promote safety from sexual offending that social workers have a role in.
- The safeguarding systems for adults and children are designed to protect from harm and to promote well-being.
- The MAPPA structures provide specific ways of managing sexual offenders in the community.
- Effective multi-agency working underpins all systems.
- Values and attitudes impact on how we approach and respond to the protection of people from sexual abuse.
- CSE has been recognised as a major problem and social work skills and values lend themselves to effective practice in this area.

Notes

[1] The other nations of the UK have their own legislation and guidance. This is subject to change, and the main current frameworks are the Social Services and Well Being (Wales) Act 2014, the Protection of Vulnerable Groups (Scotland) Act 2007 and the Protection of Children and Vulnerable Adults (Northern Ireland) Order 2003.

[2] Further guidance can be obtained from: http://www.justice.gov.uk/downloads/protecting-the-vulnerable/mca/safeguarding-policy.pdf

[3] See: https://www.gov.uk/government/uploads/system/uploads/attachment_data/file/192572/2900774_InfoGovernance_accv2.pdf

[4] MAPPA arrangements in Scotland were introduced by the Management of Offenders etc (Scotland) Act 2005 and the equivalent Public Protection Arrangements in Northern Ireland (PPANI) by the Criminal Justice (N.I.) Order 2008.

[5] Criminal Justice and Court Services Act 2000, as amended by the Domestic Violence, Crime and Victims Act 2004.

[6] This category is also relevant for those offenders who have been sentenced to 12 months or more in custody and transferred to hospital under section 47/49 of the Mental Health Act 1983 or who have been detained in hospital under section 37 of the Mental Health Act 1983 with or without a restriction order under section 41.

[7] See: http://www.legislation.gov.uk/ukpga/2003/44/schedule/15

[8] Serious harm is defined in the guidance as: 'An event, which is life-threatening and/or traumatic, from which recovery, whether physical or psychological, can be expected to be difficult or impossible' (Home Office, 2006).

5

Social work assessment of sex offenders

Introduction

The assessment of those who sexually offend has developed during the previous decades, with ever-increasing methods, technologies and approaches designed to ensure that we are able to respond effectively to this damaging behaviour, thus preventing further harm to victims. In seeking to understand how this behaviour came about and to formulate plans for managing it, some differences have developed from the more usual social work approaches to assessment. This is partly due to the dominance of this area by psychology, as discussed earlier in the book, but is also due to an understandably increased focus on 'risk'. There is a difference in assessing someone who has sexually assaulted a child to assessing someone who requires an adaptation to their home due to their physical impairment, not least the different feelings both generate, but there are also some similarities, which we will explore. Clearly, the key questions when assessing someone who has sexually offended are: 'Are they going to do it again?' and 'What will it take to prevent them doing it again?' (Shlonsky and Wagner, 2005).

In this chapter, we look at current social work approaches to assessment and how they might engage with sexual offending. We look at the development of specialist assessment tools and protocols for sexual offenders and discuss how these are located within particular ways of thinking that direct practice. Risk assessment is identified and the need for approaches that recognise and respond to complexity is highlighted.

Social work assessment

Assessment is a key task and activity of social work and social workers as they are required to seek to understand the circumstances of those that they are working with in order to intervene in ways that are helpful to the individual and society. Without an assessment, it has been argued that social workers would be merely reactive and without an informed and structured intervention (Coulshed and Orme, 2012). 'Assessment' remains a somewhat contested term and although Crisp et al (2005) found that there was no

universally agreed definition in social work, most textbooks on assessment
offer some definition related to one or more of the five stages of assessment
proposed by Milner et al (2015), which are outlined in the following.
Coulshed and Orme (2012) describe it as an ongoing process in which the
service user participates, the purpose of which is to understand people in
relation to their environment; it is the basis for planning what needs to be
done to maintain, improve and bring about change. Kemshall (1998) said
that it is a process of professional judgement or appraisal of the situation,
circumstances and behaviour of the service user and it might involve risk
assessment, while Griggs (2000) said that it is about determining need.
Healy (2012) locates it as one of the four key 'phases' of social work practice,
viewing these as Engagement, Assessment, Intervention and Evaluation/
Termination, working as a cyclical rather than a linear process.

More broadly, Smale et al (1993) held that realistic assessment has to:
encompass the whole of the assessment task; engage with all the people
involved in the situation and their possible solutions; and address the
change, care and social control tasks to avoid the individualisation of
social problems (ie marginalising the social context through emphasising
the internal psychological processes) as the focus for assessment and
intervention. Compton and Galaway (1999) described assessment as the
collection and processing of data to provide information for use in making
decisions about the nature of a problem and what is to be done about it. It
is also argued to be a cognitive process: it involves thinking about the data
and developing a plan that provides an understanding of the problem for
intervention objectives or solutions to be achieved, plus an action plan to
accomplish the objectives. For Hepworth et al (2002), assessment is a fluid,
dynamic process of receiving, analysing and synthesising new information
as it emerges through the assessment and intervention. Mainstone (2014)
makes the point that in child protection, where, for example, there may
be allegations of sexual abuse, meeting the needs of each family member
and protecting the vulnerable from harm often means that several different
assessments have to be brought together before a holistic understanding
can be reached. Specialist assessments can offer new insights but also
generate difficult and contradictory information that makes understanding
complicated. Additionally, the purpose of assessment can be unclear – is it
about the person's needs, the risk they pose others or their risk from others?
These are challenges within the assessment of sexual offending that we will
develop in this chapter.

Approaches to social work assessment

Coulshed and Orme (2012, p 22) argue that in social work (and, indeed, generally), there are 'two major distinctive approaches to assessment – positivist and constructivist'. They chart the development in social work of assessment practices that were diagnostic and underpinned by certainty, in that there was an assumption that by investigating and identifying facts about someone or a situation, you could draw accurate conclusions about their true nature. Once this has been uncovered, then it can be dealt with. In our experience, new social work students often strive to be as 'objective' as possible in their claims about working with people, assuming that this is an achievable and desirable approach. This can be particularly true for those who have an academic background in the natural sciences, such as clinical psychology, which sometimes has an uncritical positivist underpinning. A constructivist approach views the world in a different way, assuming that there are various truths about people that are competing and are created through professional and social narratives. Rather than being an exercise in finding out 'facts', constructivist assessment is seen as *creating* those facts through the ways we imagine, talk about and bring knowledge to understand situations.

This notion has also been expanded by other social work academics, such as Fook (2012), who outlines how a positivist approach takes a linear 'investigation, diagnosis and treatment' model of assessment, and is interested in finding the true causes of a problem that can then be rationally controlled. The role of the social worker (assessor) in this approach is to apply techniques to identify and gather facts, making sense of these through the application of established professional knowledge in the area. Such knowledge is viewed as the expertise of the professional, who knows what to look for and how to interpret the information gained, including what to prescribe to deal with the problem. This is what Parton and O'Byrne (2000) have described as a 'rational–technical' role for the social worker: an impartial gleaner of facts about the person's problem who then applies their superior professional knowledge to understanding it. Fook also makes the point that when assessing through professional knowledge, there will be a focus on investigating the 'facts' that are known to be relevant to that particular category of problem based on prior theoretical understanding of it, conceptualising the problem within a given framework. Thus, problems (including problem behaviours) can become reduced to the components that it is agreed are important, and these become the determining elements to investigate and quantify. This dominant way of undertaking assessments has implications across social work practice, including working with sexual offending.

Reflective exercise: Using professional judgement

Sharon is an experienced child protection social worker assessing Sean, a 14-year-old white boy who has committed a sexual assault against a similar-aged girl. Using a sex offender assessment protocol, she asks him and other significant people in his life about the factors in the protocol and is able to score these following the guidance. She is under some pressure to complete the assessment and collates the scores, reaching a number which indicates that Sean is at low risk of reoffending. Sharon is thankful that the protocol allows her to produce a clear assessment with an outcome that is defensible to her manager, the child protection conference and the courts.

Later, during a supervision session, Sharon became uncomfortable with the way she had sidelined her usually excellent analytical skills as she would usually question the information that she was receiving and make a professional judgement on this. She felt that she had been tempted by the need to be certain about a very sensitive issue and had used the protocol in a way that produced an outcome that appeared robust. On reflection, Sharon now felt that there had been some information offered that was not identified as important within the protocol, but, given her practice experience, could make Sean more dangerous than the scoring suggested (CJJI, 2013).

Fook (2012, pp 134–5) summarises that current dominant approaches to assessment contain the following:

1. A 'scientific' assumption that problems have identifiable and underlying 'causes'.
2. A rational and linear process that involves collecting data and identifying the problem, its cause and its 'cure'.
3. An assumption that the worker conducting the assessment is a passive and objective observer, whose role is simply to collect the relevant empirical 'facts' and establish the 'truth' of the problem.
4. The fitting of the problem situation into preconceived categories or labels.
5. A discursive function, in that the process undertaken and labels applied tend to reflect (and favour) the discourse of existing powerful groups, rather than the people who are experiencing the 'problem'.
6. Static definitions of problems and the identities of the people experiencing them, which attribute 'blame' to characteristics of these groups, rather than the contexts that may have created them.

As we have already seen in previous chapters, some of the broader issues here are present in the dominant explanations for sexual offending, but these factors will also be recognisable to general social work practitioners. This approach is not limited to working with sexual offenders, but we will see how the current preferred ways of making sex offender assessments tend to follow this process.

Reflective exercise: Understanding assessment practices

- Think of a recent assessment that you have successfully completed.
- Take each of the preceding points and consider how these happened in your example.
- What consequences of this were there for (a) the person being assessed and (b) you as a professional?

The 'constructive' challenge to the dominant ways of assessment has gained traction in social work during the previous decade. Rather than being located within the realm of the natural sciences, this is more influenced by postmodern, post-structural and critical perspectives, which question whether the 'traditional' approach can achieve what it aims to do and provide ideas for other types of engagement with people. The work of Foucault (1977) and Rose (1984) are examples of key theorisers in this field. Within social work, this alternative approach invites us to remember that we are actively involved as professionals in co-creating a story (narrative) about a given situation, and that there are likely to be many different stories changing over time that could quite reasonably provide explanations. This is not to say that all such stories are equally valid or that they are all 'truthful'; it recognises that when a truth-story is created about someone, it will have a particular claim to validity that is informed by ways of thinking and by the exercise of power. In this way of thinking, any assessment is the social worker constructing their own version (narrative) of the problem. This may sound dangerous and irrelevant where there is behaviour that harms others in such damaging ways and that requires a degree of certainty to ensure safety, yet there are some helpful aspects to this that we will consider.

Who we are and the types of questions we ask do influence responses, and this is important to reflect on. A child psychiatrist colleague interviewed a 16-year-old boy who had committed a sexual offence and followed a protocol that required identification of any fantasies of illegal sexual activities. She asked him what sexual fantasies he had, and after a short time of looking uncomfortable, he replied: 'Oh, suspenders and stockings, the usual stuff'. The colleague decided that having a white middle-aged, middle-class woman asking a black working-class teenager about their sexual fantasies was unlikely to produce any reliable *true* evidence and decided to discuss other issues instead. The exchange illustrates how the embodiment of the participants in this conversation impacts on the knowledge generated, which needs to be considered by practitioners in their interactions with service users.

Fook (2012, pp 135–6) summarises the constructive assessment approach as follows:

■ There is not necessarily any one 'cause' of problematic situations. Instead, situations may involve a number of factors, which may be competing and contradictory. These factors may interact with each other, bringing about a complex and changing situation.

■ The process of constructing a professional narrative may be an ongoing and integrated process. Collecting information does not necessarily precede formulating plans for action. Meanings will change and be constructed and reconstructed as relationships change with service users and new information is gained and interpreted in context.

■ The worker is actively and reflexively involved in the construction of the professional narrative. Their own assumptions and interpretations will influence how and what knowledge is selected and what narrative is created. The narrative produced represents the worker's version or perspective on the situation, which may or may not be used to the service user's advantage.

■ Existing labels and categories may need to be resisted as total ways of defining service users or problems. New labels or categories may need to be created, or existing ones modified, in order to better represent the narrative, identity or problem definition that fits the newly constructed narrative.

■ There needs to be an awareness of the discursive functions of the newly created 'assessment narrative', attempting to construct a narrative that works in favour of service users.

■ There is a need to create more open-ended service user identities and problem categories or definitions that recognise the influence of changing contexts.

This way of understanding assessment poses challenges when working with sexual offenders, but we explore how this can be done later in this chapter.

In *Assessment in Social Work*, Milner et al (2015) provided the following definition of assessment:

1. *Preparing* for the task, including defining what the purpose is.
2. *Collecting data*, including perceptions of the service user (offender), the family and other agencies of the problem and any attempted solutions.

3. *Applying professional knowledge* (practice wisdom, as well as theory) to seek analysis, understanding or interpretation of the data.
4. *Making judgements* about the relationships, needs, risks, standard of care or safety, seriousness of the situation, and people's capacities and potential for coping or for change (Is the progress good enough?).
5. *Deciding* and/or recommending what is to be done, plus how, by whom and when, and how progress will be reviewed.

In Milner et al's (2015) definition, analysis is about making sense of events and statements, arriving at an overall picture and an understanding of what is happening, and perhaps giving some thought as to how the situation has come about. This is informed by theoretical explanations of what it is to be human. Judgement is deciding what is good enough and what is not, what might be dangerous and what appears reasonably safe, what is of a reasonable quality and what is not. Decision-making is about future (in) action and aspects of that action, with a clear structure for implementing and reviewing it. This may appear straightforward, but, of course, it is anything but in most situations given the messiness of human circumstances. Even the question of what to look for, what information is relevant, when has enough been found and so on, makes starting assessment difficult and Milner et al note that many of the frameworks that have been written are little more than checklists to ensure that nothing relevant is forgotten in stages 1 and 2 of work with particular service user groups. Where it is needed most – in stages 3, 4 and 5 – there is less guidance.

Reflective exercise: Working with complexities

Consider the following scenarios:

- At age seven, Saima was sexually abused by her financially powerful uncle and fled with her mother and father to the UK from South Asia following threats of violence towards them. She attends school and has been assessed for a therapeutic project due to her sexually inappropriate and aggressive behaviour.
- George has been convicted of sexually abusing young boys over a period of 40 years when he was a church youth leader. He is 77, of white Irish heritage and has been released from custodial remand to reside in a probation hostel and to have a treatment programme.
- Slavoj, who is Croatian, has been found guilty along with several other military colleagues of being involved in the systematic rape of 'enemy' women during the break-up of Yugoslavia in the 1990s. His defence was that he was following orders during wartime.

- Harry has been suspended from school following a series of incidents where he touched girls on their bottoms. He is living with foster-carers after being neglected by his biological parents. He is 11 and of white British heritage.

Using Milner et al's first two assessment stages of 'Preparing for the task' and 'Collecting data', what ideas do you have in each scenario about how to go about doing this? What do you think you would have to take into account?

Values and attitudes

The importance of maintaining a reflexive approach to the assessment of those who commit sexual offences has practical benefits that may not at first be apparent. Social work does have a concern with the values-in-action that people bring to their work because the values and attitudes that people hold influence the outcome of their work.

Jung et al (2012) undertook a comparison between the attitudes of professionals (including probation officers and therapists) and lay people about a range of sexual offences and offenders. They found that although there were some differences between the two groups, there was a remarkable similarity in some attitudes, which were not supported by evidence. For example, both groups felt that child molesters had a higher likelihood of reoffending than rapists or exhibitionists, when the evidence is the opposite. This is particularly worrying with the professional group as it may lead to underestimating the danger that some people pose, increasing risk. It may also lead to overestimating the danger in other cases, which could have a detrimental effect on the life of the person subject to it. McAlinden (2012) notes that in England and Wales, risk is grounded in a 'wider politics of fear and insecurity' (Seddon, 2008, p 312) concerning sex offenders, where professional assessments are often subjected to emotive and sometimes misplaced assumptions about future risk.

Understandings of gender and 'race' also play their part in the (un)conscious assessment of sexual offenders. We hear no calls for an investigation into the propensity for white culture to generate sexually abusive behaviour, despite the recent revelations of historical offending by now older white men during the 1970s, but we do hear this about non-white groups. Black youth are considered vulnerable to sexist and rape-prone messages in their 'culture' of music lyrics and 'gang' behaviour, leading to enhanced sexual violence. 'Asian' grooming gangs in the UK (the UK reduces Asia to South Asia in its descriptions of ethnicity) are seen to be the products of a culture and religion (Islamophobia is woven into this discourse) that is negative about the status of women and views white girls as 'fair game' for their sexual needs. In assessing people, we need to ensure that broader social biases are acknowledged and accounted for, ensuring that we are vigilant about the story that we are constructing and questioning the ideas that we are bringing to make sense of the situation.

It is helpful to have knowledge about sexual offenders that is supported by evidence, with the proviso that this knowledge is ever-changing as further research is undertaken. Therefore, we need to ensure that we are not only up to date with current research, but also able to be discerning about the quality and nature of research produced. Dominant notions about sexual offenders do permeate our consciousness, with consequences. In an interesting paper, Lave (2011) discusses how the notion of sex offenders being highly prone to recidivism is a strong discourse within US society, including lawmakers, leading to the production of quite draconian legislation that is not based on empirical fact. This idea of inherent recidivism is a product of the way society views sexuality and offending, with a firm belief in psychopathology, fixed identity, normative sex, retributive sentencing and individualism. Responses to sexual offending are also prone to political influences as being seen to be 'tough' on sex offenders is both populist and popular. This combination excludes rational evidence that confounds it and has produced some idiosyncratic laws that are contrary to natural justice.

Risk assessment of sex offenders

Despite sociological and social work concerns about the nature and implications of risk assessment (see Milner et al, 2015), the 'science' of risk assessment and risk prediction of sexual reoffending has developed from forensic psychology and psychiatry, and has strong claims to validity through these powerful disciplines. Experts are routinely asked to make predictions about the likelihood of reoffending for different populations of individuals convicted of particular crimes, using a variety of predictive tools. The role and importance of these experts has increased in importance in managing offenders who have committed serious violent crimes, or what Lussier and Davies (2011, p 530) argue have come to be considered as 'dangerous populations'. The approaches taken are not always familiar territory for social workers, so, bearing in mind the concerns we raised in Chapter Two, we will explore some of the key issues involved in this construction of risk.

Risk assessment tools are commonly used in UK family courts, where proof is on the balance of probabilities in determining findings of fact, and they can be used to determine whether, for example, an alleged perpetrator of sexual abuse can have contact with (their) children. Risk assessment tools are not used in UK courts to determine judgements of 'beyond reasonable doubt' in criminal cases, but when an accused person is found guilty, they can be used in reports to help determine the type of sentence. The use of risk assessment tools varies internationally, for example, their use in criminal courts in the US to help establish guilt and make 'sexual predator' evaluations is controversial (Tully et al, 2013), primarily because they can lead to life imprisonment based on their outcome.

Barnett and Mann (2011) helpfully outline what they describe as 'first-', 'second-' and 'third-'generation risk assessments, which have developed over time. First-generation assessments are where only clinical experience and judgement are used by the practitioner to determine the level of risk, a process that is very subjective. The second approach moved to the use of tools and technologies and the third modified these to include more opportunities for change. We will explore these further.

Actuarial prediction

There have been a variety of techniques and technologies developed to aid professionals in making predictions to assist the criminal justice system to make decisions about sentencing, parole and so forth (eg Beech et al, 2003). One of the predominant methods in assessing sex offenders is *actuarial prediction*. Actuarial prediction for sex offenders has often been associated with the work of Quinsey and colleagues (eg Quinsey et al, 1995) and Hanson (eg Hanson, 1997). Some research has shown that actuarial prediction, which is based on a set of indicators or factors, is superior in predicting recidivism to clinical judgement (or what is often called 'unstructured clinical judgement'), which is usually premised on professional experience and judgement. The superiority of statistical prediction is claimed by many to indicate the need to abandon clinical assessment in favour of actuarial techniques (eg Quinsey et al, 1998; Bengtson and Langstrom, 2007). However, the superiority of actuarial approaches remains open to debate as although clinical assessments have evolved over the years, actuarial assessments still frequently claim the superiority of their techniques (Hanson and Morton–Bourgon, 2005; Harris and Rice, 2007; Hanson and Howard, 2010) despite research indicating that actuarial tools are too imprecise for individual decisions (Hart et al, 2007; Vrieze and Grove, 2008; Cooke and Michie, 2010). The problem of prediction error is not new (eg Auerhahn, 1999) and the limitations of the approach are becoming clearer.

In brief, actuarial risk assessment with sex offenders places an individual offender into a group of offenders sharing similar levels of known risk factors and providing a range of observed rates of sexual reoffending, based upon follow–up research with large numbers of offenders. Then, the probability of risk for relevant groups of offenders is quantified, and the individual offender's risk of reoffending is located in the context of what is known about these groups. Actuarial assessment has developed as a key approach in assessing the recidivism risk of sex offenders (Hanson, 2003; Harris and Rice, 2003). The most frequently used actuarial instruments include the Rapid Risk for Sex Offender Recidivism (RRASOR) (Hanson and Thornton, 2000), the Static-99 (Hanson and Thornton, 200), the Minnesota Sex Offender Screening Tool-Revised (MnSOST-R) (Epperson et al, 1998) and Offender Assessment System (OASys) in the UK (Ministry of Justice, 2015). Actuarial tools usually address a combination of four variables: risk factors, protective factors, static factors and dynamic factors:

- Risk factors increase the risk of reoffending.
- Protective factors decrease the risk of reoffending.
- Static factors (eg number of previous convictions, number of previous charges, history of non-sexual violence) are relatively unchanging over time.
- Dynamic factors (eg family support, employment, self-esteem) can change over time.

Most actuarial tools only address a combination of static risk factors; they rarely address the remaining three factor combinations. Most guidance does not recommend the use of available actuarial tools on their own (Campbell, 2009; Hart et al, 2007). Rather than rely exclusively on actuarial estimates of recidivism risk, the advice is to adjust the actuarial result. Adjusted Actuarial Assessment (AAA) involves a two-step procedure: obtain an actuarial quantification of recidivism risk and adjust that actuarial estimate (upward or downward) relying on risk factors that are supported by research. For example, the www.static99.org website appears to recommend the use of 'Risk Factors outside of the Static-99': sexual deviance, treatment history, general criminality, intimacy deficits, sexual self-regulation, general self-regulation, attitudes tolerating sexual assault, cooperation with supervision, and diagnosed Cluster B Personality Disorder. This can create some uncertainty about the value of the actuarial tool outcomes if the practitioner is able to modify them by additional interpreted factors. Campbell and DeClue (2010) argue that there is a lack of robust research demonstrating improved accuracy (over that obtained from static risk factors alone) by incorporating dynamic risk, dynamic protective or static protective factors, and that any changes are likely to be subject to individual bias. They suggest remaining with the substantive risk outcome based on the static factors. Howard et al (2014, p 225) raise concerns that as sexual offenders tend to 'specialise' in particular types of offending, rather than commit all forms of the behaviour, 'the use of single risk–assessment instruments to predict all types of sexual recidivism may be less effective than previously assumed'.

As highlighted, research in this field has consistently identified two main categories of risk factors: static and dynamic. Static risk factors are historical characteristics of the individual that are fixed and not amenable to change. The Static-99R[1] is one of the most popular assessment tools and uses 10 risk factors with associated coding to produce a final score (see Table 5.1; this reproduction is for information only and should not be used without the associated training provided by the creators of the tool). As can be seen, some of the risk factors are clearly open to interpretation and guidance is required before applying them.

Table 5.1: Static-99R coding

Question number	Risk factor	Codes		Score
1	Age at release	Aged 18–34.9		1
		Aged 35–39.9		0
		Aged 40–59.9		−1
		Aged 60+		−3
2	Ever lived with	Ever lived with lover for at least 2 years?		
		Yes		0
		No		1
3	Index non-sexual violence – any convictions?	No		0
		Yes		1
4	Prior non-sexual violence – any convictions?	No		0
		Yes		1
5	Prior sex offences	Charges	Convictions	
		0	0	0
		1–2	1	1
		3–5	2–3	2
		6+	4+	3
6	Prior sentencing dates (excluding index)	3 or less		0
		4 or more		1
7	Any convictions for non-contact sex offences	No		0
		Yes		1
8	Any unrelated victims	No		0
		Yes		1
9	Any stranger victims	No		0
		Yes		1
10	Any male victims	No		0
		Yes		1
	Total Score	Add up scores from individual risk factors		

Once a total score has been created, this is then translated into an overall risk category that provides a useful indication of the level of risk posed by that person (see Table 5.2).

Dynamic risk factors are those that are fairly stable aspects of psychological functioning (eg poor self-regulation), personality traits (psychopathy, personality disorders), deviant sexual arousal or preferences (eg sexual attraction to children) and cognitive distortions or beliefs that are supportive of sexual offending. These factors are potentially amenable to change through various interventions, hence *dynamic*, and are the focus of many treatment programmes. Indeed, these assessments also claim to provide key information about those factors that require a treatment focus. Some guidance also suggests the identification of *acute* dynamic risk factors, which can be subject to rapid change and significantly affect the risk within a short period of time. These can include factors such as using drugs and/or alcohol, negative emotional states, conflict with others, and gaining access to potential victims. When such factors appear, they may lead to an escalation of the potential for recidivism (Beech and Ward, 2004).

Table 5.2: Static-99R risk categories

Score	Label for risk category
−3 through 1	Low
2–3	Low–moderate
4–5	Moderate–high
6+	High

The science of actuarial risk prediction can appear rather rarified and is rich in specialised statistical argumentation, making understanding this difficult. It is not within the scope of this book to enter into these complexities, but for those who wish to develop their knowledge in this field, we would suggest further reading (eg Craig and Beech, 2010). However, the factors in the Static-99 that predict dangerousness are those that any social worker with experience of working with violence would recognise: a previous history of sexual aggression and/or violence; targeting strangers; socially and emotionally disconnected or isolated; and young. These are issues that would raise concerns (and risk) with most workers.

Lussier and Davies (2012) raise some concerns that actuarial risk assessment tools are based on the assumption that the risk of reoffending is linear, additive and relatively stable over time. As a result, actuarial instruments tend to overestimate the risk of violent/sexual recidivism for some sex offenders while underestimating this risk for others. One of the main causes of such predictive inaccuracies is the inability of current actuarial tools to account for the dynamic aspects of offending trajectories over time. The use of static factors means that the person is fixed in the category and it is difficult to recognise change within this.

It is important to remember that expert testimony is not prophecy, and actuarial conclusions rest on notions of statistical prediction, which necessarily includes uncertainty (Donaldson and Wollert, 2008). While actuarial assessments may have an air of certainty, they are not absolute. Table 5.3 represents the potential outcomes of any prediction of reoffending when someone is allocated a high- or low-risk category.

Table 5.3: Predicting outcomes

		OUTCOME	
		Re-offenders	Non re-offenders
	High risk	True positive (sensitivity) A	False positive (false alarm) B
PREDICTION			
	Low risk	False negative (misses) C	True negative (specificity) D

For every prediction of someone being assessed as high-risk, there will be a chance that the person will not reoffend (false positives). For every prediction of someone being low-risk, there will be a chance that the person will reoffend (false negative).

Reflective exercise: What are we looking for?

Imagine that you are interviewing an adult man who has committed a sexual offence against a child.

- What are the key issues you would want to discuss?
- What has led you to prioritise these?
- How will you know when you have enough information to be satisfied that each issue is dealt with?

Shlonsky and Wagner (2005), in discussing actuarialism in child protection, identified that:

Actuarial risk assessment does not assist in case specific clinical decisions, nor does it engage the family in cooperative case planning, assess their functioning, establish case plan goals, or choose treatment interventions.... Risk assessment simply informs the worker about the likelihood of future maltreatment at a given point in time. At such a transition point, the actuarial assessment is completed and the critical, clinical judgments about service interventions that may reduce the likelihood of future maltreatment must be made.

An actuarial outcome is not the end task of assessment, but requires further development. Webb (2009) discusses how actuarialism in social work (including with sexual offenders) can deskill professionals and lead to a focus on the management of risk, rather than using professional skills, knowledge and judgement within an ethical framework. He locates this within a wider social and political concern with risk and how this has consequences for working with people. He cautions that:

Inevitably actuarialism leads to a decline of intensive direct work and neutralizes core social work values of social justice and anti-oppressive practice by concentrating on harm minimization and regulation of challenging clients.... By embracing actuarial programmes social work is reconstituted as a key agency of social control and exclusion of citizens who are normatively categorized as 'challenging', 'intransigent' or 'irresponsible', thereby demarcating those who can play a full role in advanced liberal societies and those who cannot. (Webb, 2009, p 223)

This has resonance for social work's engagement with people who commit sexual offences and it is useful to reflect on how this is translated into our practices. Of course, broad socio-political concerns about control and exclusion may not override the need to prevent some sexual offenders from having the freedom to access potential victims. For example, a man with a long history of sexually abusing children may not be allowed to play a full part in society as he may pose a continuing danger to others. The need to balance social justice for offenders and for victims is a complex moral area.

The risk assessment of sexual offenders is constantly being refined to provide more robust ways of understanding and managing the behaviour. However, there are a number of caveats here: they tend to be based on aggregate populations and so cannot with certainty identify the risk that an individual offender poses; they can focus too closely on the offender and marginalise environmental factors; they provide indications but not remedies; they represent one form of (hegemonic/dominant) knowledge; they are negatively rather than positively focused; and, finally, they are a key part of one epistemological approach to understanding sex offenders and sex crimes.

Using assessment tools

Social workers may be involved in a range of settings where they may be assessing sex offenders for a range of purposes (eg accommodation, various training courses) in a range of settings (eg residential, treatment), which may include risk assessments. Risk assessments are often an inter-professional process (eg Multi-Agency Public Protection Arrangements [MAPPA]) and social workers may not be the principal profession engaged in assessing risk. However, the circumstances where social workers in England and Wales are likely to be a key risk assessor are with young offenders and possibly offenders with learning disabilities.

As discussed earlier, it is increasingly being recognised that assessment protocols need to be relevant to specific populations and that 'one size' does not 'fit all' (Howard et al, 2014). This has led to the development of more specialised approaches, and there are specific tools for boys (eg AR–RSBP; AIM2), women (eg Nathan and Ward, 2002) and people with intellectual disabilities (eg Wilcox et al, 2009). The claims made for these more structured risk assessment tools are much more limited than in previous years, and they are increasingly viewed as an aid to decision-making and a method of organising the assessment by providing a framework for investigation. For example, there are *no validated assessment tools* for use with children who commit sexual offences (CJJI, 2013), although there are helpful frameworks.

The AIM2 protocol is commonly used in the UK with boys aged 12–18 who have committed sexual offences, and it identifies offence-specific, developmental, family and environmental factors that are calculated to produce an outcome of low, medium or high risk. This tool requires specialist training to accurately understand how the factors should be interpreted and translated into the calculating matrix as there is considerable scope for individual bias and conceptual confusion. What may appear to be fairly straightforward factors can, on close investigation, turn out to be problematic. Myers (2007) raised some questions about how such factors are often not stable, with the potential for different outcomes depending on their interpretation, and warned against using the outcomes in an uncritical way. The temptation is to use assessment tools as an end in themselves, as they appear to be robust and coherent, and are privileged due to their 'scientific' appearance, providing an air of certainty about managing damaging behaviour. There is evidence that this is happening in practice, as with this quotation from the Criminal Justice Joint Investigation examining multi-agency responses to children who sexually offend (CJJI, 2013, p 27):

> Although a number of areas had made a commitment to train managers in AIM2, completed assessments were not regularly subject to any formalised or robust quality assurance process. Where completed, it was used solely as a scoring matrix with little analysis or interpretation of outcomes and it was rare for multi-agency meetings to be held following completion to agree a multi-disciplinary plan of intervention.

It is possible that social workers will find themselves being asked to coordinate an assessment where the offender is a child. Good assessment practice would encourage the collation of a range of views about the situation and the behaviour, including that of the person, as relying on just one source is unlikely to provide a rich picture of the circumstances or a robust outcome. If an assessment tool is used, then this needs to be considered and then professional judgement used to determine the significance of this, as advised by the guidance for most of the approaches. Gaining some shared understanding by the team about how to make sense of the information gathered is vital in creating a coherent narrative for managing the offender.

Structured assessment tools

Structured assessment tools that identify factors that are amenable to change include Thornton's (2002) Structured Risk Assessment, Webster et al's (2006) Structured Assessment of Risk and Need (SARN) and Hanson et al's (2007) Stable Assessment Tool, all of which are for use with adult men. We will look in more detail at Hart et al's (2003) Risk for Sexual Violence Protocol (RSVP) as a good example of how static and dynamic factors are combined to create an assessment framework:

> The RSVP is intended to help evaluators conduct comprehensive assessments of risk of sexual violence in clinical and forensic settings.... Evaluators need to characterize the risks posed by the individual in terms of the nature, imminence, severity and frequency of the sexual violence the person might commit; and also to determine what steps should be taken to minimize those risks. The task of evaluators is to speculate about how and why people chose to commit sexual violence in the past; or, put it differently, to determine whether various factors (e.g. sexual deviation, antisocial attitudes, irrational beliefs, labile affect, interpersonal

stresses) influenced their past choices about sexual violence or might influence their decisions in the future. (Hart et al, 2003, p 16)

It is recommended that use of the RSVP requires considerable professional skill and judgement and that those who are applying it should have knowledge of sexual violence, including familiarity with the literature on the nature, causes and management of sexual violence, plus expertise in individual assessment. Training and experience in the administration and interpretation of standardised tests would be required, as would expertise in the assessment and diagnosis of mental disorder (Hart et al, 2003, p 19). This 'professionalisation' of sex offender assessment makes it increasingly likely that only those who have been accredited in the use of such tools will be allowed to use them as they require specialist knowledge that, if absent, could lead to poor quality outcomes and legal liability. The protocol has five domains with associated factors to assess:

- Sexual violence history (stable or static risk factors)
  1. Chronicity
  2. Diversity
  3. Escalation
  4. Physical coercion
  5. Psychological coercion
- Psychological adjustment (dynamic risk factors)
  6. Extreme minimisation or denial
  7. Attitudes that support or condone sexual violence
  8. Problems with self-awareness
  9. Problems with stress or coping
  10. Problems resulting from child abuse
- Mental disorder (dynamic risk factors)
  11. Sexual deviance
  12. Psychopathic personality disorder
  13. Major mental illness
  14. Problems with substance abuse
  15. Violent or suicidal ideation
- Social adjustment (dynamic risk factors)
  16. Problems with intimate relationships
  17. Problems with non-intimate relationships
  18. Problems with employment
  19. Non-sexual criminality
- Manageability (dynamic risk factors)
  20. Problems with planning
  21. Problems with treatment
  22. Problems with supervision

This model combines the static factors that are not amenable to change with a series of dynamic factors that provide the opportunity for future intervention. So, for example, if factor 14 'Problems with substance abuse' is present, then a substance treatment programme could be included in the intervention plan.

Reflective exercise: Using structured risk assessments

- Choose some of the dynamic factors in the RSVP.
- What sort of behaviours would indicate that these factors are present in someone's life?
- How would you find out this information?
- How could you be certain that you have found out that each of the problems exists or not?
- How do you think your interpretation of the factors might differ from some other professionals?

The Good Lives Model (GLM) of Ward and Maruna (2007) provides a useful framework for thinking about what to consider with a view to identifying what interventions might be helpful in preventing the behaviour. The model presumes that people want to achieve a positive lifestyle and have goals that they want to reach, but because of their lack of internal and/or external resources, they use anti-social (offending) means to achieve these. It also assumes that there are 'primary goods' that people share as goals and that these are realised through the application of 'secondary goods', which are actions that help to reach them. We will explore this further in Chapter Six on interventions as the distinction between assessment and intervention (treatment) is not always clear-cut. For the purposes of assessment, Ward and Maruna have outlined the following six phases of the GLM:

- Phase 1 identifies the problems an offender presents with, and for which criminogenic (supportive of criminal behaviour) needs are evident.
- Phase 2 establishes the primary good that the offending served to achieve, and discusses which of the goods the offender values most in order to gain an idea of his/her personal identity and those things to which he/she is fundamentally committed. The GLM proposes that personal identity is defined by the things an individual values and, more specifically, by the relative priorities he/she assigns to the primary goods.
- Phase 3 involves identifying the offender's strengths: those things that will help him/her to achieve identified and valued outcomes in pro-social ways.

- Phase 4 involves identifying ways of achieving the goods in pro-social ways that are meaningful and realistic for the offender; this is essentially identifying secondary goods.
- Phase 5 considers the external factors that the offender will be subject to when restrictions are removed – the conditions under and environment in which he/she will be living, which will have an impact on the opportunities and means available through and with which to realise secondary goods.
- Phase 6 is the creation of a 'good lives' plan based on the first five phases. This should outline what measures and steps need to be taken to enable the offender to realise his/her goals. The 'good lives' plan will be based on information about existing criminogenic factors that could frustrate achievement of the plan, as well as strengths, resources, support, environment and, crucially, what the offender values and wants from life.

The GLM follows a trend in social work towards strength-based approaches (eg Saleebey, 2013), which have been argued to be a way of enabling social work values to be translated into practice when working with high-risk and mandated clients (Healy, 2012).

A similar earlier development is the Signs of Safety® (SoS) model used where there are concerns about child protection (Turnell and Edwards, 1999). This provides a framework so that everyone can be clear about what the areas of concern and strengths are. It uses solution-focused techniques with the purpose of creating a dynamic intervention plan that has the safety of actual and potential victims at its centre. It is particularly useful where there are allegations of sexual abuse within a family that are denied and the evidence is not of a standard to meet criminal thresholds, and we will explore this further in Chapter Six. The SoS uses a visual representation to clarify what people are worried about and what people would like to change, providing a document that can be used to chart change. The Junction Project (Milner and Bateman, 2011), a specialist centre for children and young people with sexually harmful or concerning behaviour, uses such a framework (see Figure 5.1) in assessing children. This provides the opportunity for all parties concerned (young person, family, professionals) to be clear about what the problems are and how these might be dealt with, drawing on the strengths of the family to assist the young person to change and to promote safety.

Figure 5.1: Signs of Safety working document for children with sexually harmful behaviour

Evidence Sheet of Safety and Concerns

Concerns ◀──▶ *Safety*

What is happening with the child/family that is worrying you?

What relevant strengths, safety measures are already in place

CHILD/YOUNG PERSON'S GOALS

What would you like your life to look like in 3–6 months time

Ideas for achieving this

CARERS' GOALS

What do the carers want to change?

Ideas for achieving this

PROFESSIONAL'S GOALS

What changes do you need to see to be able to close the case?

STRENGTHS SCALE

Scale the young person's current strengths to control the sexual behaviour

0 = low strength   10 = high strength

Agreements
Signatures   ....

Note: © Barnardos, The Junction.

Source: Adapted from Turnell and Edwards (1999).

Reflective exercise: Identifying strengths and concerns

Edward, who is a 12-year-old white boy, sexually abused his young cousin while they were playing a game. His parents and wider family are horrified and have cooperated with children's services to understand and manage this behaviour. Use the SoS framework outlined in Figure 5.1 to answer the following:

- What questions would you ask to answer the areas identified on the evidence sheet?
- How would you ask them?
- What sort of information would indicate to you that Edward had 'low strengths' in controlling his behaviour?
- What would 'high strengths' consist of?
- What evidence leads you to decide what is a 'high' or 'low' strength?

Physiological assessments

So far, we have focused on social and psychological elements in assessing sex offenders. However, as we showed in Chapter Two, multi-factorial explanations of the aetiology of sex offending all include physiological considerations. There are two principal forms of physiological assessment, both of which are carried out by specialist services: phallometry and polygraphy.

Such has been the concern about sexual offending that there have been attempts to gauge the dangerousness of offenders by some unusual means not routinely found with other criminal behaviour. Phallometry (otherwise known as penile plethysmography), where penile arousal to stimuli is measured, has been used to understand the sexual predilections of (male) offenders and what images they find sexually stimulating. The intent is to identify sexual responses that may otherwise be hidden and therefore not properly taken into account, using science to investigate and determine whether someone has a deviant and dangerous sexuality. It is premised on the notion that physical sexual arousal cannot be hidden and therefore the truth of someone's inner feelings can be found, and is located in the discourse of uncontrollable male desire. Clegg and Fremouw (2009) reviewed the evidence for the effectiveness of this approach and found that it was inconclusive, with major ethical problems that included showing people images that were illegal and offensive in order to gain the required result. This is compounded when the offender is a child or young person as there are clear concerns about showing them what are essentially pornographic images and whether this would constitute cruel and inhumane treatment under section 3 of the Human Rights Act. There has been some interest in developing vaginal photoplethysmography (which measures blood-flow induced changes in the colour of the vagina, indicating arousal) but this has limited validity (eg Chivers and Bailey, 2005).

There has been an increasing interest in the use of neuroscience to understand behaviour and this is beginning to appear in the field of sexual offending, and as we mentioned in Chapter Three, it can now be a requirement in a statutory licence for some sex offenders to submit to polygraph testing. Functional Magnetic Resonance Imaging (fMRI) has developed and allows snapshots of brain activity to be taken, which have led to claims about the physical structure and workings of sexual offenders' brains (eg on boys, see Gilderthorp et al, 2011; Longo, 2011; on adult men, see Fabian, 2012). Neuroscientific explanations are premised on understanding how different parts of the brain affect behaviours, and that the processes within the brain structure also impact on how people respond and act. There is some research support for how poor early childhood experiences have a physical impact on brain development and links have been made between this development and the attachment styles of children, which have long-lasting consequences. However, this approach is relatively new and is hotly contested. Fine (2010) outlines some of the problems with the general explanatory arguments made by neuroscience and warns of the dangers of 'neurononsense' and 'neurosexism', where the claims made are supported by limited evidence that is subject to social bias. Rose and Abi-Rached (2013) comprehensively critique the broader claims of neuroscience, concluding that these are premature and unlikely to come to fruition in the optimistic way that is argued. Social workers need to engage with 'neurosexuality' and 'neurosocialwork' approaches with a critical perspective, while respecting those who are using this approach with good intentions.

Assessing risk to whom?

An aspect of the assessment of those who commit sexual offences has to be how safe they are from retribution and their own potentially self-harming behaviour. The social location of sexual offenders (and those accused of such crimes) makes them vulnerable to violence, and there are many examples of vigilante action that have resulted in injury or death. This can occur either in the community or in closed penal institutions and a component of any assessment should explore the dangers faced by those accused, including the steps required to alleviate the risks to them. An example from our practice is the case of a 15-year-old boy from a small close-knit community accused of sexual assault against a neighbour's child. A poster campaign developed that named him and his alleged crime, and the police were concerned enough to require child welfare services to act to remove him to a safer place. Hackett et al (2015) caution about the use of community notification for young people given the danger of retribution that this created for them.

Those imprisoned can be subjected to violence, which the organising service should assess and take appropriate measures to address. Self-harm, both in the community and in secure establishments, should be considered given the social and emotional impact of shame and guilt associated with the offending (and being caught), and assessments need to ensure that there are reasonable frameworks in place to prevent any self-destructive behaviour.

Conclusion

Assessment in social work is complex, requiring a combination of skills, knowledge and values to make sense of situations and to make plans for future action. Social work balances the needs of the offender, the victim(s) and the community in undertaking assessments. It is a specialist area that includes clinical, moral and social perspectives and is more than a numerical calculation: 'Specialists must have a role in decision making that goes beyond the mere administering of the risk-assessment devices. There is a place for human judgment and experience in the decision-making process, and we must value their continued consideration' (Gottfredson and Moriarty, 2006, p 17).

Summary

- Social workers need skills, values and knowledge about people and processes to undertake assessments on sexual offending.
- Assessments focus on risk, danger and safety, ensuring that people are safeguarded from any further harm.
- Actuarial assessments have a role to play in initial stages, but have their limitations.
- Structured assessment tools or frameworks assist in thinking about what to assess and how to make sense of the information, aiding professional judgement.
- A good assessment is the basis of an intervention plan.

Note
[1] See: http://www.static99.org/pdfdocs/static-99rcodingform.pdf

Social work interventions

6

Introduction

In this chapter, we explore the various approaches to direct intervention with people who commit sexual offences and some of the systems used to manage their behaviour. We look at the importance of who we, the social workers, are and how this can affect our work with people, and we argue for a reflexive approach that asks us to think about our knowledge and values. The ways in which sexual offending has been understood has affected the ways in which the behaviour has been responded to, and we look at these changes to gain some perspective on current practices. As we have already seen in this book so far, sexual offending is complicated and we explore some of these complexities through discussion and reflective exercises.

As an example, during the writing of this book, there was recognition of sexual offending by some high-profile individuals in the UK during previous decades. Contemporary reports of investigations into this behaviour demonstrated a lack of willingness to recognise the seriousness of it, often dismissing it as young women and girls developing their sexual interests or as men simply behaving as expected. The predatory and exploitative nature of these relationships and assaults was not clear to observers, and victims were often viewed as active participants in their abuse. This has echoes of the controversy around the seduction theory of Freud, where the sexual abuse of girls by their fathers was reframed as a developmental psychic fantasy (Masson, 1984) following what appears to be shock and denial at the scale and implications of such behaviour. The accounts of abuse by girls and women were dismissed (by Freud) as hysterical projections of their inner conflicts, and, of course, the louder they protested, the more deep-rooted their problem was diagnosed.

Intervening to prevent further abusive behaviour has to be a key task of any social work action, and promoting behaviour change is the often unstated aim of much social work practice. The dominance of psychological approaches to understanding and intervening in sexual offending poses some puzzles for social work, although social work has a strong relationship with psychology through the use of various psychosocial theories and models in engaging with people. Dominant ways of working are influenced by what is popular at the time in the particular location of practice, and as social work draws on other areas of subject knowledge, it is prone to incorporating whatever is the most convincing mode of thinking. The history of social work intervention demonstrates an initial use of Freudian psychodynamic ideas that informed casework (psychotherapy-lite), which concentrated on the inner failings and deficits of people who were behaving in socially unacceptable ways. Subsequently, social work absorbed behavioural and cognitive behavioural approaches, plus the more sociological critiques of how society influences life chances and delimits opportunities. Social work, in many ways, has come full circle and practice is currently heavily influenced by understanding the inner world through psychosocial theorising about attachment and loss.

Sex offender treatment has reflected the dominant understandings and approaches of its time and place, reflected in the very use of the term 'treatment' to describe interventions, which implies a medicalised way of thinking about this behaviour. Further to this, there are differences in responses based on social structures and culture, with evidence that mainland European approaches have been premised much more on the curing and integration of 'sick' people back into the community (Petrunik and Deutschmann, 2007). This may indicate the different relationship between the individual and the state in the traditional social solidarity models of (West) European political-economic systems, compared with the more individualised, economically (neo-)liberal anglophone approach. Recent changes in the approach to sexual offenders in continental Europe towards more surveillance and control could demonstrate a changing political and socio-economic context (McAlinden, 2012).

The direct interventions outlined here focus on criminal behaviour that transgresses Western norms of what constitutes a crime, rather than some of the expanded definitions of non-Western cultures. Non-Western states do legislate against and respond to sexual crimes in ways that are recognisable to Western criminal justice, and may also criminalise behaviours that are outside some Western expectations, such as consenting same-sex sexual behaviour, broader consanguinity and extramarital sexual relations (*Zina* in Islam). It is questionable whether the interventions discussed here are appropriate for these types of sexual crimes (Aili et al, 2012).

Reflective exercise: Explaining sexual violence

Zoran has been convicted of rape, which he committed during the armed conflicts that followed the break-up of Yugoslavia in the 1990s. He described being carried along by the general brutality and ethnic hostility to assault women from national groups different from his own. As a soldier, he was encouraged both by senior officers and his comrades to join in acts of mass sexual assault as part of the offensive against perceived 'mothers of the enemy'.

He considered the 'enemy' to be deserving of their fate as they had committed similar atrocities against his own people, including his mother. He committed several acts of rape and is unrepentant about his actions, claiming that he was following orders and that he was only doing what others were doing.

Zoran would like to go and live with his sister, who has two young daughters. You are asked to assist in assessing whether he can live there.

- How do theoretical explanations help you to understand his behaviour?
- What are the key issues you might want to raise with him about his behaviour?
- How likely do you think it is that he will reoffend?
- What dangers does he pose to women?

The use of the self in interventions

Before we explore the different theoretical and practice approaches, it is worth considering the importance of how the worker goes about engaging with those who have committed sexual offences. Some ways of working, particularly cognitive behavioural programmes, have viewed the worker/therapist as merely a vector to deliver the prescribed, manualised method in a way that maintains 'treatment integrity', reducing their skills to the ability to meet programme scripts. The rationale for this is that it lends itself to evaluation, enabling each intervention to be measured, quantified and directly compared to others, thus discovering just 'what works'. We view this as underutilising the skills and knowledge of workers and treating clients as simple and simplistic machines to be inputted with generalised actions that will effect change. Marshall (2009) outlines some of the problems with such an approach, including: failing to effectively implement therapeutic skills; reducing the ability of the worker to meet the responsivity principle (managing the specific and individual responses made by clients – workers may follow a script but clients do not); reducing the flexibility to change to meet new evidence as it emerges; and preventing any innovative working practices to develop. Moreover, such an approach fails to recognise that workers are people with a range of intersecting identities and that these identities will be a crucial part in the dynamic between worker and offender (eg Gilligan and Akhtar [2006] have pointed to difficulties experienced by South Asian women when interviewed by workers from their own community). Increasingly, the qualities of the worker have been recognised as important in making a difference, and the ability to develop a good working relationship based on respect, genuine interest, honesty and other values-in–action has been demonstrated to improve the outcomes for treatment (eg Hanson et al, 2009). Indeed, Yates (2013, p 91) makes it clear that 'it is essential that treatment is delivered in a positive manner that is motivating to clients'. In short, if those who have committed sexual offences are treated with actions that flow from established social work values, then their danger of reoffending may be reduced. We have highlighted the impact of this work on individual social workers in Chapter One, the ability to be appropriately challenging yet supportive can be an emotionally demanding task but one that social work has long experience of in the wide range of situations in which it operates.

Reflective exercise: Using the self

- Find 10 different words to describe your identity using 'I am ...'
- How might each of these aspects of your identity impact on your work with the range of people who sexually offend?

One example of worker behaviour that impacts on outcomes is illustrated by the work of Prescott (2009), who discusses how Motivational Interviewing (where the worker uses techniques and methods to energise the client into co–constructing change) is helpful in keeping the client engaged with treatment. Workers are more than just deliverers of a treatment dose; how they go about their interaction with people is a crucial factor in outcomes, and it is important to remember this when faced with dominant approaches that can feel deskilling.

Reflective exercise: Professional skills and knowledge

James was reflecting on his involvement with delivering a cognitive behavioural therapy (CBT) sex offender programme that had been video-recorded and assessed to ensure programme integrity. He had approached the work with an enthusiastic commitment to help change the participants and prevent future offences, but he felt that his therapeutic skills had been underused due to having to follow the required programme script in the accompanying guidance. The programme supervisor explained to James that a new set of skills was required to work in this way and that this approach was evidence-based and empirically validated. Deviation from the programme script would compromise the impact and success of the work and may lead to an increased risk of offending, as well as making it difficult to measure the programme outcome. James wondered whether he could effectively carry out this scientific way of working as his personal approach was more responsive to individual need and personal dynamics than that of the programme.

- What are the benefits of such a programme approach?
- What are the potential problems with such an approach?

There is ample evidence that the quality of the relationship between the worker and the offender does have an impact on the outcome. Having a positive therapeutic relationship in any counselling situation improves the treatment outcome and this is also the case for sexual offenders (eg Yates, 2007; Hanson et al, 2009). Workers who treat people with respect and honesty, are direct, and actually demonstrate that they are interested in them as *people worth doing business with* are valued by clients. They stay with treatment longer and are more prepared to engage with the difficult and challenging work of accepting what they have done and what this says about them. All interventions are voluntary in the sense that offenders have to make a decision to engage even when they have been mandated; therefore, creating the climate where this can be achieved is a skill that workers need to develop. Very practically, there is evidence that offenders who drop out of treatment early may be at higher risk of reoffending, so any methods that reinforce attendance are helpful for preventing this. Marshall and Marshall (2012, p 77) summarise this evidence:

> When sexual offenders are offered a place in treatment many refuse (Jones, Pelissier, & Klein-Saffran, 2006; Mann & Webster, 2002; Seager, Jellicoe, & Dhaliwal, 2004) and of those who enter treatment too many withdraw or are removed typically because they are deemed uncooperative or resistant (Lee, Proeve, Lancaster, & Jackson, 1996; McPherson, Chein, Van Maren, & Swenson, 1994; Shaw, Herkov, & Greer, 1995). These are serious problems because refusers have high recidivism rates (Seager et al., 2004) and treatment drop-outs have even higher reoffense rates than do sexual offenders who do not enter treatment (Abel, Mittelman, Becker, Rathner, & Rouleau, 1988; Browne, Foreman, & Middleton, 1998; Lee et al., 1996; McGrath, Cumming, Livingston, & Hoke, 2003).

We do not know how many people have been judged as being at 'higher risk' and incarcerated because they withdrew from a treatment programme that they found unwelcoming, disrespectful and over-confrontational.

Interventions: modes of delivery

The interventions explored in the following may be delivered in individual or groupwork formats. Some of the issues relating to workers have been addressed earlier. However, it is also important to be aware that anti-oppressive practice needs to engage with the various dynamics that may occur in groups in relation to race, ethnicity, gender, ability and sexuality. As we have previously mentioned, Ahmad (1992) highlights the need for (white) workers to address, with confidence, issues related to diversity, particularly when challenging people with different identities. The recent inquiries in Rotherham (Jay, 2014; Casey, 2015) and Oxford (Bedford, 2015) have highlighted the failure of social work to effectively engage with issues of race and ethnicity. White anxieties about being thought racist may produce racist practice through disengagement, effectively withdrawing services from people due to exaggerated notions of 'difference'. Anti–racism requires workers to be informed and confident about issues relating to cultures, faiths, power and abuse, knowing the limitations of their knowledge and retaining a commitment to respecting others and being able to ask questions. Of course, it is impossible to 'know' another's culture in totality, and claims to this should be treated with caution as a form of colonialism. In terms of groupwork, anti-oppressive perspectives may inform: how groups are constituted (eg no lone members of a social minority in a group on their own); the nature of the programme that is being followed (for example, does the programme contain heterosexist or ethnocentric assumptions?); and the dynamics of the group itself (for example, are discriminatory statements or behaviours challenged and, if so, how?). One way of beginning to address these issues is for workers to be clear about their values and how they shape their practice.

Psychodynamic theory

Wood et al (2000) outline the development of treatment approaches in the US, recognising that sexual offences have been a focus of concern since the 1930s, when the first legislation identifying 'sexual psychopaths' was enacted, which led to the incarceration of people for some form of treatment. Brown (2005) argues that these offences were deemed to be 'abnormal', requiring a different approach to non–sexual offenders and having a focus on mental health. Although not viewed as a mental illness, sexual offending was treated as a disorder that could be cured or at least modified. The period up to the 1970s seems to have been primarily dominated by what Wood et al (2000, p 30) called 'insight-oriented, psychoanalytic or humanistic treatment', and they cite the Atascadero programme in California (Frisbie, 1958, 1969) as an example of such programmes. The lack of robust data about the programmes and the outcomes, partly due to historical distance and different recording protocols, makes clarity about this very problematic. It appears that the centre treated men who had been diagnosed as sexual psychopaths, which possibly made them a higher-risk group than those who had not received the label, and it was recognised that they were not representative of the broad range of sexual offenders. Treatment appears to have been based on patient-led groupwork designed to develop psychoanalytic insight, with little in the way of the monitoring of progress or assessment of dangerousness. Participants left the programmes in a fairly random way and follow-up was not consistent. The success rates of these early programmes were not particularly impressive, and there was some indication that they could actually have worse reoffending rates than people who were untreated (Frisbie and Dondis, 1965; Romero and Williams, 1983; Laws and Marshall, 2003). This approach could be seen to reflect the dominant values and methods of the time, with such group and user-led activities designed to be introspective and psychodynamically developmental; yet, the evidence did not support the effectiveness of their use. Criticisms of these approaches fitted the move in the 1960s and 1970s towards behavioural and cognitive behavioural practices, moving towards a 'what works' agenda.

In recent years, the application of psychodynamic ideas and interventions has returned to work with sexual offending, particularly but not exclusively with children and young people. Gilderthorp et al (2011), for example, discuss the ways in which attachment theory (which is psychodynamically derived) is used to explain and intervene with sexually inappropriate behaviour through their work with adolescents. In brief, attachment theory is a normative model of classifying behaviours linked to parent–child relationships that describes how the individual develops different ways of relating to others – an internal working model – and it has become the dominant way of understanding interpersonal relationships (Simonelli et al, 2004), particularly in social work. As Bretherton (1992) points out, the basics of attachment theory are actually quite simple and appeal to common sense. If an infant most often experiences responsiveness from the parent, then they will become 'securely attached'; if they most often experience rejection, then they will become 'avoidant'; and if they receive inconsistent experiences of both, then they will become anxious and 'ambivalent'. The resulting internal working models are viewed as a stable schema about relationships that the child carries into adulthood, leading to assessments that seek confirming evidence of the type of model that the person holds. If the diagnosed model is a problematic one (ie not 'secure'), then actions may be taken to rectify this, or to locate this as a risk factor in any prognosis (for a fuller discussion of attachment theory and its application to social work practice, see Howe, 2011; Milner et al, 2015). Rich (2006) applies attachment theory to understanding and treating sexual offending (for an outlining of the evidential, scientific and practical limitations of attachment theory, see Kagan, 2000; Berghaus, 2011; Wastell and White, 2012).

The evidence for the link between attachment style and sexual offending is not well developed, and tends to be seen as one rather general element in the pathways to offending. For example, Milner et al (2015), in their study of adolescent boys, and McKillop et al's (2012) study of adult men found little or no convincing evidence that attachment problems were causally related to offending. Creeden (2013, p 13) states that 'The presence or absence of secure attachment relationships has not been identified through research as directly determining those individuals who will engage in sexually abusive behavior or differentiating individuals who commit sexual offenses from non-sexual offenders'.

As the theory proposes that those who have problematic attachment styles may be less able to understand other people's perspectives and feelings, this *could* be a factor in committing sexually abusive behaviours and is argued as such by, for example, Fonagy et al (1997) and Marshall and Marshall (2000). Attachment deficits may lead to social deficits, which, in turn, make someone more vulnerable to sexual offending. There appears to be a correlation between insecure attachment and sexual victimisation, where such styles are more prevalent in those people (children) who are sexually assaulted, although whether this causes the abuse or is a product of it is difficult to unravel, and leads to the difficult arena of making the victim at least partly responsible for their abuse. If being the victim of sexual abuse increases the likelihood of becoming an abuser, then this would be a more substantive argument for intervention.

Ward (2003) hypothesised that one of what he described as the 'pathways' to sexual offending against children was insecure attachments, specifically those who are subcategorised as 'preoccupied' or 'fearful-dismissively' attached. He felt that the reason for this was that 'child molesters experience problems with intimacy and may turn to sex with children if their adult relationships are compromised or unsatisfactory' (Ward, 2003, p 12). Ward (2003, p 12) also argued that 'offenders following this route to becoming a sex offender will expect intimate relationships with adults to be unsuccessful and so develop maladaptive interpersonal strategies to escape from, or avoid, this outcome'.

Such deficits in emotional and social skills are potentially difficult to change due to the theoretical stability of attachment styles and internal working models, and generally require intensive work to resolve some of the early traumatic experiences that have led to this. Interventions tend to be longer-term and psychodynamic, exploring feelings and childhood relationships to try to bring about more healthy attachments that are trusting and not abusive. However, this is a contested area and the stability of attachment patterns and associated claims about the 'hardwiring' of the brain have been challenged (eg Wastell and White, 2012), making the imagining, opportunity and success of change much more feasible. If it is hypothesised that sexual offending behaviour is located in fixed physical or psychical schema, then this leads to certain ways of approaching the problem; if the schema is less embedded, then this will lead to a different approach.

Psychodynamic approaches have gained traction within sex offender treatment programmes such as the 'Extended Sex Offender Treatment Programme' delivered by the National Offender Management Service (NOMS), which is designed as an additional input for those deemed to be at the highest risk of offending (NOMS, 2013). Within this six-month, nine-block, 76-session programme, at least five blocks are concerned with the direct exploration of an individual's attachment ('Life maps', 'Understanding and modifying schema', 'Emotion regulation', 'Attachment styles', 'Sex and intimacy') in order to promote attitude and behaviour change. Psychodynamic therapy generally tends to be longer-term, recognising that when the therapy unearths distressing memories and feelings, there is a moral and ethical obligation to support people through the processing of these at their own pace. Psychodynamic approaches in sex offender work tend to be located within the time constraints of a fixed programme and have a functional role in informing the required cognitive changes about relating to adults. The issues raised are not managed for the emotional health of the offender, but to inform their treatment – psychodynamic theory is used to identify disordered attachment styles that are then included in a CBT programme. This mixing of theoretical perspectives may lead to conceptual confusion and ethical dilemmas, not least whether the emotional needs of the person can be met within the rigid framework of the programme. To insist that someone shares painful emotional experiences yet fail to provide adequate support in managing this distress raises ethical questions and issues of human rights as Article 3 of the Human Rights Act 1998 prohibits inhumane or degrading treatment or punishment, which includes mental suffering and humiliation.

With young people who abuse, there are significant differences in how this behaviour is managed as adolescence is a time of developing, rather than fixed, moral reasoning and the ability to understand and respond to the needs of others. This is seen as an opportunity to intervene with some reasonable hope of effecting change and also brings young people who have sexually offended back into the primacy of a welfare-oriented approach that addresses their emotional needs, not just their abusive behaviour. Of course, this is true in practice with adults, where individuals who have been damaged by their early experiences are recognised as needing attention to their emotional health in order to live non-offending lives. Exploring how people can 'do' positive relationships and gain insight into why they view the world (and the people in it) in the way that they currently do are key elements of work to be done. As young people have quite low reoffending rates (eg Reitzell and Carbonell, 2006), it is helpful to see this approach as assisting in their overall development to strengthen their resilience against any further offending, rather than being driven by anxiety to prevent further 'inevitable' offending. A measured, longer-term developmental intervention can promote both healthy individual growth and pro-social behaviours.

Although psychodynamic ideas can remind us that sexual offenders are complicated people with histories that are worthy of recognition, there are some potential pitfalls in its application, not least the tendency to focus on intra-psychic rather than social issues. This means that patriarchy, heteronormativity, racism and other influences on the social construction of behaviour tend to be neglected.

Reflective exercise: Using theory

A student social worker was involved in an assessment of a man who had sexually abused a girl child in his extended family. Keen to demonstrate the use of a range of theoretical perspectives informing his practice, and mindful of the need to provide robust evidence for his assessment, the student chose to use attachment theory to understand the offender. He asked probing questions about the man's childhood, looking at the nature and quality of the relationship between him and his prime care-giver (mother). The man was able to engage with this and to give an account of what was clearly a damaging relationship with his mother that was diagnosed by the student as leading to an anxious-avoidant attachment style. The student fed back to the man that he had obviously had a very difficult time as a child and that his offending was due to his unconscious internal working model.

- How do you think the man felt when this was explained to him?
- How does this approach understand issues of power, gender and age?
- With whom do you think responsibility for the offending behaviour lies?

Cognitive behavioural approaches

CBT, in different guises, has been the dominant way of working with sexual offenders for at least the previous two decades and has a reasonable evidence base to support its application. Offending is viewed as learned and reinforced through attitudes, thinking distortions and patterns of behaviour that support the continuance of sexually harmful actions. CBT is designed to break the patterns that lead to and reinforce the unwanted behaviour, replacing them with behaviours that are pro-social and 'normal', through various techniques and by focusing on the evidence-based dynamic risk factors. The development of CBT approaches in the 1980s mirrors the general turn to behaviourism of this time and includes the challenging of attitudes, beliefs and distorted thinking, and the development of skills in managing the self and relationships in a more constructive way. This model required the offender to accept how cognitive processes work, taking ownership of these and practising alternative ways of thinking to reduce problematic behaviour and increase non–offending behaviour. The approach presumes that sexual offending is a product of development, where distorted ways of thinking have been learned through a variety of causes (eg poor attachment), although the aetiology of the behaviour is of less interest than focusing on change. People may have learned to offend through family, peer or social influences, but the key is to understand how their behaviour works and to change these patterns rather than analyse their development. CBT remains the most popular model of work with sexual offenders. The research base is emerging and the current situation is one of cautious optimism, rather than *the* answer that has sometimes been promoted. Ho and Ross (2012) warn against some of the hyperbolic claims for CBT and question interpretations of research that make exaggerated statements. CBT seems to have some noticeable effect, but on who, when and how is not yet completely known.

CBT has been used across different types and typologies of offenders, including gender, 'race', age and ability (Yates et al, 2010). Common practices in most CBT programmes include: understanding the cycle of offending behaviour, including triggers; modifying deficits in relationships and intimacy; increasing empathy for victims; responsibility building; and planning to prevent relapses. Some of these areas have been subject to debate about their importance, for example, as victim empathy does not have strong research support as an indicator of lower recidivism (eg Hanson and Morton-Bourgon, 2005), it is therefore argued that it should not be a major component of intervention (Mann and Barnett, 2012). A central approach has been to challenge cognitive distortions, which are those ways of thinking that support someone's offending. An example would be if an adult male offender thought that his young prepubescent girl victim was consenting to him sexually abusing her by her behaviours. He may be consciously or unconsciously reading these behaviours to support his offending, thus minimising his role and responsibility. CBT would question his reading of this and also question the cognitive schema that supports this distortion. Cognitive schemas are those broader attitudes and beliefs that can produce specific distortions (Beck et al, 2004), so holding views that children are competent to engage in sexual activity, or that women of all ages should submit to male sexual desire, are schemas that can lead to specific actions and require challenging. Initial CBT programmes tended to focus on the cognitive distortions rather than the schemas, thus failing to deal with the underlying attitudes that supported distortions, which simply re-emerged in a different form (Gannon, 2009).

CBT has provided the impetus for the development of further models, which we now discuss.

Risk, Need and Responsivity

Interventions with sexual offending during the previous three decades have been led by the three principles of Risk, Need and Responsivity (RNR), which outline what needs to be considered for a method to be effective (Andrews and Bonta, 2010). Within this framework, a wide variety of approaches can be used as long as they consider and conform to these principles. It is useful to think of this as *who* to work with (Risk), *what* to focus on (Need) and *how* to do this (Responsivity).

Risk is explained by the need to reserve treatment for higher-risk offenders, often using actuarial methods to determine who is in this group. The more risky (dangerous) a person is assessed as being, the longer, more intensive and frequent the treatment and supervision should be (Hanson and Yates, 2013). Those deemed to be low-risk should have the minimum level of supervision and intervention as there is evidence that over-involvement may lead to an increased danger of reoffending (eg Andrews and Bonta, 2010). Of course, this requires a robust assessment, which, as we have seen in Chapter Five, does have some difficulties. There have been attempts to quantify just what is meant by 'high', 'medium' and 'low' intervention, and Yates (2013) outlines the contact hours recommended by different intervention programmes. So, it is suggested that the bottom 10–20% of riskiness may not require any specialised intervention (Hanson and Yates, 2013), whereas the top 10–20% are more likely to require at least 300 hours of contact (Hanson et al, 2012). There is a presumption here that 'dosage' (contact hours) is similar to a medical procedure, where if something is serious, it requires more 'medicine' to counter it. Whether this is a sound principle for psychological interventions designed to change behaviour is open to discussion (Wampold, 2011).

Riskiness, or just who needs to be prioritised to be worked with, has changed over time. The days when all children and young people were worked with in quite intrusive ways to ensure that they did not become adult sexual offenders (Chaffin, 2008) have, by and large, disappeared, with a much more nuanced approach that recognises the changing understanding of the problem (Looman and Abracen, 2013a).

Need refers to those needs that are empirically associated with recidivism (criminogenic) and susceptible to change (dynamic). Andrews and Bonta identify eight major criminogenic factors that create and sustain offending: a history of anti-social behaviour; an anti-social personality (eg disregard for others; weak impulse control); attitudes and values that are favourable to crime; anti-social networks; problematic domestic circumstances; problematic work/education circumstances; few positive leisure activities; and substance misuse.

Treatment should focus on these intrapersonal, interpersonal and social areas as they are empirically evidenced as significant, and it is claimed that two factors in particular – 'sexual deviance' and 'anti-social lifestyle' – are very strongly linked to recidivism (Hanson and Morton-Bourgon, 2005). Most interventions are premised on the identification of such needs and these have changed over time as research has developed. Hanson et al (2007) identified the following dynamic risk factors that appeared in those who sexually reoffended: a lack of positive social influences; problems with sexual and general self-regulation; attitudes supportive of sexual assault; intimacy deficits; deviant sexual preferences; and problems cooperating with supervision. The same principle is used for other populations of sexual offenders (although unstated, the aforementioned dynamic risk factors are for adult men), for example, with young people (eg Leversee, 2011), and the range of dynamic risk factors are similar in breadth, although the detail may differ.

This approach also informs the construction of typologies of offenders to link with types of treatment. Leversee (2011), when discussing young people, identifies three types of offender: those with deficits in psychosocial functioning; those with general conduct problems and delinquency; and those with paedophilic interests. Each of these categories has different dynamic risk factors and so requires a different treatment approach. For example, a young person who has deficits in psychosocial functioning will be socially isolated, have significantly higher than usual general and social anxieties, and have low self-esteem. Treatment would include sex offence-specific work, skills building and providing opportunities for emotional and coping strategy growth in their families and schools and with peers. Focusing the work on the dynamic factors does make conceptual sense, although this raises questions of working holistically and artificially delineating the factors as many of these issues are interlinked and their definition can be vague and contestable. Hall (2011) discusses the complexities of working holistically with young people, recognising that this includes the need to use a range of creative practices relevant to them, rather than necessarily following preferred theoretical models. Hall's research found that experienced practitioners are wary of claims for particular methods to be 'evidence-based' as they understand that the research base is often limited, partial or politically motivated within a managerialist, measurable and target-driven culture. This recognises the dependent location of young people as situated in families and communities, with obvious limitations to the use of psychological therapies for social development.

Reflective exercise: Exploring attitudes and values

Discuss the following in a group or in pairs:

- What do you consider to be indicators of someone who has 'low self-esteem'?
- What do you consider to be 'deviant sexual preferences'?
- What attitudes in society are supportive of sexual offending?
- What differences in your group did you hold about these topics and what are the implications for practice?
- Undertake an internet search for definitions of the aforementioned terms. What are the similarities and differences between what you have found and your ideas?

The inclusion and exclusion of specific risk needs is itself a value-laden act based on an understanding of the world. Andrews and Bonta (2010) highlight several needs that are not empirically associated with sexual recidivism; therefore, they suggest that these are not addressed and the resource is used to focus on those factors that are known to have significance in the research. These non-criminogenic needs are dismissed as being of little significance, yet include elements that we may consider worthy of attention from a holistic and, indeed, humane perspective, including: the distress of the offender; their self-esteem; their empathy for the victim; and their denial of the offence. These are all very powerful issues, yet because there is no direct evidence to link them to recidivism, they are not considered important to work with. This raises questions about the reductionism of this approach and the breaking down of the person into discrete parts that are then made measurable. Looking back at the previous list of criminogenic factors, it is not hard to argue that there is some influence, overlap and interaction between these two lists, and filtering them out is quite a challenge.

Responsivity refers to the general approaches that have been demonstrated to have some effect, such as cognitive, behavioural and social learning theoretical perspectives, and also the specific approaches that are relevant to the particular person (Smith et al, 2009; Looman and Abracen, 2013b). It is what Yates (2013, p 90) calls 'the interaction between the individual and treatment', recognising the specifics of the person and ensuring that the intervention is as effective as possible within that context. So, gender, age, culture, religion, language, cognitive ability, learning and personality styles, and general intelligence (Smith et al, 2009) need to be taken into account to maximise the opportunity for the offender to engage. For example, the application of CBT might pose serious questions for people who have difficulty in processing and understanding information and concepts, and some of the ideas involved in these approaches may not be held within non-Western cultures. In addition to this, the CBT sex offender programme manuals often contain material that is culturally specific, with case examples of stereotyped white working-class heterosexual men that are irrelevant to a broader population (Cowburn and Bains, 2008). This opens up the space for considering the skills of the worker in engaging with people, rather than simply applying a technocratic and mechanistic model. Encouraging and motivating offenders to change are key skills that social workers can apply.

For example, Powell (2011) describes the use of strengths-based approaches with young people who have sexually offended, recognising that their lives are often saturated with stories of despair and deficit and that this can have an iatrogenic effect on change. Taking an approach that acknowledges that these young people have positives as well as having behaved badly assists in motivating and creating solutions to the problem, thus fitting with the responsivity principle. There can be a lack of conceptual congruence between the various approaches (eg CBT is very different to solution-focused therapy) but finding a way of working that meets the needs of the person as well as allowing the offending to be addressed is a key professional skill.

RNR underpins much offender work and there is some research evidence to support its effectiveness with sexual offending, although there is clearer evidence for its use in general offending. Hanson et al (2009) undertook a meta-analysis of the impact of RNR principles on offender work and recommended cautious optimism about applying RNR to sex offenders. Despite the lack of definitive evidence about the effectiveness of RNR, it remains a strong plank of practice principles, and is a framework that practitioners can work within. We will look at some of the criticisms of the approach later in this chapter.

Relapse Prevention

Psychological interventions with sexual offenders have drawn from the experience of working with other problematic behaviours, and Relapse Prevention (RP) has been a significant tool in most of the sex offender treatments that emerged in the 1980s and 1990s. RP was developed as a method of supporting alcoholics who were struggling to continue with their post-programme abstinence or control over their drinking (Marlatt, 1985). This addiction model of behaviour had some attractions in explaining the strength of deviant sexual arousal and recidivism, locating it in a bio-psychological discourse, and at the time (the 1980s), it was a framework that gave some structure to practice in a relatively new area. RP with alcoholism focused on identifying, anticipating and preventing situations that could lead someone to lapse temporarily back into unwanted drinking behaviour after they have stopped, or into a total relapse back into destructive alcoholism. Treatment assisted people to deal with critical situations and developed their skills in managing these.

The RP model has been criticised in sex offender work as being too simplistic as it tends to view all problem behaviour as requiring the same response, even though there are many different ways into (and out of) offending, and there is no evidence that sexual offending is 'addictive' in the medical sense. Conceptually, there are also problems as someone lapsing into an isolated drinking episode is unfortunate, whereas someone lapsing back into the sexual abuse of a child is on an altogether different scale (Yates and Ward, 2008); lapsing is not an acceptable option. The model presumes a passivity and inadequacy about the person that does not fit the known heterogeneity of sexual offenders, particularly those who actively plan their offences. RP remains an influential way of working but there is little evidence to support its use with sexual offenders.

Reflective exercise: The implications of theory

Following a search of the internet for explanations for his offending, Henry described his sexual offending as compulsive and addictive behaviour that he thought had a genetic component, as his father had been an alcoholic.

- How does this affect Henry's view of his ability to stop offending?
- How does this affect the worker's view of his ability to stop offending?
- What responsibility is Henry taking for his behaviour?
- What are the implications for his treatment?

The Self-Regulation Model

The Self-Regulation Model (SRM) has been recognised as an increasingly popular method of understanding and responding to sexual offending (Ward and Hudson, 1998); it frames the development of the behaviour into four pathways. Each of the pathways has a goal and is associated with specific ways of regulating the self to achieve these goals. The model claims the following pathway typology:

1. *Avoidant-passive pathway*. The person wants to stop offending (avoidance goal) but does not have the skills or capacity to change their behaviour to meet this goal (under-regulation).
2. *Avoidant-active pathway*. The person takes actions to deal with their desire to offend but these are ineffective or make the situation worse. This misregulation could, for example, include using pornography to divert from actual hands-on victims; however, this actually reinforces the sexually undesirable behaviour and leads to the potential for further offences. Realising that they have a problem, the person develops a strategy to manage their propensity to offend but it fails.
3. *Approach-automatic pathway*. The person does not want to stop offending and there is under-regulation, which means that they take advantage of pro-offending situations. Offending can be rapid from opportunity to action, which can appear spontaneous.
4. *Approach-explicit pathway*. The person is aware of their capacity to offend and works towards this goal (self-regulation), supported by pro-offending beliefs and explicit planning.

This model recognises that there are different ways in which people act out their offending, which is more reflective of what is known about its heterogeneity, and therefore allows for a more individualised assessment and treatment of the risk factors. Yates (2013) rehearses the evidence supporting the validity of the pathways, including their strong association with risk factors and recidivism. The 'Approach' pathways are clearly linked with people who are more committed to their offending behaviour, whereas the 'Avoidant' pathways indicate that there is recognition of wrongdoing and evidence of wanting to prevent this. Rather than viewing all offenders as entirely motivated by meeting deviant sexual gratification needs, there is a more nuanced understanding that there are differences that require different responses.

The Good Lives Model

The RNR approach outlined previously has been criticised for its narrow focus on deficits and risks, rather than providing constructive ways forward that motivate the person to change (Ward and Gannon, 2006). The Good Lives Model (GLM) is argued to be a strengths-based approach that addresses these concerns (Purvis et al, 2011), being underpinned by a commitment to human dignity and a recognition of *agency*, that is, the ability to take part in determining one's own future. GLM presumes that sexual offenders, like other people, desire what are called *primary human goods*, that is, the 'actions, experiences and activities that are intrinsically beneficial to individual well–being and that are sought for their own sake' (Yates, 2013, p 92). Purvis (2010) identified 11 classes of primary human goods (sometimes called goals): quality of life, knowledge, excellence in play, excellence in work, excellence in agency, inner peace, relatedness to others, relatedness to community, spirituality, pleasure and creativity. These are the core areas that people desire and they are achieved through the application of *secondary goods*, where actions are taken to reach them. If someone is good at a team sport, practises regularly, builds friendships, wins matches and enjoys the experience, then they will be using this secondary good to achieve several of the primary goods.

Reflective exercise: Problematic identities

Ian (a 15-year-old white boy) and James (a 14-year-old mixed-heritage boy) were prosecuted for a sexual offence while in a children's home. The behaviour had been consenting but against the law and a decision was made to charge. Although not academically very able, Ian was a promising footballer who had been signed up for his local team juniors, winning acclaim for his skill and team spirit. He was popular with teammates and fans alike and was said to have a potential professional future.

As he had committed a sexual offence, Ian was forced to leave the team on the grounds that he was a potential threat to the other young players. The social worker said that she thought he was using football as an excuse to groom potential victims.

- What do you think of this scenario?
- How does the GLM inform your understanding of this?
- What might be the consequences of the action taken?

GLM understands sexual offending as the maladaptive use of secondary goods to achieve primary ones, so that the desire to be intimate with someone may be transferred into sexual activity with a child, or violence may be used to achieve agency. The problem lies not with the primary goals, but with the (damaging) ways in which people try to achieve them.

This leads to interventions that focus on developing pro–social and harmless ways of attaining the primary goals, encouraging new skills to build a positive life rather than focusing on the avoidance of poor, destructive or harmful behaviours. In practice, this could mean exploring how someone who has offended against a child can develop a healthy sexual relationship with another adult, thus replacing the abusive behaviour with more desirable ones, whereas RNR and RP approaches would focus more on diminishing the unwanted behaviour. This links into the SRM discussed previously, where it is easier to attain and sustain approach goals (doing something) than avoidance goals (the absence of something) (Mann et al, 2004). This model is recommended to be integrated with approaches that include risk factors and risk management to reduce the chance of recidivism.

Ward and Fisher (2005) discuss how people hold a 'life plan', mapping out how they would like to live their life, which is often at odds with the life that they are living. They identify four general problem areas that impinge on achieving the ideal life plan – capacity, scope, means and coherence – and suggest that these can be helpful in constructing treatment plans. *Capacity* can be either internal – whether someone has the emotional, psychological or cognitive resources required – or external – whether the familial, social, economic and cultural structures are available to meet the goals. Someone may wish to achieve socio-economic autonomy but may be constrained, for example, by the lack of employment opportunities or racist barriers. These capacity obstacles are the criminogenic needs of previous models as they are changeable. *Scope* refers to the situation where people are unable to achieve the 11 primary goods at any reasonable level. This is disheartening and can lead to emotional problems and unhappiness. *Means* refers to the appropriateness of strategies to achieve the primary goods, where anti-social methods are used to gain them, for example, sexual intimacy through violence. *Coherence* refers to the requirement that the primary goods are in balance with and complement each other, ensuring that there is no conflict between them. For example, achieving excellence in play, agency and work by being a physically aggressive boxer could lead to problems if this approach is taken with some of the other primary goods.

The GLM is regarded by many practitioners as being helpful in motivating offenders to engage with treatment, to stay in treatment longer and to complete treatment, and also to improve pro-social and problem-solving skills (Yates et al, 2009), particularly when compared with RP, although the evidence is not conclusive or robust (Harkins et al, 2012). Looman and Abracen (2013b) propose that the lack of evidence supporting the GLM should lead to a return to a modified RNR approach that has some research base, and it appears that the debate between the two approaches will continue for some time.

The recent revision in the provision of accredited groupwork for sex offenders in England and Wales clearly shows the influence of both RNR and GLM. Moreover, these revisions also show an awareness that one therapeutic programme does not 'fit' all types of offenders. Table 3.2 in

Chapter Three summarises the groupwork programmes currently available for sex offenders in England and Wales; such innovative developments, taking into account recent research, are to be applauded.

The psychodynamic and cognitive behavioural approaches discussed earlier are dominant in sex offender treatment. We will now look at other interventions that have been developed, some of which have similarities to what has gone before, while others are based on very different assumptions about people.

Mindfulness

Jennings et al (2013) chart the development of what have been described as the 'third wave' of CBT (Baer, 2006), influenced by the notion of Mindfulness, and discuss how this can be applied with sexually abusive adolescents. Mindfulness is a concept that encourages the acceptance of the self in the immediate here and now, without judging who the person is, thus enabling greater awareness of negative thoughts and feelings. It also claims that it enables the person to gain more control over problematic cognitions. Workers approach the person non-judgementally (with similarities to Rogerian therapy) and encourage reflection on the problematic feelings, thoughts and behaviour. It has influences from Buddhist philosophy, although it tends to incorporate these into a more Western cognitive schema that is about the individualised internal world rather than the social context.

There are different models of Mindfulness, including: Mindfulness Based Stress Reduction (MBSR) (Kabat-Zinn, 1982); Acceptance and Commitment Therapy (ACT) (Gutierrez and Hagedorn, 2013); Dialectical Behaviour Therapy (DBT) (Linehan et al, 2001); Mindfulness Based Cognitive Therapy (MBCT) (Segal et al, 2002); and Mode Deactivation Therapy (MDT) (Apsche et al, 2005). There is some support for their ability to manage emotional states that are considered to be part of the pathways to offending through Mindfulness techniques such as breathing exercises that improve emotional regulation (Gillespie et al, 2012). Apsche and DiMeo (2012) reviewed the use of MDT with adolescent sexual offenders and found promising results, and the approach seemed to enhance the effectiveness of other therapeutic interventions. Jennings et al (2013) support the inclusion of Mindfulness principles with all interventions with adolescent sexual offenders as this helps to develop good (and successful) therapeutic relationships. There is little research on whether Mindfulness approaches are effective across age, ethnicity and gender and this is an area that would benefit from further investigation.

Strengths-based approaches

Strengths-based approaches have gained traction in social work practice across the range of people-problems (Saleebey, 2013). Solution-Focused Brief Therapy (SFBT) (Myers, 2007) is focused on identifying often hidden strengths and exceptions to the problem behaviour that can be used to develop a problem-free future, recognising that people can become subsumed into the group category of 'sex offender', which compromises the ability to imagine and achieve change. Indeed, Hudson (2005) described how participants in a programme resisted the 'master status' sex offender label that the CBT approach required of them. A solution-focused worker would be keen to use and build on this resistance rather than view it as 'denial' or 'failure to engage'. SFBT uses a series of principles, processes and techniques to encourage the development of skills, attitudes and behaviours that are pro-social, creating ways of being that do not sustain the problem behaviour. These include: the 'Miracle' question; scaling questions; coping questions; complimenting the client; setting homework tasks; looking for strengths and solutions; setting goals; and finding exceptions to the problem.

Milner and Bateman (2011) outline how this has been applied with children and young people who have sexual behaviour problems, and a solution-focused Signs of Safety® framework (Turnell and Edwards, 1999) has been used to highlight, manage and reduce risk.

Reflective exercise: Questioning problematic identities

Gary, a 17-year-old white male, was released back into the community following two years in a residential programme after committing a sexual offence. The residential treatment followed a RP/CBT model and Gary had been taught to understand the triggers of his cycle of abusive behaviour. When he came for his first community supervision and was asked to talk about himself, Gary immediately described himself as a sex offender with a clear and detailed cycle that he was able to monitor and respond to. After a pause, the solution-focused worker asked him to tell her about all the ways in which he was not like a sex offender, and the therapeutic conversation began.

Narrative therapy (White and Epston, 1990) has similarities with SFT in some of its practices but has a more theorised approach to work based on postmodern and deconstructivist ideas. Premised on the notion that people live their lives through stories that are not always of their making, narrative therapy enables workers to explore with people how they came to be ensnared by abusive attitudes and behaviours, rather than positive and pro-social ways of being. Behaviour is viewed as the problem, rather than the problem being located within the person (an *essentialised* approach), which means that the person can be separated from the behaviour and it can be deconstructed. Therapy is designed to co-create a new problem-free preferred identity through increased responsibility-taking. Jenkins (1993) has used this approach with adult men and adolescent boys, although it has not been widely applied.

Both SFBT and narrative therapy share a common assumption that sexually abusive behaviour is socially constructed through stories of gender and power, and that interventions open up the space for this to be reconstructed into new less harmful ways of being. Rather than seeing the problem behaviour as located in wrong feeling (psychodynamic), wrong thinking or wrong hardwiring (cognitive), or just genetic, which are all explanations that totalise and conflate the person with the problem and make change hard to imagine, it is viewed as being performed through discourses that are amenable to influence. There are always exceptions to the poor behaviour that are the basis for questioning totalising stories, whether these are held by the person, professionals or wider society.

Multisystemic Therapy

Multisystemic Therapy (MST®) (Henggeler et al, 2009) is an approach that has been used with offending young people, including those who offend sexually, with some success. Claimed to be a distinct therapy, MST promotes a coordinated, intensive and focused approach that brings together family, community and professional resources to manage the problem behaviour. The direct work can include strengths-based therapy, systemic family therapy and CBT, including working with the parents or carers to increase their capacity to reduce the offending behaviour. Pro-social behaviours are encouraged through peers, school and constructive leisure activities. This approach is holistic in orientation, rather than focusing solely on the internal psychology of the offender, and takes into account their social circumstances, recognising that people are located in wider situations that are worthy of intervention. Letourneau et al (2013) found in their randomised control trial that MST had a significant effect in improving problem sexual behaviour and reducing the need for incarceration of the young people.

Engaging with families and communities

A distinctive feature of social work is that it not only engages with individuals, but also works with families, social networks and communities.

This may be a particularly positive way of working with offenders from some minority ethnic groups, but this will require culturally sensitive and actively engaged practice (in relation to some South Asian Muslim issues that require consideration, see, eg, Gilligan and Akhtar, 2006; Cowburn et al, 2015). Both family and community work require workers engaging with people who sexually offend to consider ways of involving a wider network of people in helping the sex offender to reintegrate into the community in a safe and harm-free manner. We have previously highlighted the value of restorative justice approaches to sex offenders, and ensuring that these approaches do not unwittingly support the power of the offender over victims. Restorative justice initiatives require engagement with key stakeholders in the community and (sometimes) with the victims of the offender. Engagement with the community carries the possibility of ensuring that offenders are reintegrated safely into communities and that communities are aware of the ex-sex offender in their midst (eg through sensitive use of the public notification scheme). There have been indications that some communities are beginning to address sex crime/exploitation-related issues. In evidence to the House of Commons Home Affairs Committee (Great Britain, 2013, p 57, para 119), a councillor from Rochdale, a northern English town, commented on a recently established community forum:

> Although the forum was initially set up through the mosques, at the first meeting there were women from the Asian community, women from the white community and men from the white community.... So although it came up from the grassroots from within the BME community, they were determined to widen that right across the area.... All faith groups and both sexes, but also the age ranges were to be brought in.

We do not know whether this initiative has continued, but clearly by engaging with communities actively, social work may help to lay the foundations for enabling more victims to feel able to report the abuse that they are experiencing and help develop local strategies for countering the potential for sexually abusive behaviour through campaigns and discussions.

A more sex offender-focused community-based initiative is Circles of Support and Accountability (CoSAs). The approach of CoSAs (Wilson and McWhinnie, 2013) grew out of concern that offenders were being released back into communities without having the appropriate support to integrate safely into what could be a hostile environment. The stigma and isolation experienced by offenders increased the danger that they may reoffend or come to harm, and local initiatives were taken by voluntary sector organisations to provide care and control for them in the community. Research indicated that this approach was successful in reducing reoffending (eg Wilson et al, 2008) and it developed into a more formalised system, where the offender is a member of a core group of four to six lay community volunteers who commit to regular meetings to monitor and promote safe integration. Professionals (probation officers, psychologists, etc) in an 'outer circle' provide guidance as and when appropriate, supporting the core group to maintain a focus on safety and accountability.

McAlinden (2007, p 44) suggests that CoSAs are a positive example of how communities can deal with sex offenders in a reintegrative manner. A key feature of COSAs as they operate in Britain is that volunteers from local communities staff them. Circles UK[1] is the national coordinating body, with regional branches across England and Wales. A 'Circle' is made up of one convicted sex offender, known as the 'core member', and approximately six volunteers from the community (see Figure 6.1).

Circles are coordinated locally/regionally and probation officers who are responsible for supervising the offender's statutory licence refer potential core members to the local Circle's coordinator. The outer circle shown in Figure 6.1 is made up of professionals involved with the core member and could include probation officers, psychologists, health service staff and social workers. The inner circle meets regularly (at least once a week) and offers the core member help to reintegrate into his community while holding him accountable for his actions. To date, CoSAs have received positive evaluations on both sides of the Atlantic (Hanvey et al, 2011).

Circles UK sees itself following a restorative justice approach; while it does not bring victims and offenders together, it does involve local community members and it sees restoring the relationship between offenders and their community as a fundamental part of its work (Hanvey and Höing, 2013).

This approach allows for an individually tailored engagement that recognises the heterogeneity of offenders and the uniqueness of each person, rather than subjecting them to models that assume one causality and treatment. It also allows for a strong focus on the social supports necessary for stability and living a problem-free life.

Which intervention?

The variety of interventions available all have some research evidence to support their use, and this evidence is changing and subject to different interpretations. Certainly, CBT has become the most dominant approach, possibly because it lends itself more easily to measurement than some other ways of working, as well as fitting with a prevailing correctional culture.

Most of the approaches have an unstated assumption that the offender is a white adult male located in Western societies without any intellectual disability. Complications arise when we are faced with sexual offenders who

Figure 6.1: Circles of Support and Accountability

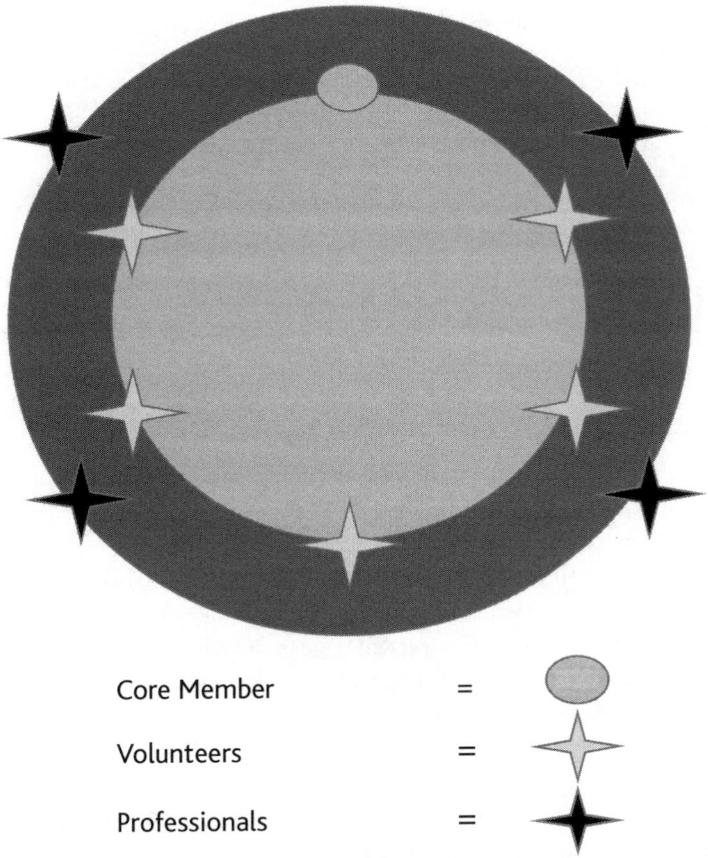

Core Member	=	⬭
Volunteers	=	✦
Professionals	=	✦

Reprinted, with permission, from Wilson et al (2007)

are young, disabled or female, or from cultures that are different from an often assumed white norm. It is important to note that an issue that has not been adequately resolved is the under-participation of black and minority ethnic (BME) sex offenders in these groupwork programmes (Cowburn et al, 2008). The reasons for this non-involvement are complex and will involve programme content, programme process, community and cultural issues (see Cowburn et al, 2015).

Reflective exercise: Choosing appropriate approaches

Aysha, aged 14, is a refugee from a war-torn Middle Eastern country. She has sexually abused her younger boy cousins, bribing them with presents and threatening them with violence to ensure their compliance. She is intellectually disabled and has a history of being sexually abused by a family member. She is prone to violent outbursts at school and refuses to accept that she has done anything.

- How would the different approaches outlined earlier influence practice with Aysha?
- How would you go about planning intervention with Aysha?

Corabian et al (2011), in their overview of systematic reviews, formed the following conclusion:

> It is still not clear whether all sex offenders require treatment or whether current therapeutic interventions are appropriate for all subgroups of offenders. There also remains much disagreement concerning what are the most useful components and elements of SOT [sex offender treatment] programs that would ensure meaningful rehabilitation for convicted adult male sex offenders and limit the number of future victims. Neither does the available research on SOT outcomes provide clear answers on whether program location matters. More and better designed, conducted, and reported primary and secondary research is warranted to resolve these uncertainties.

Lacombe (2008, p 72) argued that most sex offender treatment approaches reinforce difference, creating a sex offender identity of heightened uncontrollable dangerousness where 'they teach offenders to recognize, acknowledge and internalize what Becker (1963) refers to as a Master Status – a set of characteristics that over-determines identity and overshadows all other aspects of an offender's character'. This is a salutary warning that some approaches may actually create and accentuate sexual offending by emphasising 'otherness', rather than attending to the range of needs that people, including those who sexually offend, have. Models that over-psychologise the behaviour at the expense of social and community influences and solutions may not provide any long-term management. Social work locates the individual within their family, community and society, recognising that these are important aspects that need to be taken into account. This perspective increasingly seems relevant to effective, accountable and humane intervention in the lives of sexual offenders.

Social workers find themselves working in many different locations and this will influence the methods that they are allowed to use and the purpose of their interventions. Some may work with adults with learning disabilities in the community; others may work with young people in the criminal justice system; still others may work with parents in children's social care. Each of these will have preferred and/or prescribed ways of working that are relevant to the task and have a multi-professional approach. There are potential difficulties with eclectic practice as the approaches outlined in this chapter have very different assumptions about people, knowledge and practice, and so bringing them together in any coherent way is a challenge, particularly if they are linked to specific professional bases. For example, there are conceptual differences between the problem-based psychodynamic approach and strengths-based solution-focused working.

All interventions are in context, so we suggest that the following questions may be helpful when undertaking direct work with someone who has sexually offended:

1. What is it that you are trying to do?
2. What are you focusing on?
3. How do you intend to achieve this?
4. How does it fit in with what other profession(al)s are doing?
5. What will you do next?
6. How do your plans relate to what has gone before?
7. How will you and others know when you have achieved the goals?

Social workers can have a key role to play in interventions with sexual offenders, bringing their skills, values and knowledge together to provide effective change for the person and safety for the community.

Summary

- Treating sex offenders with respect and humanity has a positive impact on their offending behaviour.
- There are different ways of understanding offending behaviour and these can lead to different practices.
- There has been a move to more positive, holistic working that addresses the range of needs of the offender.
- Interventions often require specialist skills and knowledge.
- Treatment generally has good outcomes and practise can be hopeful.
- Social and familial, as well as psychological, interventions are important in ensuring continuing safety.

Note
[1] See: http://www.circles-uk.org.uk

7

Developing reflexive and reflective practice with sex offenders

Introduction

In many ways, we are circumspect about using the terminology in this chapter's title. Potentially, it takes us into a semantic swamp, and an extensive review of other authors' attempts at defining these concepts will, we fear, only take us further into the mire of meaning(s). However, the issues of thinking about, and thinking in and after, action are very important, and lie at the heart of this book. We must tread carefully across the prominent landscape of reflective practice, leaving fresh footprints to add to the many that have come before us. In our final chapter, we explore the landscape of reflective/reflexive practice in more detail, with a view to demonstrating the contribution that this book makes to social work practice with sex offenders.

The terms 'reflective' and 'reflexive' are concerned with thinking; in connection with practice, they point to *thoughtful* practice. In his seminal work *The Reflective Practitioner: How Professionals Think in Action*, Schön (1983) described the thinking of some professions whose work was primarily engaged with the inanimate material world as 'technical rationality'. Observation, measurement and (mathematical) calculation were the foundational methods of these professions. However, for those professions engaged with people – for example, planning, psychotherapy and social work – abstracted scientific calculation was seen as insufficient to inform the complexities of the professional task. Schön (1983, pp 76–104) suggested that reflection – on the task, relevant theories and research – was required. He identified two types of reflection: 'on action' and 'in action'. These two aspects of thinking about social work practice before, during and after direct work have had various manifestations and proponents: 'reflective thinking', 'reflexive thinking' and 'critical thinking'. Thompson and Thompson (2008, p 19) identify two usages for the word 'reflect': a colloquial 'let me reflect on that' and a more precise usage meaning 'looking back on ourselves'. They consider both usages as relevant to 'reflective practice', which 'involves both thinking/analysis and self-awareness' (Thompson and Thompson, 2008, p 19). The term 'reflexive' largely overlaps with the second usage;

they suggest that 'reflective practice needs to be reflective in both senses of the word: thoughtful (analytical and well-informed) as well as self-aware or reflexive. Thompson and Thompson (2008, p 31) further comment that:

> Reflection is the ability to think and consider 'experiences, percept[ion]s, ideas [values and beliefs], etc. with a view to the discovery of new relations or the drawing of conclusions for the guidance of future action' (Quinn, 1998; p 122). In other words, reflection enables individuals to make sense of their lived experiences through examining such experiences in context.

> Reflection, although a cornerstone of reflective practice, is not the only skill needed. Reflective practice is more than just a thoughtful practice. It is the process of turning thoughtful practice into a potential learning situation 'which may help to modify and change approaches to practice' (Schober, 1993; p 324). Reflective practice entails the synthesis of self-awareness, reflection and critical thinking (Brechin, Brown and Eby, 2000; p 52).

Of interest here is that reflection enables the social worker to review the interrelationship of emotional, behavioural, cognitive, theoretical and ideological/theological components of the 'lived experiences' of social work practice. The overall process is construed as educational ('a potential learning situation') and transformational (to 'modify and change approaches to practice'). Clearly, (social work) practice is not merely 'technical-rational' in its orientation, particularly because it includes 'self-awareness' as part of the endeavour. By focusing on personal aspects of the thinking process, Thompson and Thompson (2008) point towards notions of 'reflexivity'. Reflexive practice focuses on the self as a worker and a human being; it addresses the interplay of feelings, values, thoughts and actions, and is part of the wider activity of reflective practice – a key consideration for social work practitioners at all levels of practice, with all service users. Fook and Gardner (2007, p 28) note that 'in order to be reflexive, we need to be aware of the many and varied ways in which we might create, or at least influence, the type of knowledge we use'. Put another way, reflexivity is 'our intrinsic ability to attend to what we are saying and doing in everyday situations' (White, 2013, p 219). Reflection incorporates critical thinking and reflexivity. Payne (2014, p 85), drawing on the work of Fook, states that 'Reflexive thinking tries to understand different perspectives on a situation. Reflective thinking, however, is a process of working things through.'

It is not profitable to explore further the definitional nuances of these terms, or to consider whether social work practice without thought is possible, or, indeed, whether the term 'reflective practice' has lost critical purchase and instead become an unquestioned tautology. However, as this book is premised on the notion of the thinking practitioner, in this chapter, we focus on how the social worker critically engages in social work practice with sex offenders. This concept is illustrated by Fook and Gardner (2007, p 28), who state:

> the idea of reflexivity alerts us to the fact that knowledge does not necessarily exist in some independent form, separate from our experiences and own sense of who we are. We are often responsible for interpreting, selecting, prioritising, sometimes seeing and not seeing, and using knowledge in particular ways that are to do with a myriad of things about ourselves and our and historical social situations.

In our opening discussion of terminologies in Chapter One, we highlighted the *constructive* nature of language; this approach assumes a postmodern epistemology that recognises, particularly with social phenomena, that there is not one 'true' definition – definitions are socially and historically located, and knowledge deriving from them is similarly created. Fook and Gardner (2007, p 28) identify four dynamic dimensions of knowledge creation:

1. Knowledge is both embodied and social (as well as emotionally and intellectually influenced).
2. Knowledge is subjectively mediated.
3. There is a reactivity element (the tools used to discover knowledge influence what is found).
4. Knowledge is created interactively (influenced by the specific situation).

These dimensions offer a useful structure from which to further explore pertinent issues raised by this book. The chapter concludes with an exploration of reflexivity on the values and human rights necessarily underpinning social work with sex offenders.

Knowledge is both embodied and social (as well as emotionally and intellectually influenced)

> Knowledge ... is mediated by who we are physically and socially, and by the consequent lenses through which we experience our world. So our physical and bodily state of being, and our social positions will influence how we interpret and select information,

and indeed how we are socially interpreted and interacted with by others. (Fook and Gardner, 2007, p 28)

Throughout this book, we have highlighted that social workers' knowledge is shaped by who they are and how people respond to them – a person's physical appearance, for example, gender, age, ethnicity or (dis)ability, will centrally affect how they 'read' a situation (whether it is this book or an active practice situation).

This has particular implications for considering information gathered during assessment and treatment interventions. In considering key areas in undertaking assessments with sex offenders, we highlighted that the process was inevitably influenced by the various identities of the worker and offender. This is more clearly appreciated if we consider the nature of the interview; Franklin (1997) identifies three distinct approaches to research interviewing, which have relevance to the social work interview, and the ensuing construction of knowledge. The approaches are: information extraction, shared understanding and the discourse model. The information extraction model clearly locates the interviewer as the person with power and expert knowledge: the interview is a mechanical instrument of data collection, the process of the interview is characterised by separateness and distance, and the (social) worker is an objective collector of facts (possibly using structured interview protocols or standardised questionnaires) from the sex offender. In the 'shared understanding' approach, the interviewer attempts to gain understanding of how the interviewee experiences aspects of her/his own life/world and other people in it. The approach is interpersonal; both parties acknowledge each other's humanity and, where necessary, the interviewer will participate in conversation. The 'discourse model' recognises power relations, is more conversational and both interviewer and interviewee have active roles in knowledge construction. While the 'information extraction' model is undoubtedly the most common in work with sex offenders, it only produces information prescribed by the structure and content or the interview (in most cases, information related to risk). The two other approaches allow for a wider exploration of issues, and, as such, they are more congruent with interventions that recognise the offender as being human, with rights and needs (eg the Good Lives Model and various community-based initiatives such as Circles of Support and Accountability). The knowledge that these approaches produce may well challenge and change firmly held views of sex offenders and sex offending. However, this knowledge will be shaped by the various embodied identities of both the worker and offender.

Consideration of embodiment and social context is key to understanding interview dynamics relating to gender, as well as to race and ethnicity. Social work, internationally, is a profession dominated by women, except in the senior management grades (Huppatz, 2012, pp 40–1). It is therefore necessary to address the gendered nature of interviewing sex offenders. The dominant format will be a female social worker interviewing a male offender. In qualitative research, there has been consideration of the gender dynamics when women interview men; while this is not exactly the same as social work interviewing, it points to issues that are likely to be common to both. Pini (2005) reports on the research of 'a young, female doctoral student' interviewing male leaders of an Australian agricultural organisation. She noted that the men emphasised their heterosexuality, their power and their expertise and superior knowledge. However, she also noted that focusing on gendered activity was a key factor in the dynamics; thus, she stated that 'we need to go beyond a simple focus on the gender of the interviewer and interviewee, and undertake a more sophisticated analysis which explores the intersection of the mediating influences of "who, whom, what and where"' (Pini, 2005, p 201). Gailey and Prohaska (2011, p 376) interviewed men about sex and sexually degrading practices; this quotation, from women researchers, highlights potential gendered problems in talking about such issues:

> Watching a man smile and listening to him laugh as he described how he and his friends humiliated women sexually was almost unbearable, especially because the interviewer thought it was important that he felt at ease and if she reacted negatively he would have felt uncomfortable and potentially ended the interview. Both of us became emotional after a number of the interviews because we felt horrible about remaining silent, because we did not challenge the abuse, and because we could only imagine how the women who were treated in this manner must have felt. We repeatedly put our own comfort aside to protect the men we were interviewing because we needed them to open up to us.

Concluding their article, they commented that 'The interview experiences analysed above clearly indicate that conducting cross-gender, in-depth interviews about sex and, specifically, sexually degrading practices puts a female researcher in a trying situation' (Gailey and Prohaska, 2011, p 377).

To offset these negative experiences, Gailey and Prohaska (2011) made a number of suggestions in relation to clothing, place of interview and the need to debrief after the interview. Issues relating to male researchers interviewing men are different; here, the issue is how to respond to invitations to participate in sexist/misogynistic dialogue and how such a response affects the progress of the interview (Cowburn, 2007, 2013; Blagden and Pemberton, 2010). What is clear is that in both cases, the 'data' constructed in the interviews are likely to be different; attention to gender dynamics assists understanding of what is happening and what is being said in interviews.

Earlier in the book, we introduced the concept of 'intersectionality' as useful in recognising the dimensions of individual identities that intersect and are variously emphasised at different times and locations. Apart from gender, the other key aspect of embodied identity that shapes knowledge from interviews is race (and ethnicity). As we have discussed, race is the concept that foregrounds physical appearance, prompting responses based on physiognomy and skin colour. We have highlighted the reluctance of black and minority ethnic (BME) victims, offenders and communities to engage with white criminal justice organisations; Angela Davis (1981) and others have suggested that this may be because of the perceived (and actual) racist nature of these organisations. To ignore issues of race and ethnicity in working with offenders, victims, families and communities, at best, perpetuates misunderstanding and, at worst, endorses a racial hierarchy.

Critical knowledge of sex crimes and sex offenders necessarily incorporates consideration of gender, race and all other aspects of identities. The social worker has to apply a reflexive approach in working with offences involving sexual harm in order to uncover how dominant (white, male, etc) identities shape and influence the creation of both self and other in the offender. With these dimensions explicitly acknowledged, it may be that unresolved issues relating to sex offender treatment in the UK could be more sensitively addressed (ie the under-representation of BME sex offenders on treatment programmes, the cultural appropriateness of these programmes and the disengagement of BME communities with most criminal justice initiatives).

Knowledge is subjectively mediated

The *subjective* mediation of knowledge points to how people's personal histories influence and affect how they use professional knowledge – for example, a worker who has been a victim of sexual harm may need to explicitly process her/his experiences in order to engage in work with sex offenders: 'Being reflexive by taking into account subjectivity will involve a knowledge of who I am as a whole being (social, economic, political) and an understanding of the effects this has on the knowledge I perceive and create' (Fook and Gardner, 2007, p 29).

Reflexivity requires self-awareness, a key concept in this book, particularly in considering how personal values influence professional practice and the impacts (on social workers) of working with people who commit acts of sexual harm. Thompson and Thompson (2008, p 157) note that 'Work pressures can lead us into losing sight of who we are, what impact we are having on the situations we are dealing with and what impact they are having on us'. In most official inquiries and serious case reviews of sex offender-related matters, scant attention is paid to this area; greater concern is given to whether or not procedures were followed. Throughout this book, we emphasise the human-ness of the social worker at the centre of practice. Without the opportunity to engage critically in holistic reflection, Thompson and Thompson (2008, p 157) take the view that 'if we adopt an unthinking, non-reflective approach to our work, then we may find that this human dimension slips away, with the result that people experience our efforts to help as mechanistic and dehumanising'.

Ferguson (2005), in analysing the death of eight-year-old Victoria Climbié in 2000, argued that where social workers suppressed the emotional content of their practice, it compromised their decision-making; moreover, they failed to recognise that the management of risk is not a straightforward rational exercise, but complicated by the inherent 'messiness' of people. Munro (2011), in her review of child protection services in the UK, also suggested that a rational-technical approach to social work intervention struggles to encompass the emotional components of everyday practice, which can increase, rather than decrease, risk.

In Chapter One, we outlined the possible adverse consequences for those working with people convicted of sexually harming others. Some of the reasons why this work is potentially so problematic are fairly obvious and shared, whereas others are somewhat nuanced and very individual. Personal perspectives on sex, sexuality and violence are often closely held, and not open to discussion, leading to approaches that lack the reflexivity required to ensure thoughtful practice. Strongly held views can provide security when faced with assaults on our emotional being, but they can also affect the way we go about our work. In addition to this, working with sex offenders is often mandated rather than voluntary, operating through legal or other processes, which creates a further dynamic where clients may be resistant, resentful and lacking responsibility (Connolly and Ward, 2008; Hatcher and Noakes, 2010). Hearing intimate and detailed stories of sexual activities, violence, abuse and degradation on a regular basis is stressful for workers and challenges personal value systems and moral codes, generating understandable feelings of disgust, anger and sadness.

It has been suggested that this work creates a paradoxical dilemma, whereby the professional requirement to develop a relationship with the offender is countered by personal revulsion at the behaviour and a desire to create distance (Lea et al, 1999). This creates tensions for the worker that can be hard to manage, and can lead to behaviours that compromise emotional and physical health, as identified in Chapter One. Without regular opportunities for reflection on the personal (and professional) impacts of work with this client group, the worker in this situation may also find their professional judgement is compromised.

Recognising the influence of the subjective mediation of knowledge in relation to social work with sex offenders can be facilitated through supervision. Munro (2011) identified the need for organisations to operate in ways that support workers to reflect on their practice, encouraging openness, transparency and discussion – a supervision structure that values staff through the encouragement of reflective space and creative practices. This is not, however, as straightforward as it might appear. Much of the literature about social work and organisations has identified the anxieties felt by practitioners about the blaming nature of many of their employing agencies (Kemshall, 2010), and this can be seen in the ways in which individual social workers have been treated following high-profile child death investigations (for an analysis of the 'Baby P' tragedy, see Jones, 2014). The fear of being blamed by their organisation for events that are difficult to predict, plus being held to account for inadequate institutional systems and processes, is experienced by social workers as impacting on their ability to undertake the job.

Social workers are, indeed, 'held to account' for their practice, in terms of both meeting professional and ethical codes of conduct, and working in line with legal requirements. Worker responsibility and accountability are important aspects of professionalism that need to be encouraged rather than imposed, and high-quality supervision can provide the mechanism to achieve this. Supervision can be about professional development as well as a mechanism for the surveillance of professional practice, and these two understandings can create tensions. Certainly there have been concerns expressed that supervision has moved away from its focus on education, administration and support (eg Kadushin and Harkness, 2002): 'the sole goal of supervision is in danger of becoming the elimination of risk through the micro-management and surveillance of practitioners and their outcomes' (Peach and Horner, 2007, p 229). The balance between professional and managerial agendas is often played out in supervision, and there can be different interpretations of what it is for. Is it about accountability and monitoring performance, or facilitating professional development? Is it about professional education, or meeting organisational needs? Beddoe (2010, p 1280) summarised this discussion as leading to two types of supervision: 'a professional approach, anchored in social work and with a focus on practitioner learning and development, and a second approach emerging from the risk-management imperatives so prevalent in social care'. In order to avoid the latter dominating and narrowing the goals of supervision, Beddoe (2010) proposed that supervision should:

- explore emotions;
- facilitate critical inquiry of practice and issues;

■ support practitioners' self-confidence when faced with uncertainty and in the face of conflicting or competing demands; and

■ enable trust to develop in the supervision relationship.

The subjective pressures of managing 'risk' permeate work with sex offenders; this places a huge burden of expectation on the worker, which has personal consequences. Stanford (2011, p 1526, emphasis in original) identifies fear as '*the* emotion of risk' in social work, which indicates the powerful feelings at play when practising. Culpitt (1999, p 132) highlights the 'terrible fear that is driven by overwhelming risk'. Practice can become 'very defensive, overly proceduralized and narrowly concerned with assessing, managing and insuring against risk' (Parton and O'Byrne, 2000, p 1). Yet, in spite of this, social workers can and do resist the powerful invitations to work in such limited ways. Webb (2006, p 203) describes social workers as having 'an ethical disposition to do the best for clients and insofar as they have the resources to do so, they try to use these to maximize ethical ends', in other words, they want to 'do good', but, of course, this raises questions about what is 'good' for the sexual offender, the victim and society, creating tensions and the need to make judgements about risk. Risks can never be completely eliminated (and it is a dangerous illusion to believe that they can be), and decisions on risk are always being made. Creative, constructive, *just* practice requires risk-taking and this needs personal, professional and organisational commitment and support.

Despite the difficulties and dangers of working with sexual offenders, there is also an emerging evidence base which recognises that it is a valuable, rewarding and positive experience for workers. A key aspect valued by workers is the feeling of personal and professional pride in effecting change as sex offender work has generally positive outcomes. Research (eg Huffam, 2001; Scheela, 2001; Slater and Lambie, 2011) indicates the practice of workers taking an optimistic approach based on their values-in-action is validated by positive outcomes. The commitment to 'make a difference' (Slater and Lambie, 2011, p 330) helps workers to maintain energy and focus, which is, in turn, reinforced by successful outcomes: 'It fulfils the idealist in me. That says the world can be a better place and that people can have, live happy lives' (Slater and Lambie, 2011, p 327). In particular, workers often feel greatest pride in using role models – clients who had changed and were able to promote non-abusive ways of being to their communities. They also appreciated the strengths of their teams, which were often made up of many disciplines but created a helpful, supportive and safe atmosphere. The shared ethos of wanting to effect change brought together people and created a team culture where feelings and ideas could be shared, often with a strong use of humour in the face of potentially depressing situations. Such settings recognise that the subjective creation of knowledge can be nurtured and developed intersubjectively when teams are coherent and supportive.

A reactivity element (the tools used to discover knowledge influence what is found)

> Being reflexive from this perspective … means being aware of what methods we are using, the setting and purpose of the information being gathered, the effects this has on the information obtained, and, of course, making an assessment about whether they are mutually appropriate. (Fook and Gardner, 2007, p 29)

In terms of social work with sex offenders, this can be applied to interviews and groupwork, and the need for the social worker to be critically aware of the way in which s/he is approaching and engaging in the work. Awareness of how the objective of the interview relates to wider understandings of sex offending is important (eg inquiring into an offender's early relationships and attachments, as we discussed earlier, could be done to identify how early patterns of attachment shape current cognitions about relationships, or it could be the beginning of an in-depth psychotherapeutic exploration). Thus, if the social worker's intention is to understand current patterns of attachment and how they relate to offending behaviour, this would need to be made clear. In-depth disclosure about unhappy childhood events would need to be kept to a minimum, and the focus of the interview resolutely fixed on how these events relate to present patterns of behaving. Without this clarity, the danger of a confused and potentially very distressing interview is high. Thus, there needs to be a constant interplay between three elements: theoretical frameworks that provide a justification for the intervention; ethics to monitor that the approach is not harmful and is respectful of human rights; and attention to the detail of what is happening in the interview. Awareness of these elements comprises the foundations of a reflexive/reactive stance for social work with sex offenders. In many ways, the critical interplay of these elements forms part of an ongoing internal dialogue, which interrelates micro-detail with macro-theory; as such, it can be likened to the processes of hermeneutics or interpretation.

Originally, hermeneutics was primarily concerned with the interpretation of texts, principally biblical texts. The process of interpretation is characterised as circular (hermeneutic circle). The interpreter (in this case, the social worker) begins with a general theory and then examines fine details of practice, the consideration of which changes the original hypothesis. From the changed general hypothesis, the interpreter/social worker returns to the detail of practice, and again changes in the interpretation of the detail, and consequently of the whole, occurs. This process of continual change through critique and counter-critique points to the extent to which knowledge creation is dynamic and unending. It is also an illustration of the concept of 'turning back' as part of being reflexive.

Hermeneutics, therefore, offers a perspective of social work as always incomplete and uncertain, responding to new questions and problems in the quest for (new/better) meaning. While there is a range of hermeneutic schools, the work of Gadamer (1974) is of relevance here, in that he recognises the active role and involvement of the interpreter (for our purposes – social worker) in creating new knowledge. The values, epistemological standpoint, practice experience and emotional responses of the interpreter are all-important, and if explicitly recognised, become part of the new knowledge. Thus, in relation to understanding the reactivity element of knowledge creation in relation to sex offending, it is necessary to be aware of the starting point of the worker in terms of knowledge, values, emotions and practice experience. In trying to identify starting point knowledge and values, Figure 7.1 may offer some suggestions.

This book addresses all of the areas in Figure 7.1, and hopefully early reflective exercises have helped readers identify issues for themselves in relation to the five tiers of the triangle. Figure 7.2 represents the dynamic interaction of knowledge and practice; the (hermeneutic) circle is continuous and there is no end point. The starting point is purely notional; the practitioner comes to a practice situation largely influenced by dominant forms of knowledge. In the case of social work with sex offenders, this may be a mixture of media representations, some psychological information and safeguarding protocols. In the process of engaging in reflexive practice, the

Figure 7.1: Identifying starting points for critical reflection

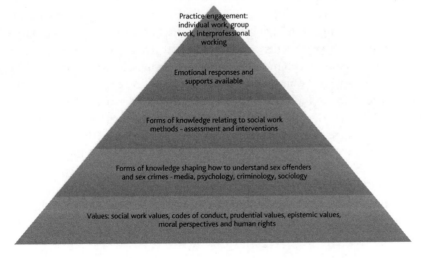

Practice engagement: individual work, group work, interprofessional working

Emotional responses and supports available

Forms of knowledge relating to social work methods – assessment and interventions

Forms of knowledge shaping how to understand sex offenders and sex crimes – media, psychology, criminology, sociology

Values: social work values, codes of conduct, prudential values, epistemic values, moral perspectives and human rights

Figure 7.2: A reflective circle – knowledge, change and practice

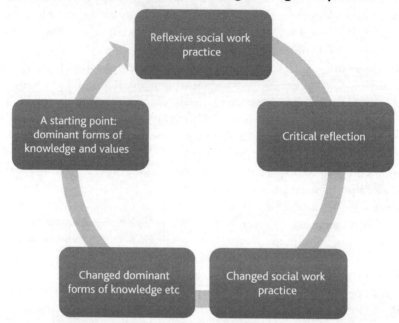

practitioner develops more effective ways of engaging with the offender, and issues that s/he considers relevant. Critical reflection (with and without a supervisor) after meeting with a client enables the worker to reflect in greater depth on issues, particularly those relating to forms of knowledge and values, and thus both are changed. The process does not have an end point, but may come to a halt for a range of practical reasons.

Addressing responsibility and victim empathy as parts of therapy have long been central components of therapeutic programmes. This could, for example, be a notional starting point for critical reflection. A social worker is aware that addressing these issues is an established part of cognitive working. Yet, new thinking, prompted by meta-analysis of reconviction data (referred to in Chapter Two), points to the (statistical) irrelevance of these areas in relation to reducing offending. Moreover, proposals have been made to remove responsibility and victim empathy from correctional programmes, and instead focus more directly on criminogenic issues. The dominant form of knowledge is challenged; reflection needs to occur in relation to the relevance of these subject areas for social work with sex offenders. This may involve reflection on what the social worker is trying to do – for example, if s/he was working as part of a restorative justice project (see Chapter Three), while accepting that responsibility for offending and victim empathy may be irrelevant to any likelihood of reoffending, it would be of central importance to the processes of reparation and restoration. Thus, the social worker would need to examine the new information critically and in the overall context of the work being undertaken. Moving from small detail to bigger picture(s), and back, helps to clarify the relevance of both.

Knowledge is created interactively (influenced by the specific situation)

> Being reflexive from this perspective means understanding how any knowledge may in fact represent only limited perspectives, from the particular point in time or a particular standpoint. This means being open to the possibility of other perspectives. (Fook and Gardner, 2007, p 30)

By highlighting various forms of knowledge in relation to sex crimes and sex offenders, we have indicated the *constructed* nature of values and knowledge. For example, while acknowledging the influence of psychological research in relation to thinking about how to respond to the convicted population, we have drawn attention to unconvicted populations and to issues of identities that are beyond the parameters of clinical utility. We have particularly pointed to the importance of gender and ethnicity in developing a wider understanding of sex offenders and sex crime. However, while sociological critiques of dominant forms of masculinity may not fit within a clinical psychological approach to sex offenders, social workers may need to consider how unquestioned ways of *being a man* endorse attitudes and values that can be understood as supportive of rape (sex crime). A large proportion of sex crimes can be viewed as misogynistic acts, and through sociological analysis, misogyny has been shown to be an influential part of *becoming a man*.

Understanding female sex offenders presents challenges to both sociological and psychological understandings of sex offenders; an initial reluctance by some feminist theorists to move from a simple analysis of sex crimes as embodiments of patriarchal values may have delayed the development of theory in this area. It may be that the growing presence of this group of offenders, and practitioner involvement with them, forced reflective engagement and nurtured the development of more sophisticated understandings; models relating to men were clearly inappropriate for women offenders, yet central to the development of theory in this area was the concept of responsibility – women could be, and were accountable and responsible for, committing offences.

Furthermore, the voices of victims, which we have drawn attention to in Chapter Two, are an important counterbalance to therapeutic approaches that may be marginalising the need to hear of the harms perpetrated by sex offenders. While attempting victim empathy may no longer be considered a prime component in cognitive-behavioural programmes designed to reduce reoffending, the voices of victims are of prime concern to wider community initiatives, and it is in (and for) communities that social workers engage with sex offenders. However, a key requirement of including victim-survivors in interactive knowledge development of sex offenders and sex crimes is that they retain power and agency to contribute (or not). Voluntary participation underscores the point that knowledge creation is a non-coercive partnership endeavour.

As we mentioned earlier, Ward and Beech (2015) point to 'integrative pluralism' as a way of consciously synthesising different perspectives about sex offenders and sex crime. As Fook and Gardner (2007) recognise, a reflexive stance towards established forms of knowledge and new potentials is a prerequisite in developing theory and practice. Integrative pluralism potentially provides a way for 'constructing local theories at multiple levels of analysis and across different domains of inquiry (e.g. psychological, developmental, cultural, biological, etc.) loosely incorporating them within an overall conceptual structure' (Ward and Beech, 2015, p 110). Reflexive social work clearly has a contribution to make to this development.

Values, rights and reflexivity

Thompson and Thompson (2008, p 47) note that 'Values shape not only our thoughts and feelings, but also our actions.' However, as we have shown, values are not easily defined or distinguished. In considering values that influence the rehabilitation of offenders, Siegert et al (2007, p 1609) identify:

> a variety of different types of values including, but not limited to, prudential values (what is in the best interest of individual clients), utilitarian values (what is in the best interests of the community), and epistemic or knowledge-based values (what are our methods of best practice).

This book started by highlighting the *constructive* importance of values in understanding sex offenders, sex crimes and how social workers respond to such. Utilitarian values inform theories of punishment in considering what is the best way for societies and communities to respond to sex offending; epistemic values reach beyond treatment effectiveness and have been shown to be of central concern to this book, in that we have presented a variety of ways of understanding sex offenders and sex crimes. We have not focused epistemic concerns solely on pariah (forensic) populations. Sex offenders are not *out there* beyond the pale of communities, they are part of communities, and sex offending is a community problem requiring a complex and multilayered response. Diversity presents a challenge to an essentialist account of sex offending; potentially, within such an account are hierarchies of knowledge and, implicitly, gender, class and race/ethnicity. By focusing on 'social divisions', we have highlighted that sex offenders are not an homogeneous group, and that in penal responses to sex offenders, particularly rehabilitative responses, one cannot assume that 'one size fits all'. For example, prudential values underpin the Good Lives Model and are foundational to human rights law.

Historically, social work is a value-driven profession; however, unlike medicine and many other health-care-based professions (including psychology), social work has, from its outset, retained a central concern for issues of social justice (Banks, 2006, p 45), and has concerned itself with vulnerable and oppressed groups in society. In its earliest years, in both the UK and the US, social work developed out of Christian faiths and was motivated by a desire to ameliorate social hardships and reform wayward individuals. In the UK, social work with people who have committed offences was initially practised by Christian 'police court missionaries', who later, in 1907, became the probation service. Social work, voluntary and statutory, has generally seen its aim as to do 'good' and to minimise social 'harms'. By including issues of social justice and focusing on issues relating to power and oppression within its value framework, social work, as a profession, is seen to be operating from a different *epistemic* base than other caring professions. While other professions may seek to ameliorate the impact of social/psychological hardship by focusing exclusively on individuals and their immediate context (eg family), social work locates these 'problems' within a wider context that includes victims and communities. The reflective exercise that follows is concerned with using the information from this book to develop a wider, and conceptually clearer, value base relevant to 21st-century social work.

Reflective exercise: Developing an integrated value base for practice

1. Social work values – write down the social work values that underpin your practice with sex offenders.
2. Identify the justifications for different practice approaches with sex offenders.
3. Identify prudential values that inform your work with sex offenders – self- and offender-related.
4. Epistemic values – identify the knowledge bases that inform and shape your practice with sex offenders (substance and interpretations).

5. How do these values accord with the aims and objectives of institutionalised
    social work?

The 'Ethics in Social Work, Statement of Principles' of the International
Federation of Social Workers and International Association of Schools of
Social Work (IFSW and IASSW, 2004) explicitly acknowledges the relevance
to social work practice of six international conventions on human rights.
In addressing human rights and human dignity, the IFSW and IASSW
(2004) stress that 'Social work is based on respect for the inherent worth
and dignity of all people'. The concept of dignity is foundational in human
rights law (Rainey, 2013), although it is also a contested and debated
concept. McCrudden (2008, p 698, cited in Rainey, 2013, p 20) suggests
that 'human dignity … is exposed as culturally relative, deeply contingent on
local politics and values, resulting in significantly diverging, even conflicting,
conceptions'. However, he acknowledges three minimum core components
of human dignity: 'the recognition of the intrinsic worth of every human
being, that this intrinsic worth is recognised and respected by others and
that the state should recognize and exist for the sake of individual worth'
(Rainey, 2013, p 20). Human dignity is protected and sustained by national
and international human rights legislation, and Connolly and Ward (2008,
p 50), among others, argue 'that human rights are based on abstract values
that can be meaningfully translated into local norms that protect conditions
for people to live minimally worthwhile lives'.

While we do not provide legal commentary on human rights law and
sex offender legislation (for further information, see Rainey, 2013), the
area of potential conflict relates to risk management. Potentially restrictive
requirements in supervisory licences, sex offender registers and public
notification schemes threaten or breach the convicted sex offender's
human right to a 'private and family life'. For example, as was shown in
Chapter Three, Article 8 of the UK Human Rights Act has been used to
successfully challenge the 'indefinite' period for which a person may be
required to remain on the sex offender register without any review of his/
her circumstances. Other areas where human rights legislation may be
used to challenge sex offender legislation are in the areas of indeterminate
sentences (life sentences), public disclosure of (private) information relating
to criminal convictions and the use of pharmacotherapeutic treatments
(anti-libidinal drugs) (Rainey, 2013).

For social workers, an awareness of the human rights of sex offenders is
a reflexive counterbalance to an over-preoccupation with the sex offender
as an embodiment of risk. As Loraine Gelsthorpe (2007, pp 41–2) states:

a human rights approach incorporates values of equality, respect for diversity, concern for community, victims and offenders. Prioritising rights entails managing risk, because it involves the duty of seeing that all are enabled to live their lives freely and securely. Risk control – over emphasizing risk, dividing people into the risked and the risky – would leave the criminal justice system mired in the zero-sum approach. Although it might seem obvious that victims' and the public's rights to safety are more important than the offenders' rights to as much liberty as possible and to respectful treatment, it would be a mistake to think that the former are everything and the latter are but nothing. If both sets of views and needs are 'rights', then they are the same category of thing, and must be held in careful balance, rather than one being everything and the other nothing.

Conclusion

This chapter brings together personal, theoretical and skill-focused issues in a reflective consideration of the social construction of social work knowledge of sex offenders and sex crimes. It asserts the interdependence of emotive, cognitive and value–based components in understanding sex offenders and sex crimes.

This book problematises various forms of knowledge about both the sex offender and sex crimes. Dominant forms of knowledge separate people convicted of sexual offences from those who are not convicted; we suggest that this bifurcation is arbitrary and that knowledge gleaned from convicted populations is, at best, partial. We have presented the importance of recognising difference in terms of aspects of identities (eg gender, ethnicity, sexualities, faith and abilities) in relation to both offenders and workers, and a social work response to sex offenders necessarily integrates diversity into developing practice. This recognition (of difference) is not to be noted and dismissed; it is central in the construction of knowledge about sex offenders and their victims, families and communities. Social work practice with sex offenders is necessarily reflexive, integrating a variety of forms of knowledge and values.

References

Abel, G.G., Mittelman, M., Becker, J.V., Rathner, J. and Rouleau, J.L. (1988) Predicting Child Molesters' Response to Treatment. *Annals of the New York Academy of Sciences*, 528, 223–34.

Ahmad, B. (1992) *Black Perspectives in Social Work*. Birmingham: Venture Press.

Aili, H.H., Manveen, K.S., Pillai, S.K., Muhsin, M. and Salwina, W. (2012) *Clinical and developmental characteristics of sex offenders in Malaysian prisons*, Available at: http://www.academia.edu/8034414/Clinical_and_developmental_characteristics_of_sex_offenders_in_Malaysian_prisons (accessed 20 October 2015).

Allen, H. (1998) Rendering Them Harmless: The Professional Portrayal of Women Charged with Serious Violent Crimes. In K. Daly and L. Maher (eds) *Criminology at the Crossroads: Feminist Readings in Crime and Justice* (pp 54-68). New York, NY: Oxford University Press.

Alleyne, E., Gannon, A.T., Ciardha, Ó. and Wood, L.G. (2014) Community Males Show Multiple-Perpetrator Rape Proclivity: Development and Preliminary Validation of an Interest Scale. *Sexual Abuse: A Journal of Research and Treatment*, 26, 82–104.

Andrews, D.A. and Bonta, J. (2010) Rehabilitation Through the Lens of the Risk-Needs Responsivity Model. In: McNeil, F., Raynor, P. and Trotter, C. (eds) *Offender Supervision: New Directions in Theory, Research and Practice*. Cullompton: Willan Publishing.

Andrews, D.A., Bonta, J. and Hoge, R.D. (1990a) Classification for Effective Rehabilitation: Rediscovering Psychology. *Criminal Justice and Behavior*, 17(1), 19–52.

Andrews, D.A., Zinger, I., Hoge, R.D., Bonta, J., Gendreau, P. and Cullen, F.T. (1990b) Does Correctional Treatment Work? A Clinically Relevant and Psychologically Informed Meta-Analysis. *Criminology*, 28, 369–404.

Andrews, D.A., Bonta, J. and Wormwith, J.S. (2011) The Risk-Need-Responsivity Model: Does Adding the Good Lives Model Contribute to Effective Crime Prevention? *Criminal Justice and Behavior*, 38(7), 735–55.

APA (American Psychiatric Association) (2013) *Diagnostic and Statistical Manual of Mental Disorders – DSM-5* (5th edn). Arlington. VA: American Psychiatric Publishing.

Apsche, J. and DiMeo, L. (2012) *Mode Deactivation Therapy for Aggression and Oppositional Behavior in Adolescents: An Integrative Methodology Using ACT, DBT & CBT.* Oakland, CA: New Harbinger.

Apsche, J.A., Bass, C.K., Jennings, J.L., Murphy, C.J., Hunter, L.A. and Siv, A.M. (2005) Empirical Comparison of Three Treatments of Adolescent Males with Physical and Sexual Aggression: Mode Deactivation Therapy, Cognitive Behavioral Therapy, and Social Skills Training. *International Journal of Behavioral Consultation and Therapy*, 1(2), 101–13.

Araji, S.K. (1997) *Sexually Aggressive Children: Coming to Understand Them*. London: Sage.

Ashley Montagu, M.F. (1942) *Man's Most Dangerous Myth: The Fallacy of Race*. New York, NY: Columbia University Press.

Aspinall, P.J. (2002) Collective Terminology to Describe the Minority Ethnic Population: The Persistence of Confusion and Ambiguity in Usage. *Sociology*, 36(4), 803–16.

ATSA (Association for the Treatment of Sexual Abusers) (no date) Children with Sexual Behavior Problems: Fact Sheet. Available at: http://www.atsa.com/children-sexual-behavior-problems (accessed 21 September 2015).

ATSA (2012) Adolescents Who Have Engaged in Sexually Abusive Behavior: Effective Policies and Practices. Available at: http://www.atsa.com/adolescents-engaged-in-sexually-abusive-behavior (accessed 21 September 2015).

ATSA (2015) Symposium: Rape-Supportive Cognition and Sexual Aggression against Adults. Proceedings from 'Breaking New Ground: Understanding and Preventing Sexual Abuse', Montreal, Quebec.

Auerhahn, K. (1999) SelectiveIncapacitation and the Problem of Prediction. *Criminology* 37, 703–34.

Baer, R.A. (ed) (2006) *Mindfulness-Based Treatment Approaches: A Clinician's Guide*. San Diego, CA: Elsevier.

Banks, S. (2006) *Ethics and Values in Social Work* (3rd edn). Basingstoke: Palgrave Macmillan.

Barnett, G.D. and Mann, R.E. (2011) Good Lives and Risk Assessment: Collaborative Approaches to Risk Assessment with Sexual Offenders. In: Kemshall, H. and Wilkinson, B. (eds) *Good Practice in Assessing Risk: Current Knowledge, Issues and Approaches*. London: JKP.

Basdekis-Jozsa, R., Turner, D. and Briken, P. (2013) Pharmacological Treatment of Sexual Offenders and Its Legal and Ethical Aspects. In K. Harrison and B. Rainey (eds) *The Wiley-Blackwell Handbook of Legal and Ethical Aspects of Sex Offenders' Treatment and Management* (pp 302–20). Chichester: Wiley-Blackwell.

Bauman, Z. (1993) *Postmodern Ethics*. Oxford: Blackwell.

BBC News India (2014) Mumbai Gang Rape: Death Sentences for India Rapists. Available at: http://www.bbc.co.uk/news/26887723 (accessed 15 July 2014).

BBC News UK (2013) 'Sarah's Law' Sees 700 Paedophiles Identified. Available at: http://www.bbc.co.uk/news/uk-25489541 (accessed 24 June 2014).

Beck, A.T., Freeman, A. and Davis, D.D. (eds) (2004) *Cognitive Therapy of Personality Disorders* (2nd edn). New York, NY: Guilford.

Becker, H.S. (1963) *Outsiders: Studies in the Sociology of Deviance*. London and New York, NY: Free Press.

Beddoe, E. (2015) Making a Moral Panic – 'Feral Families', Family Violence and Welfare Reforms in New Zealand: Doing the Work of the State? In V.E. Cree (ed) *Gender and Family* (pp 31–42). Bristol: The Policy Press.

Beddoe, L. (2010) Surveillance or Reflection: Professional Supervision in the 'Risk Society'. *British Journal of Social Work*, 40(4), 1279–96.

Bedford, A. (2015) *Serious Case Review into Child Sexual Exploitation in Oxfordshire: From the Experiences of Children A, B, C, D, E, and F. Approved by the OSCB February 26th 2015*. Oxford: Oxfordshire Safeguarding Children Board.

Beech, A.R. and Fisher, D.D. (2004) Treatment of Sex Offenders in the UK in Prison and Probation Settings. In H. Kemshall and G. McIvor (ed) *Managing Sex Offender Risk* (pp 137–63). London: Jessica Kingsley.

Beech, A.R. and Ward, T. (2004) The Integration of Etiology and Risk in Sexual Offenders: A Theoretical Framework. *Aggression and Violent Behavior*, 10, 31–63.

Beech, A.R., Fisher, D.D. and Thornton, D. (2003) Risk Assessment of Sex Offenders. *Professional Psychology: Research and Practice*, 34(4), 339–52.

Bengtson, S. and Långström, N. (2007) Unguided Clinical and Actuarial Assessment of Re-Offending Risk: A Direct Comparison with Sex Offenders in Denmark. *Sex Abuse*, 19, 135–53.

Berelowitz, S., Clifton, J., Firimin, C. and Edwards, G. (2013) *'If Only Someone Had Listened': Office of the Children's Commissioner's Inquiry into Child Sexual Exploitation in Gangs and Groups – Final Report*. London: Office of the Children's Commissioner.

Berghaus, B.J. (2011) A New Look at Attachment Theory & Adult 'Attachment' Behavior. *Behaviorology Today*, 14(2) 3–10.

Bhatti-Sinclair, K. (2011) *Anti-Racist Practice in Social Work*. Basingstoke: Palgrave Macmillan.

Bickley, J.A. and Beech, A.R. (2001) Classifying Child Abusers: Its Relevance to Theory and Clinical Practice. *International Journal of Offender Therapy*, 45, 51–69.

Bird Edmunds, S. (1997) The Personal Impact of Working with Sex Offenders. In S. Bird Edmunds (ed) *Impact: Working with Sexual Abusers* (pp 11–29). Brandon, VT: Safer Society Press.

Blacker, K. and Griffin, L. (2010) Megan's Law and Sarah's Law: A Comparative Study of Sex Offender Community Notification Schemes in the United States and the United Kingdom. *Criminal Law Bulletin*, 46, 987–1008.

Blagden, N. and Pemberton, S. (2010) The Challenge of Conducting Qualitative Research with Convicted Sex offenders. *The Howard Journal*, 49(3), 269–81.

Bonnycastle, K.D. (2012) *Stranger Rape: Rapists, Masculinity, and Penal Governance*. Toronto, Canada: University of Toronto Press.

Bradley, K. (2009) *The Bradley Report: Lord Bradley's Review of People with Mental Health Problems or Learning Disabilities in the Criminal Justice System*, www.dh.gov.uk/prod_consum_dh/groups/dh_digitalassets/documents/digitalasset/dh_098698.pdf

Brechin, A., Brown, H. and Eby, M.A. (2000) 'Introduction'. In A. Brechin, H. Brown and M.A. Eby (eds) *Critical Practice in Health and Social Care*, London: Sage.

Bretherton, I. (1992) The Origins of Attachment Theory: John Bowlby and Mary Ainsworth. *Developmental Psychology*, 28, 759–75.

Breuil, B.C.O., Siegel, D., Van Reenan, P., Beijer, A. and Roos, L. (2011) Human Trafficking Revisited: Legal, Enforcement and Ethnographic Narratives on Sex Trafficking to Western Europe (Report). *Trends in Organized Crime*, 14(1), 30–46.

Briere, J. and Elliott, D.M. (2003) Prevalence and Psychological Sequelae of Self-Reported Childhood Physical and Sexual Abuse in a General Population Sample of Men and Women. *Child Abuse & Neglect*, 27, 1205–22.

Briggs, D., Doyle, P., Gooch, T. and Kennington, R. (1998) *Assessing Men Who Sexually Abuse: A Practice Guide*. London: Jessica Kingsley.

British National Party (2013) Oxford Grooming Gang Convicted of Appalling Acts of Depravity on Children. Who Is at Fault, You Decide. Available at: http://www.bnp.org.uk/news/national/oxford-grooming-gang-convicted-appalling-acts-depravity-children-who-fault-you-decide (accessed 10 October 2015).

Brown, S. (2005) *Treating Sex Offenders: An Introduction to Sex Offender Treatment Programmes*. Cullompton: Willan Publishing.

Brown, S. (2015) The Wrong Type of Mother: Moral Panic and Teenage Parenting. In V.E. Cree, G. Clapton and M. Smith (eds) *Revisiting Moral Panics* (pp 39–47). Bristol: The Policy Press.

Browne, K.D., Foreman, L. and Middleton, D. (1998) Predicting Treatment Dropout in Sex Offenders. *Child Abuse Review*, 7, 402–19.

Brownmiller, S. (1975) *Against Our Will: Men, Women & Rape*. London: Secker & Warburg.

Bruenig, E.S. (2015) Sex is Serious: Affirmative Consent Laws Miss the Point. *Boston Review*, 12 January.

Bryant, S., Peck, M. and Lovbakke, J. (2015) *Reoffending Analysis of MAPPA Eligible Offenders: Ministry of Justice Analytical Series*. London: Ministry of Justice.

Burman, M. and Cartmel, F. (2006) *Young People's Attitudes to Gendered Violence*. Edinburgh: NHS Health.

Burton, S., Kitzinger, J.W., Kelly, L. and Regan, L. (1998) *Young People's Attitudes Towards Violence, Sex and Relationships: A Survey and Focus Group Study*. Edinburgh: Zero Tolerance Charitable Trust.

Caldicott, F. (2013) *Information: To share or not to share? The Information Governance Review*, https://www.gov.uk/government/uploads/system/uploads/attachment_data/file/192572/2900774_InfoGovernance_accv2.pdf. Accessed 20.01.2016.

Campbell, A.M. (2009) False Faces and Broken Lives: An Exploratory Study of the Interaction Behaviours Used by Male Sex Offenders in Relating to Victims. *Journal of Language and Social Psychology*, 28(4), 428–40.

Campbell, T.W. and DeClue, G. (2010). Flying Blind with Naked Factors: Problems and Pitfalls in Adjusted Actuarial Sex-Offender Risk Assessment. *Open Access Journal of Forensic Psychology*, 2, 75–101.

Casey, L. (2015) *Report of Inspection of Rotherham Metropolitan Borough Council* (HC1050). London: Her Majesty's Stationery Office.

Chaffin, M. (2008) Our Minds Are Made Up – Don't Confuse Us with the Facts: Commentary on Policies Concerning Children with Sexual Behavior Problems and Juvenile Sex Offenders. *Child Maltreatment*, 13(2): 110–21.

Chamallas, M. (2013) Vicarious Liability in Torts: The Sex Exception, 48 *Val. U. L. Rev.* 133. Available at: http://scholar.valpo.edu/vulr/vol48/iss1/4 (accessed 2 October 2015).

Chambers, J.C., Horvath, M.A.H. and Kelly, L. (2013) Reconstructing and Sequencing Behaviours in Multiple Perpetrator Rape. *Psychology, Crime & Law*, 19(3), 253–75.

Chivers, M.L., and Bailey, J.M. (2005). A Sex Difference in Features that Elicit Genital Response. *Biological Psychology*, 70: 115–20.

Cipriani, D. (2009) *Children's Rights and the Minimum Age of Criminal Responsibility: A Global Perspective*. Farnham: Ashgate Publishing Ltd.

Clark, C. (2015) Integration, Exclusion and the Moral 'Othering' of Roma Migrant Communities in Britain. In V.E. Cree, G. Clapton and M. Smith (eds) *Revisiting Moral Panics* (pp 231–42). Bristol: The Policy Press.

Clegg, C. and Fremouw, W. (2009) Phallometric Assessment of Rapists: A Critical Review of the Research. *Aggression and Violent Behavior*, 14: 115–25.

Cockbain, E. (2013) Grooming and the 'Asian Sex Gang Predator': The Construction of a Racial Crime Threat. *Race & Class*, 54(4), 22–32.

Code, L. (2006) *Ecological Thinking. The Politics of Epistemic Location*. Oxford: Oxford University Press.

Cohen, S. (1972) *Moral Panics: The Social Construction of Deviance*. Oxford: Martin Robertson.

Cohen, S. (2001) *States of Denial: Knowing About Atrocities and Suffering*. Cambridge: Polity.

Collins, P.H. (1991) *Black Feminist Thought: Knowledge, Consciousness, and the Politics of Empowerment*. London: Routledge.

Collins, W.H. (1918) *The Truth About Lynching and the Negro in the South: In Which the Author Pleads That the South Be Made Safe for the White Race*. New York, NY: The Neale Publishing Company.

Compton, B.R. and Galloway, B. (1999) *Social Work Processes* (6th edn). Pacific Grove CA: Brooks/Cole.

Comptroller and Auditor General (2013) *Ministry of Justice and National Offender Management Service: Managing the Prison Estate – a Report by the Comptroller and Auditor General.* London: National Audit Office.

Connolly, M. and Ward, T. (2008) *Morals, Rights and Practice in the Human Services: Effective and Fair Decision-Making in Health, Social Care and Criminal Justice.* London: Jessica Kingsley Publishers.

Cooke, D.J. and Michie, C. (2010) Limitations of Diagnostic Precision and Predictive Utility in the Individual Case: A Challenge for Forensic Practice. *Law and Human Behaviour,* 34, 259–74.

Corabian, P., Dennett, L. and Harstall, C. (2011) Treatment for Convicted Adult Male Sex Offenders: An Overview of Systematic Reviews. *Sexual Offender Treatment,* 6(1), online edition. Available at: http://www.sexual-offender-treatment.org/93.html (accessed 21 October 2015).

Cortoni, F., Hanson, R.K. and Coache, M.E. (2010) The Recidivism Rates of Female Sexual Offenders Are Low: A Meta-Analysis. *Sexual Abuse: A Journal of Research and Treatment,* 22, 387–401.

Cortoni, F., Sandler, J.C. and Freeman, N.J. (2015) Women Convicted of Promoting Prostitution of a Minor Are Different from Women Convicted of Traditional Sex Offenses. *Sexual Abuse: A Journal of Research and Treatment,* 27(3), 324–34.

Cossar, J., Brandon, M., Bailey, S., Belderson, P., Biggart, L. and Sharpe, D. (2013) *'It Takes a Lot to Build Trust' Recognition and Telling: Developing Earlier Routes to Help Children and Young People.* London: Office of the Children's Commissioner.

Coulshed, V. and Orme, J. (2012) Social Work Practice (fifth edition). Basingstoke: Palgrave Macmillan.

Cowburn, M. (2012) Reflections on the Jimmy Savile Disclosures: Grooming and Denial Behind the Masks of Masculinities. *British Society of Criminology Newsletter,* 71(Winter), 17–20.

Cowburn, M. (2013) Men Researching Violent Men: Epistemologies, Ethics and Emotions in Qualitative Research. In B. Pini and B. Pease (eds) *Men, Masculinities and Methodologies* (pp 183–96). Basingstoke: Palgrave Macmillan.

Cowburn, M. and Bains, H. (2008) Diversity Review on: Thinking Skills Programme. Unpublished report for HM Prison Service.

Cowburn, M. and Dominelli, L. (2001) Masking Hegemonic Masculinity: Reconstructing the Paedophile as the Dangerous Stranger. *British Journal of Social Work,* 31, 399–414.

Cowburn, M. and Lavis, V. (2009) Race Relations in Prison: Managing Performance and Developing Engagement. *British Journal of Community Justice,* 17(3), 77–89.

Cowburn, M., Lavis, V. and Walker, T. (2008) BME Sex Offenders in Prison: The Problem of Participation in Offending Behaviour Groupwork Programmes – A Tripartite Model of Understanding. *British Journal of Community Justice*, 6(1), 19–34.

Cowburn, M., Gill, A.K. and Harrison, K. (2015) Speaking About Sexual Abuse in British South Asian Communities: Offender, Victims and the Challenges of Shame and Reintegration. *Journal of Sexual Aggression*, 21(1), 4–15.

Craig, L. and Beech, A.R. (2010) Towards a Guide to Best Practice in Conducting Actuarial Risk Assessments with Sex Offenders. *Aggression and Violent Behaviour*, 15, 278–93.

Cree, V.E., Clapton, G. and Smith, M. (eds) (2015a) *Revisiting Moral Panics*. Bristol: The Policy Press.

Cree, V.E. Clapton, G. and Smith, M. (2015b) Preface. In V.E. Cree, G. Clapton and M. Smith (eds) *Revisiting Moral Panics* (pp xi–xvi). Bristol: The Policy Press.

Creeden, K. (2013) Taking a Developmental Approach to Treating Juvenile Sexual Behavior Problems. *International Journal of Behavioral Consultation and Therapy*, 8(3/4), 12–16.

Crenshaw, K. (1991) Mapping the Margins: Intersectionality, Identity Politics, and Violence Against Women of Color. *Stanford Law Review*, 43(6), 1241–99.

Criminal Justice Joint Inspection (2014) *A Joint Inspection of the Treatment of Offenders with Learning Disabilities within the Criminal Justice System – Phase 1 from arrest to sentence*, https://www.justiceinspectorates.gov.uk/cjji/wp-content/uploads/sites/2/2014/04/LearningDisabilities_Jan14_thm_rpt.pdf. Accessed 21.01.2016.

Crisp, B., Anderson, M.A., Orme, J. and Lister, P.G. (2007) Assessment Frameworks: A Critical Reflection. *British Journal of Social Work* 37(6): 1059-77.

Critcher, C. (2002) Media, Government and Moral Panic: The Politics of Paedophilia in Britain 2000–1. *Journalism Studies*, 3(4), 512–35.

Critcher, C. (2003) *Moral Panics and the Media*. Maidenhead: Open University Press.

Crombie, I.K. and Davies, H.T.O. (2009) What is meta-analysis? Available at: http://www.medicine.ox.ac.uk/bandolier/painres/download/whatis/meta-an.pdf (accessed 28 June 2014).

Culpitt, I. (1999) *Social Policy and Risk*. London: Sage.

Daly, K. (2002) Sexual Assault and Restorative Justice. In H. Strang and J. Braithwaite (eds) *Restorative Justice and Family Violence* (pp 62–88). Cambridge: Cambridge University Press.

Davidson, J.C. (2008) *Child Sexual Abuse: Media Representation and Government Reactions*, London: Routledge.

Davis, A. (1981) *Women, Race and Class*. London: Women's Press.

DCSF (Department of Children, Schools and Families) (2009) *Safeguarding Children and Young People from Sexual Exploitation: Supplementary Guidance to Working Together to Safeguard Children.* London: HM Government.

Death Penalty Information Center (2014) Death Penalty for Offences Other Than Murder. Available at: http://www.deathpenaltyinfo.org/death-penalty-offenses-other-murder (accessed 15 July 2014).

Deering, R. and Mellor, D. (2011) An Exploratory Qualitative Study of Self-Reported Impact of Female-Perpetrated Childhood Sexual Abuse. *Journal of Child Sexual Abuse*, 20(1), 58–76.

Denov, M.S. (2004) *Perspectives on Female Sex Offending: A Culture of Denial.* Farnham: Ashgate.

Department of Education (2015) *Working Together to Safeguard Children.* London: HM Government.

Department of Health (2014) Annual Report by the Chief Social Worker of Adults: One YEAR ON. Available at: https://www.gov.uk/government/uploads/system/uploads/attachment_data/file/368485/Annual_report_2014_web_final.pdf (accessed 25 September 2015).

Doel, M. and Kelly, T. (2014) *A-Z of Groups and Groupwork.* Basingstoke: Palgrave.

Dominelli, L. (1988) *Anti-Racist Social Work*, London: BASW/Macmillan.

Donaldson, T. and Wollert, R. (2008) A Mathematical Proof and Example that Bayes's Theorem is Fundamental to Actuarial Estimates of Sexual Recidivism Risk. *Sexual Abuse: A Journal of Research and Treatment*, 20, 206–17.

Donat, P.L.N. and D'Emilio, J. (1992) A Feminist Redefinition of Rape and Sexual Assault: Historical Foundations and Change. *Journal of Social Issues*, 48(1), 9–22.

Douglas, M. (1985) *Risk Acceptability According to the Social Sciences.* New York, NY: Russell Sage Foundation.

Douglas, M. (1992) *Risk and Blame: Essays in Cultural Theory.* London: Routledge.

Droisen, A. (1989) Racism & Anti-Semitism. In E. Driver and A. Droisen (eds) *Child Sexual Abuse: Feminist Perspectives.* London and Basingstoke: MacMillan.

Duff, R.A. and Garland, D. (1998) Introduction: Thinking About Punishment. In R.A. Duff and D. Garland (eds) *A Reader on Punishment* (pp 1–43). Oxford: Oxford University Press.

Ellerby, L. (1997) Impact on Clinicians: Stressors and Providers of Sex Offender Treatment. In S. Bird Edmunds (ed) *Impact: Working with Sexual Abusers* (pp 51–60). Brandon, VT: Safer Society Press.

Epperson, D.L., Kaul, J.D. and Hesselton, D. (1998) Final Report on the Development of the Minnesota Sex Offender Screening Tool—Revised (MnSOST–R). Paper presented at the 15th Annual Research and Treatment Convention of the Association for the Treatment of Sexual Abusers, Vancouver, British Columbia, Canada.

ESRC (2012) Revisiting Moral Panics: A Critical Examination of 21st Century Social Issues and Anxieties. ESRC-funded research seminar series, 1 October 2012–31 October 2014, ES/J021725/1. Available at: https://moralpanicseminars.wordpress.com

Fabian, J.M. (2012) Neuropsychology, Neuroscience, Volitional Impairment and Sexually Violent Predators: A Review of the Literature and the Law and Their Application to Civil Commitment Proceedings. *Aggression and Violent Behavior*, 17: 1–15.

Falselyaccused.co.uk (2015) Homepage. Available at: http://www.falselyaccused.co.uk

Farrall, S. (1995) Why Do People Stop Offending? *The Scottish Journal of Criminal Justice Studies*, 1, 1, 51–9.

Farrenkopf, T. (1992) What Happens to Therapists Who Work with Sex Offenders? *Journal of Offender Rehabilitation*, 18, 217–23.

Featherstone, B., White, S. and Morris, K. (2014) *Re-Imagining Child Protection Towards Humane Social Work with Families*. Bristol: The Policy Press.

Feinberg, J. (1965) The Expressive Function of Punishment. *The Monist*, 49(3), 397–423.

Ferguson, H. (2005) Working with Violence, the Emotions and the Psycho-Social Dynamics of Child Protection: Reflections on the Victoria Climbié Case. *Social Work Education*, 24(7), 781–95.

Ferguson, I. and Lavalette, M. (2006) Globalization and Global Resistance: Towards a Social Work of Resistance. *International Social Work*, 49(3), 309–18.

Fine, C. (2010) *Delusions of Gender: How our Minds, Society, and Neurosexism Create Difference*. London: W.W. Norton

Finkelhor, D. (1984) *Child Sexual Abuse: New Theory and Research*. New York, NY: The Free Press.

Finkelhor, D., Ormrod, R. and Chaffin, M. (2009) *Juveniles Who Commit Offences Against Minors*. Rockville, MD: Office of Juvenile Justice and Delinquency Prevention, US Department of Justice.

Fisher, D. and Mair, G. (1998) *A Review of Classification Schemes for Sex Offenders: Home Office Research and Statistic Directorate Research Finding No. 78*. London: Great Britain Home Office Research Development and Statistics Directorate.

Fonagy, P., Target, M., Steele, M., Steele, H., Leigh, T., Levinson, A. and Kennedy, R. (1997) Morality, Disruptive Behaviour, Borderline Personality Disorder, Crime, and Their Relationships to Security of Attachment. In L. Atkinson and K.J. Zucker (eds) *Attachment and Psychopathology* (pp 223–74). New York, NY: Guilford Press.

Fook, J. (2012) *Social Work: A Critical Approach to Practice*. London: Sage.

Fook, J. and Gardner, F. (2007) *Practising Critical Reflection: A Resource Handbook*. Maidenhead: Open University Press.

Foucault, M. (1977) *Discipline and Punish: The Birth of the Prison.* London: Allen Lane.

Foucault, M. (1984) *The History of Sexuality: An Introduction* (vol I) (trans R. Hurley). London: Peregrine.

Frances, A. and First, M.B. (2011) Paraphilia NOS, Nonconsent: Not Ready for the Courtroom. *Journal of American Academy of Psychiatry Law,* 39, 555–61.

Franklin, M.B. (1997) Making Sense: Interviewing and Narrative Representation. In M.M. Gergen and S.N. Davis (eds) *Toward a New Psychology of Gender.* London: Routledge.

Fricker, M. (2007) *Epistemic Injustice: Power & the Ethics of Knowing.* Oxford: Oxford University Press.

Frisbie, L. (1958) The Treated Sex Offender. *Federal Probation,* 22, 18–24.

Frisbie, L. (1969) *Another Look at Sex Offenders in California.* California Mental Health Research Monograph No 12. Sacramento, CA: California Department of Mental Hygiene.

Frisbie, L.V. and Dondis, E.H. (1965) *Recidivism Among Treated Sex Offenders.* Sacramento, CA: California Department of Mental Hygiene.

Fulton, R. and Richardson, K. (2014) *Equality and Inclusion for Learning Disability Workers.* Exeter: Sage

Furedi, F. (2015) The Moral Crusade Against Paedophilia. In V.E. Cree, G. Clapton and M. Smith (eds) *Revisiting Moral Panics* (pp 201–10). Bristol: The Policy Press.

Futa, K.T., Hsu, E. and Hansen, D.J. (2001) Child Sexual Abuse in Asian American Families: An Examination of Cultural Factors That Influence Prevalence, Identification and Treatment. *Clinical Psychology: Science and Practice,* 8, 189– 209.

Gabbidon, S. (2010) *Race, Ethnicity, Crime and Justice: An International Dilemma.* Thousand Oaks, CA: Sage.

Gadamer, H. (1974) *Truth and Method.* New York, NY: Seabury Press.

Gailey, J.A. and Prohaska, A. (2011) Power and Gender Negotiations During Interviews with Men About Sex and Sexually Degrading Practices. *Qualitative Research,* 11(4), 365–80.

Galeste, M.A., Fradella, H.F. and Vogel, B. (2012) Sex Offender Myths in Print Media: Separating Fact from Fiction in U.S. Newspapers. *Western Criminology Review,* 13(2), 4–24.

Gannon, T.A. (2009) Social Cognition in Violent and Sexual Offending: An Overview. *Psychology, Crime & Law,* 15(2/3) 97–118.

Gannon, T.A., Wood, J., Pina, A., Vasquez, E. and Fraser, I. (2012) *The Evaluation of the Mandatory Polygraph Pilot.* London: Ministry of Justice.

Gannon, T.A., Waugh, G., Taylor, K., Blanchette, K., O'Connor, A., Blake, E. and Ciardha, C. (2013) Women Who Sexually Offend Display Three Main Offense Styles: A Re-Examination of the Descriptive Model of Female Sexual Offending. *Sexual Abuse: A Journal of Research and Treatment,* 26, 207–24.

Garland, D. (2008) On the Concept of Moral Panic. *Crime Media Culture,* 4(1), 9–30.

Garside, R. (2013) Does Sarah's Law Work? Available at: http://www.crimeandjustice.org.uk/resources/does-sarahs-law-work (accessed 29 August 2014).

Gavey, N. (2005) *Just Sex: The Cultural Scaffolding of Rape.* London: Routledge.

Gelsthorpe, L. (2007) Probation Values and Human Rights. In L. Gelsthorpe and R. Morgan(eds) *Handbook of Probation* (pp 485–517). Cullompton: Willan Publishing.

Gerry, F., Sjölin, C. and Harris, L. (2014) *Sexual Offences Handbook: Law, Practice and Procedure.* London: Wildy, Simmonds and Hill.

Gilderthorp, N., Whittaker, M. and Dunn, J. (2011) Past Caring? Issues of After Care, Attachment and Mental Health for Young People who Have Displayed Harmful Sexual Behaviour. In M. Calder (ed) *Contemporary Practice With Young People Who Sexually Abuse: Evidence-Based Developments* (pp 173–90). Lyme Regis: Russell House.

Gill, A.K. and Harrison, K. (2015) Child Grooming and Sexual Exploitation: Are South Asian Men the UK Media's New Folk Devils? *International Journal for Crime, Justice and Social Democracy,* 4(2), 34–49.

Gillespie, S., Mitchell, I., Fisher, D. and Beech, A. (2012) Treating Disturbed Emotional Regulation in Sexual Offenders: The Potential Applications of Mindful Self-Regulation and Controlled Breathing Techniques. *Aggression and Violent Behavior,* 17, 333–343.

Gilligan, P. and Akhtar, S. (2006) Cultural Barriers to the Disclosure of Child Sexual Abuse in Asian Communities: Listening to What Women Say. *British Journal of Social Work,* 36, 1361–77.

Gottfredson, S.D. and Moriarty, L.J. (2006) Statistical Risk Assessment: Old Problems and New Applications. *Crime and Delinquency,* 52(1): 178–200.

Grabham, E., Cooper, D., Krishnadas, J. and Herman, D. (eds) (2009) *Intersectionality and Beyond: Law, Power and the Politics of Location.* Abingdon: Routledge-Cavendish.

Great Britain (2013) House of Commons, Home Affairs Committee – Second Report, Child Sexual Exploitation and the Response to Localised Grooming. Available at: http://www.publications.parliament.uk/pa/cm201314/cmselect/cmhaff/68/6802.htm (accessed 9 December 2013).

Greer, C. (2003) *Sex Crime and the Media: Sex Offending and the Press in a Divided Society.* Cullompton: Willan Publishing.

Gregory, M. and Holloway, M. (2005) Language and the Shaping of Social Work. *British Journal of Social Work,* 35, 37–53.

Griggs, L. (2000) Assessment in Community Care. In M. Davies (ed) *The Blackwell Encyclopaedia of Social Work* (pp 22–3). Oxford: Blackwell.

Groth, A.N., Burgess, A.W. and Holmstrom, L.L. (1977) Rape: Power, Anger and Sexuality. *American Journal of Psychiatry,* 134, 1239–43.

Grubin, D. (1999) Actuarial and Clinical Assessment of Risk in Sex Offenders. *Journal of Interpersonal Violence*, 14(3), 331–43.

Gutierrez, D. and Hagedorn, W. (2013) The Toxicity of Shame Applications for Acceptance and Commitment Therapy. *Journal of Mental Health Counseling*, 35, 43–59.

Hackett, S., Masson, H., Balfe, M. and Phillips, J. (2015) Community Reactions to Young People who have Sexually Abused and their Families: A Shotgun Blast, Not a Rifle Shot. *Children and Society* 29(4): 243–54.

Hall, G.C.N. and Hirschman, R. (1991) Towards a Theory of Sexual Aggression: A Quadripartite Model. *Journal of Consulting and Clinical Psychology*, 59, 662–9.

Hall, S. (2011) Evidence for Working Holistically with Young People Who Have Sexually Harmed. In M. Calder (ed) *Contemporary Practice With Young People Who Sexually Abuse: Evidence-Based Developments*. Lyme Regis: Russell House.

Hanson, R.K. (1997) *The Development of a Brief Actuarial Risk Scale for Sexual Offense Recidivism* (User Report 97-04). Ottawa: Department of the Solicitor General of Canada.

Hanson, R.K. (2003). Who is dangerous and when are they safe? Risk assessment with sexual offenders. In B.J. Winick and J.Q. La Fonds (eds), *Protecting Society from Sexually Dangerous Offenders: Law, Justice, and Therapy*. Washington, DC: American Psychological Association.

Hanson, R.K. and Bussiere, M.T. (1998) Predicting Relapse: A Meta-Analysis of Sexual Offender Recidivism Studies. *Journal of Counselling and Clinical Psychology*, 66(2), 348–62.

Hanson, K.R. and Howard, P.D. (2010) Individual Confidence Intervals do not Inform Decision Makers about the Accuracy of Risk Assessment Evaluations. *Law and Human Behaviour*, 34, 275–81.

Hanson, R.K. and Morton-Bourgon, K.E. (2005) The Characteristics of Persistent Sexual Offenders: A Meta-Analysis of Recidivism Studies. *Journal of Counselling and Clinical Psychology*, 73(6), 1154–63.

Hanson, R.K. and Thornton, D. (2000). Improving Risk Assessments for Sex Offenders: A Comparison of Three Actuarial Scales. *Law and Human Behavior*, 24, 119–136.

Hanson, R.K. and Yates, P.M. (2013) Psychological Treatment of Sex Offenders. *Current Psychiatry Reports*, 15, 1–8.

Hanson, R.K., Harris, A.J.R., Scott, T.L., and Helmus L. (2007) *Assessing the Risk of Sexual Offender on Community Supervision: The Dynamic Supervision Project*. (Corrections Research User Report 2007-05). Ottawa: Public Safety Canada.

Hanson, R.K., Bourgon, G., Helmus, L. and Hodgson, S. (2009) The Principles of Effective Correctional Treatment Also Apply to Sexual Offenders: A Meta-Analysis. *Criminal Justice and Behavior*, 36, 865–91.

Hanson, R.K., Lloyd, C.D., Helmus, L. and Thornton, D. (2012) Developing Non-Arbitrary Metrics for Risk Communication: Percentile Ranks for the Static-99/R and Static-2002/R Sexual Offender Risk Scales. *International Journal of Forensic Mental Health*, 11, 9–23.

Hanvey, S. and Höing, M. (2013) A More Ethical Way of Working: Circles of Support and Accountability. In K. Harrison and B. Rainey (eds) *The Wiley-Blackwell Handbook of Legal and Ethical Aspects of Sex Offender Treatment and Management* (pp 373–87). Chichester: Wiley-Blackwell.

Hanvey, S., Philpot, T. and Wilson, C. (2011) *A Community-Based Approach to the Reduction of Sexual Offending: Circles of Support and Accountability*. London: Jessica Kingsley Publishers.

Harding, S. (1991) *Whose Science? Whose Knowledge? Thinking from Women's Lives*. Milton Keynes: Open University Press.

Harding, S. (2006) *Science and Social Inequality: Feminist and Postcolonial Issues*. Urbana and Chicago, IL: University of Illinois Press.

Harkins, L., Flak, V.E., Beech, A.R. and Woodhams, J. (2012) Evaluation of a Community-Based Sex Offender Treatment Program using a Good Lives Model Approach. *Sexual Abuse: A Journal of Research and Treatment*, published online 30 January 2012.

Harris, A.J.R. and Hanson, R.K. (2004) *Sex Offender Recidivism: A Simple Question*. West Ottawa, Ontario: Public Safety and Emergency Preparedness Canada.

Harris, D. (2010) Theories of Female Sexual Offending. In T. Gannon and T. Cortoni (eds) *Female Sexual Offenders: Theory, Assessment and Treatment* (pp 31–51). Chichester: John Wiley and Sons.

Harris, G.T. and Rice, M.E. (2003) Actuarial Assessment of Risk among Sex Offenders. In R.A. Prentky, E. Janus, and M.C. Seto (eds), *Understanding and Managing Sexually Coercive Behaviour* (pp. 198–210). New York: Annals of the New York Academy of Sciences.

Harris, G.T. and Rice, M.E. (2007) Adjusting Actuarial Violence Risk Assessments Based on Aging or the Passage of Time. *Criminal Justice and Behavior*, 34(3), 297–313.

Hart, S., Kropp, P.R. and Laws, D.R., with Klaver, J., Logan, C. and Watt, K.A. (2003) *The Risk for Sexual Violence Protocol (RSVP): Structured Professional Guidelines for Assessing Risk of Sexual Violence*. Vancouver, BC: The Institute Against Family Violence.

Hart, S., Michie, C., and Cooke, D. (2007) Precision of Actuarial Risk Assessment Instruments: Evaluating the 'Margins of Error' of Group v. Individual Predictions of Violence. *The British Journal of Psychiatry*, 190, s60-s65.

Hatcher, R. and Noakes, S. (2010) Working with Sex Offenders: The Impact on Australian Treatment Providers. *Psychology, Crime & Law*, 16, 145–67.

Hayes, S. and Baker, B. (2014) Female Sex Offenders and Pariah Femininities: Rewriting the Sexual Scripts. *Journal of Criminology*, Article ID 414525, 1–8.

Healy, K. (2012) *Social Work Methods and Skills: The Essential Foundations of Practice*. Basingstoke: Palgrave Macmillan.

Henggeler, S.W., Schoenwald, S.K., Borduin, C.M., Rowland, M.D. and Cunningham, P.B. (2009) *Multisystemic Therapy for Antisocial Behavior in Children and Adolescents* (2nd edn). New York, NY: The Guilford Press.

Henshaw, M., Ogloff, J.R.P. and Clough, J.A. (2015) Looking Beyond the Screen: A Critical Review of the Literature on the Online Pornography Offender. *Sexual Abuse: A Journal of Research and Treatment*, September, 1–30.

Hepworth, D.H., Rooney, R.H. and Larsen, J.A. (2002) *Direct Social Work Practice: Theory and Skills*. Pacific Grove, CA: Brooks/Cole.

HM Government (2015a) Information Sharing: Advice for practitioners providing safeguarding services to children, young people, parents and carers. Available at: https://www.gov.uk/government/uploads/system/uploads/attachment_data/file/419628/Information_sharing_advice_safeguarding_practitioners.pdf

HM Government (2015b) Tackling Child Sexual Exploitation. Available at: https://www.gov.uk/government/uploads/system/uploads/attachment_data/file/408604/2903652_RotherhamResponse_acc2.pdf (accessed 11 October 2015).

Ho, D. K. and Ross, C. C. (2012) Editorial: Cognitive Behaviour Therapy for Sex Offenders. Too Good to be True?, *Criminal Behaviour and Mental Health*, 22: 1–6.

Home Office (2001) *Initial Guidance to the Police and Probation Services on Sections 67 and 68 of the Criminal Justice and Court Services Act 2000 (HOC 10/2001)*. London: Home Office.

Home Office (2006) *OASys Manual*. London: Home Office

Home Office (in cooperation with Barnardos, NSPCC, The Lucy Faithfull Foundation and Stop it Now! UK and Ireland) (2007) *Keeping Children Safe from Sex Offenders: How Sex Offenders Are Managed*. London: COI on behalf of the Home Office.

Home Office (2013) Guidance: Domestic Violence and Abuse. Available at: https://www.gov.uk/guidance/domestic-violence-and-abuse (accessed 21 October 2015).

Home Office (2014) *Multi Agency Working and Information Sharing Project Final report*. London: Home Office.

Howard, P.D., Barnett, G.D. and Mann, R.E. (2014) Specialization In and Within Sexual Offending in England and Wales. *Sexual Abuse: A Journal of Research and Treatment*, 26(3), 225–51.

Howe, A. (2008) *Sex, Violence and Crime: Foucault and the 'Man' Question*. Abingdon, Oxon: Routledge-Cavendish.

Howe, D. (2011) *Attachment Across the Lifecourse: A Brief Introduction*. Basingstoke: Palgrave Macmillan.

Hudson, K. (2005) *Offending Identities: Sex Offenders' Perspectives on Their Treatment and Management*. Cullompton: Willan Publishing.

Huffam, L. (2001) A Balancing Act: Impact on Therapists of Working With Sex Offenders. Unpublished Master's thesis, Victoria University of Wellington.

Humphrey, M. (2007) Culturalising the Abject: Islam, Law and Moral Panic in the West. *Australian Journal of Social Issues*, 42(1), 9–25.

Huppatz, K. (2012) *Gender Capital at Work: Intersections of Femininity, Masculinity, Class and Occupation*. Basingstoke: Palgrave Macmillan.

IFSW (International Federation of Social Workers) and IASSW (International Association of Schools of Social Work) (2004) Ethics in Social Work, Statement of Principles. Available at: http://www.iassw-aiets.org/uploads/file/20130506_Ethics%20in%20Social%20Work,%20Statement,%20IFSW,%20IASSW,%202004.pdf (accessed 15 May 2014).

Institute of Race Relations (2015) Criminal Justice System Statistics. Available at: http://www.irr.org.uk/research/statistics/criminal-justice/ (accessed 1 September 2015).

International Federation for Human Rights (2009) *IRAN/Death Penalty: A State Terror Policy*. Paris: Fédération internationale des ligues des droits de l'Homme.

Jackson, K.E., Holzman, C., Barnard, T. and Paradis, C. (1997) Working with Sex Offenders: The Impact on Clinicians. In S. Bird Edmunds (ed) *Impact: Working with Sexual Abusers* (pp 61–73). Brandon, VT: Safer Society Press.

Jackson, R.L. and Covell, C.N. (2013) Sex Offender Civil Commitment: Legal and Ethical Issues. In K. Harrison and B. Rainey (eds) *The Wiley-Blackwell Handbook of Legal and Ethical Aspects of Sex Offender Treatment and Management* (pp 406–23). Oxford: John Wiley & Sons.

Jay, A. (2014) *Independent Inquiry into Child Sexual Exploitation in Rotherham 1997–2013*. Rotherham: Rotherham Metropolitan Borough Council.

Jehle, J.-G. (2012) Attrition and Conviction Rates of Sexual Offences in Europe: Definitions and Criminal Justice Responses. *European Journal of Criminal Policy & Research*, 18, 145–61.

Jenkins, A. (1993) *Invitations to Responsibility: The Therapeutic Engagement of Men Who Are Violent and Abusive*. Adelaide, South Australia: Dulwich Centre Publications.

Jenkins, P. (1998) *Moral Panic: Changing Concepts of the Child Molester in Modern America*, New Haven and London: Yale University Press.

Jennings, J.L., Apsche, J.A., Blossom, P. and Bayles, C. (2013) Using Mindfulness in the Treatment of Adolescent Sexual Abusers: Contributing Common Factor or a Primary Modality? *International Journal of Behavioral Consultation and Therapy*, 8(3/4) 17–22.

Jewkes, Y. (2011) *Media & Crime* (2nd edn). London: Sage Publications Ltd.

Jones, N., Pelissier, B. and Klein-Saffran, J. (2006) Predicting Sex Offender Treatment Entry Among Individuals Convicted of Sexual Offence Crimes. *Sexual Abuse: A Journal of Research and Treatment*, 18, 83–98.

Jones, R. (2014) *The Story of Baby P: Setting the Record Straight*. Bristol: The Policy Press.

Jung, S., Jamieson, L., Buor, K. and Decesare, J. (2012) Attitudes and Decisions about Sexual Offenders: A Comparison of Laypersons and Professionals. *Journal of Community & Applied Social Psychology*, 22: 225–38.

Kabat–Zinn, J. (1982) An Outpatient Program in Behavioral Medicine for Chronic Pain Patients Based on the Practice of Mindfulness Meditation: Theoretical Considerations and Preliminary Results. *General Hospital Psychiatry*, 4, 33–47.

Kadushin, A. and Harkness, D. (2002) *Supervision in Social Work*. New York, NY: Columbia University Press.

Kagan, J. (2000) *Three Seductive Ideas*. Harvard, MA: Harvard University Press.

Kelly, L. (1988) *Surviving Sexual Violence*. Oxford: Polity Press.

Kelly, L. and Lovett, J. (2009) *Different Systems, Similar Outcomes? Tracking Attrition in Reported Rape Cases in Eleven Countries (European Briefing)*. London: Child & Woman Abuse Studies Unit, London Metropolitan University.

Kelly, L., Lovett, J. and Regan, L. (2005) *A Gap or a Chasm? Attrition in Reported Rape Cases*. London: Home Office Research, Development and Statistics Directorate.

Kemshall, H. (1998) Risk in Probation Practice. Farnham: Ashgate.

Kemshall, H. (2010) Risk Rationalities in Contemporary Social Work Policy and Practice. *British Journal of Social Work*, 40(4), pp 1247–62.

Kemshall, H. and Weaver, B. (2012) The Sex Offender Public Disclosure Pilots in England and Scotland: Lessons for 'Marketing Strategies' and Risk Communication with the Public. *Criminology and Criminal Justice*, 12(5), 549–65.

Kemshall, H., Wood, J., Westwood, S., Stout, B., Wilkinson, B., Kelly, G. and Mackenzie, G. (2010) *Research Report 32. Child Sex Offender Review (CSOR) Public Disclosure Pilots: A Process Evaluation* (2nd edn). London: Home Office Research, Development and Statistics Directorate.

Kenny, M.C. and McEachern, A.G. (2000) Racial, Ethnic, and Cultural Factors of Childhood Sexual Abuse: A Selected Review of the Literature. *Clinical Psychology Review*, 20(7), 905–22.

Kingston, D. and Yates, P.M. (2012) The Self-Regulation Model of Sexual Offending: The Relationship to Risk and Need. *Law and Human Behavior*, 36, 215–24.

Kirby, M. (2013) The Sodomy Offence: England's Least Lovely Criminal Law Export? In C. Lennox and M. Waites (eds) *Human Rights, Sexual Orientation and Gender Identity in the Commonwealth: Struggles for Decriminalisation and Change*. London: Human Rights Consortium, Institute of Commonwealth Studies, School of Advanced Study, University of London.

Kitzinger, J. (1999) The Ultimate Neighbour from Hell: Media Framing of Paedophiles. In B. Franklin (ed) *Social Policy, the Media and Misrepresentation* (pp 207–21). London: Routledge.

Kitzinger, J. (2004) *Framing Abuse: Media Influence and Public Understanding of Sexual Violence Against Children*. London: Pluto Press.

Knight, R.A., Carter, D.L. and Prentky, R.A. (1989) A System for the Classification of Child Molesters. *Journal of Interpersonal Violence*, 4, 3–23.

Krafft-Ebing, R. (2011/1886) *Psychopathia Sexualis, with Especial Reference to the Antipathic Sexual Instinct: A Medico-Forensic Study* (D. Falls, Trans.). Chicago; University of Chicago Press

Lacombe, D. (2008) Consumed with Sex: The Treatment of Sex Offenders in Risk Society. *British Journal of Criminology*, 48(1), 55–74.

Lave, T.R. (2011) Inevitable Recidivism—The Origin and Centrality of an Urban Legend. *International Journal of Law and Psychiatry*, 34, 186–94.

Laws, D.R. and Marshall, W.L. (2003) A Brief History of Behavioral and Cognitive Behavioral Approaches to Sexual Offenders, Part 1: Early Developments. *Sexual Abuse: A Journal of Research and Treatment*, 15(2), 75–92.

Laws, R.D. (2003) The Rise and Fall of Relapse Prevention. *Australian Psychologist*, 38(1), 22–30.

Lawson, C. (1993) Mother–Son Sexual Abuse: Rare or Underreported? A Critique of the Research. *Child Abuse & Neglect*, 17, 261–9.

Lea, S., Auburn, T. and Kibblewhite, K. (1999) Working with Sex Offenders: The Perceptions and Experiences of Professionals and Paraprofessionals. *International Journal of Offender Therapy and Comparative Criminology*, 43: 103–19.

Lee, J.K.P., Proeve, M.J., Lancaster, M. and Jackson, H.J. (1996) An Evaluation and 1-Year Follow-Up Study of a Community-Based Treatment Program for Sex Offenders. *Australian Psychologist*, 31, 147–52.

Le Grand, E. (2015) Moralising Discourse and the Dialectical Formation of Class Identities: The Social Reaction to 'Chavs' in Britain. In V.E. Cree, G. Clapton and M. Smith (eds) *Revisiting Moral Panics* (pp 159–68). Bristol: The Policy Press.

Leicht, S.K.C. (2008) The Impact on Professionals of Working with Sex Offenders. In J. Houston and S. Galloway (eds) *Sexual Offending and Mental Health: Multi-Disciplinary Management in the Community* (pp 263–79). London: Jessica Kingsley Publishers.

Letourneau, E.J., Henggeler, S.W., McCart, M.R., Borduin, C.M., Schewe, P.A. and Armstrong, K.S. (2013) Two-Year Follow-Up of a Randomized Effectiveness Trial Evaluating MST for Juveniles Who Sexually Offend. *Journal of Family Psychology*, 27, 978–85.

Leversee, T. (2011) Understanding and Applying Typologies in the Context of a Holistic Model for the Treatment of Sexually Offending Juveniles. In M. Calder (ed) *Contemporary Practice With Young People Who Sexually Abuse: Evidence-Based Developments*. Lyme Regis: Russell House.

Le Vrai, B. (2010) Mods, Rockers, Folk Devils, Deviants. Available at: http://www.vice.com/en_uk/read/mods-rockers-folk-devils-deviants (accessed 11 November 2015).

Linehan, M., Cochran, B. and Kehrer, C. (2001) Dialectical Behavior Therapy for Borderline Personality Disorder. In C. Barlow (ed) *Clinical Handbook of Psychological Disorders: A Step by Step Treatment Manual* (3rd edn) (pp 470–522). New York, NY, and London: Guilford Press.

Lines, N. (2013) Insidetime Legal Factsheet (England) 2014 Sex Offenders' Register Notification & Review Mechanism. Available at: http://insidetime.org/wp-content/uploads/resources/Factsheets2014/Sex-Offenders-Register-Lines-Chivers-2014.pdf (accessed 15 January 2016).

Locke, P. (2013) The Wrongly Convicted Sex Offender. Available at: http://wrongfulconvictionsblog.org/2013/09/02/the-wrongfully-convicted-sex-offender/

Looman, J. and Abracen, J. (2013a) The Static-99R: Are There Really Differences between the Normative Groups? *International Journal of Offender Therapy and Comparative Criminology*, 57(7), 888–907.

Looman, J. and Abracen, J. (2013b) The Risk Need Responsivity Model of Offender Rehabilitation: Is There Really a Need For a Paradigm Shift? *International Journal of Behavioral Consultation and Therapy*, 8(3/4) 30–36.

Lukes, S. (2005) *Power: A Radical View*. Basingstoke: Palgrave.

Lussier, P. and Davies, G. (2011) A Person-Oriented Perspective on Sexual Offenders, Offending Trajectories, and Risk of Recidivism: A New Challenge for Policymakers, Risk Assessors, and Actuarial Prediction? *Psychology, Public Policy, and Law*, 17, 4,530–561.

Maguire, M. and Kemshall, H. (2004) Multi-Agency Public Protection Arrangements: Key Issues. In H. Kemshall and G. McIvor (eds) *Managing Sex Offender Risk* (pp 209–24). London: Jessica Kingsley Publishers.

Mainstone, F. (2014) *Mastering Whole Family Assessment in Social Work*. London: Jessica Kingsley.

Mair, G. (2011) The Community Order in England and Wales: Policy and Practice. *Probation Journal: The Journal of Community and Criminal Justice*, 58(3), 214–32.

Malamuth, N.M., Heavey, C.L. and Linz, D. (1996) The Confluence Model of Sexual Aggression: Combining Hostile Masculinity and Impersonal Sex. *Journal of Offender Rehabilitation*, 20(3/4), 13–37.

Mann, R.E. and Barnett, G.D. (2012) Victim Empathy Intervention with Sexual Offenders: Rehabilitation, Punishment, or Correctional Quackery? *Sexual Abuse: A Journal of Research and Treatment*, 25(3), 282–301.

Mann, R.E. and Webster, S.D. (2002) Understanding Resistance and Denial. Paper presented at the 21st Annual Research and Treatment Conference of the Association for the Treatment of Sexual Abusers, Montreal, Canada, October.

Mann, R.E., Webster, S.D., Schofield, C. and Marshall, W.L. (2004) Approach Versus Avoidance Goals in Relapse Prevention with Sexual Offenders. *Sexual Abuse: A Journal of Research and Treatment*, 16, 65–75.

Mannay, D. (2015) Myths, Monsters and Legends: Negotiating an Acceptable Working Class Femininity in a Marginalised and Demonised Welsh Locale. In V.E. Cree, G. Clapton and M. Smith (eds) *Revisiting Moral Panics* (pp 19–29). Bristol: The Policy Press.

Marlatt, G.A. (1985) Relapse Prevention: Theoretical Rationale and Overview of the Model. In G.A. Marlatt and J.R. Gordon (eds) *Relapse Prevention: Maintenance Strategies in the Treatment of Addictive Behaviors* (pp 208–50). New York, NY: Guilford Press.

Marshall, W.L. (2009) Manualization: A Blessing or a Curse? *Journal of Sexual Aggression*, 15(2), 109–20.

Marshall, W.L. and Barbaree, H.E. (1990) An Integrated Theory of the Etiology of Sexual Offending, in W.L. Marshall, D.R. Laws and H.E. Barbaree (eds) *Handbook of Sexual Assault: Issues, theories and treatment of the offender* (pp 257–75), New York: Plenum.

Marshall, W.L. and Marshall, L.E. (2000) The Origins of Sex Offending. *Trauma Violence and Abuse*, 1(3), 250–63.

Marshall, W.L. and Marshall, L.E. (2012) Treatment of Sexual Offenders: Effective Elements and Appropriate Outcome Evaluations. *Advances in Program Evaluation*, 13, 71–94.

Marshall, W.L., Smallbone, S. and Marshall, L.E. (2015) A Critique of Current Child Molester Subcategories: A Proposal for an Alternative Approach. *Psychology, Crime and Law*, 21(3), 205–18.

Masson, J.M. (1984) *The Assault on Truth: Freud's Suppression of the Seduction Theory*. New York, NY: Farrar, Straus and Giroux.

McAlinden, A. (2007) *The Shaming of Sexual Offenders: Risk, Retribution and Reintegration*. Oxford: Hart Publishing.

McAlinden, A.-M. (2012) The Governance of Sexual Offending Across Europe: Penal Policy, Political Economies and the Institutionalization of Risk. *Punishment & Society*, 14(2), 166–92.

McAlinden, A.-M. (2013) Reintegrative and Disintegrative Shaming: Legal and Ethical Issues. In K. Harrison and B. Rainey (eds) *The Wiley-Blackwell Handbook of Legal and Ethical Aspects of Sex Offender Treatment and Management* (pp 113–28). Chichester: Wiley-Blackwell.

McCann, I.L. and Pearlman, L.A. (1990) Vicarious Traumatization: A Framework for Understanding the Psychological Effects of Working with Victims. *Journal of Traumatic Stress*, 3, 131–49.

McCrudden, C. (2008) Human Dignity and Judicial Interpretation of Human Rights. *European Journal of International Law*, 19(4), 655–724.

McFadden, P., Campbell, A. and Taylor, B. (2015) Resilience and Burnout in Child Protection Social Work: Individual and Organisational Themes from a Systematic Literature Review. *British Journal of Social Work*, 45(5), 1546–63.

McGlynn, C., Westmarland, N. and Godden, N. (2012) 'I Just Wanted Him to Hear Me': Sexual Violence and the Possibilities of Restorative Justice. *Journal of Law and Society*, 39(2), 213–40.

McGrath, R., Cumming, G.F., Livingston, J.A. and Hoke, S.E. (2003) Outcome of a Treatment Program for Adult Sex Offenders: From Prison to Community. *Journal of Interpersonal Violence*, 18, 3–17.

McGrath, R., Cumming, G., Burchard, B., Zeoli, S. and Ellerby, L. (2010) *Current Practices and Emerging Trends in Sexual Abuser Management: The Safer Society 2009 North American Survey*. Brandon, VT: Safer Society Press.

McKendrick, D. (2015) Internet Radicalisation and the 'Woolwich Murder'. In V.E. Cree, G. Clapton and M. Smith (eds) *Revisiting Moral Panics* (pp 149–58). Bristol: The Policy Press.

McKillop, N., Smallbone, S., Wortley, R. and Andjic, I. (2012) Offenders' Attachment and Sexual Abuse Onset: A Test of Theoretical Propositions. *Sexual Abuse: Journal of Research and Treatment*, 24(6), 591–610.

McNeill, F. (2012) Four Forms of 'Offender' Rehabilitation: Towards an Interdisciplinary Perspective. *Legal and Criminological Psychology*, 17(1), 18–36.

McPherson, M., Chein, D., Van Maren, N. and Swenson, D. (1994) *Sex Offender Treatment Programs*. Saint Paul, MN: Program Evaluation Division, Office of the Legislative Auditor, State of Minnesota.

Mellor, D. and Deering, R. (2010) Professional Response and Attitudes Toward Female-Perpetrated Child Sexual Abuse: A Study of Psychologists, Psychiatrists, Probationary Psychologists and Child Protection Workers. *Psychology, Crime & Law*, 16(5), 415–38.

Meloy, M., Saleh, Y. and Wolff, N. (2007) Sex Offender Laws in America: Can Panic Driven Legislation Ever Create Safer Societies? *Criminal Justice Studies*, 20(4), 423–43.

Messerschmidt, J.W. (1993) *Masculinities and Crime: Critique and Reconceptualization of Theory*. Lanham, MD: Rowman and Littlefield Publishers, Inc.

Messerschmidt, J.W. (2000) *Nine Lives*. Boulder, CO: Westview Press.

Messerschmidt, J.W. (2011) The Struggle for Heterofeminine Recognition: Bullying, Embodiment and Reactive Sexual Offending by Adolescent Girls. *Feminist Criminology*, 6(3), 203–33.

Messerschmidt, J.W. (2012) *Gender, Heterosexuality, and Youth Violence: The Struggle for Recognition*. Lanham, MD: Rowman & Littlefield Publishers, Inc.

Milner, J. and Bateman, J. (2011) *Working with Children and Teenagers Using Solution Focused Approaches*. London; Jessica Kingsley Publishers.

Milner, J., Myers, S. and O'Byrne, P. (2015) *Assessment in Social Work* (4th edn). London: Palgrave MacMillan.

Ministry of Justice: National Offender Management Service (2010) *What Works with Sex Offenders?*, London: Ministry of Justice, National Offender Management Service.

Ministry of Justice (2012) *Restorative Justice Action Plan for the criminal Justice System*. London: Ministry of Justice.

Ministry of Justice (2014) Press Release – Compulsory Lie Detector Tests for Serious Sex Offenders. Available at: https://www.gov.uk/government/news/compulsary-lie-detector-tests-for-serious-sex-offenders (accessed 22 July 2014).

Ministry of Justice (2015) A Compendium of Research and Analysis on the Offender Assessment System (OASys); Studies completed between 2009 and 2013. Available at https://www.gov.uk/government/publications/research-and-analysis-on-the-offender-assessment-system (accessed 21 January 2016).

Ministry of Justice and Youth Justice Board (2015) *Youth Justice Statistics 2013/14: England and Wales*. London: Ministry of Justice, Youth Justice Board and National Statistics.

Ministry of Justice, Home Office and Office for National Statistics (2013) *An Overview of Sexual Offending in England and Wales: Statistics Bulletin*. London: Ministry of Justice, Home Office and Office for National Statistics.

Munro, E. (2011) *The Munro Review of Child Protection: Final Report: A Child-Centred System (Cm 8062)*. London: Department of Education.

Myers, S. (2007) *Solution Focused Approaches*. Lyme Regis: Russell House.

Mythen, G. and Walklate, S. (2006) Introduction: Thinking Beyond the Risk Society. In G. Mythen and S. Walklate (ed) *Beyond the Risk Society: Critical Reflections on Risk and Human Security* (pp 1–10). Maidenhead: Open University Press.

National Policing Improvement Agency (2010) *Guidance on Protecting the Public: Managing Sexual and Violent Offenders 2010* (2nd edn, Version 2 ed). London: National Policing Improvement Agency (on behalf of Association of Chief Police Officers).

NOMS (National Offender Management Service) (2013) *Offending Behaviour Programmes (OBPs)*, https://www.justice.gov.uk/offenders/before-after-release/obp (accessed 20 October 2015).

NOMS (2014) *Licence Conditions, Polygraph Examinations and temporary Travel Abroad (PI 11/2014)*. London: National Offender Management Service.

NSPCC (National Society for the Prevention of Cruelty to Children) (2013) Vicarious Trauma: The Consequences of Working with Abuse. NSPCC research briefing. Available at: http://www.nspcc.org.uk/Inform/research/briefings/consequences-working-abuse_wda97769.html (accessed 4 March 2014).

OED (Oxford English Dictionary) (2015) Homepage . Available at: http://www.oed.com (accessed 10 October 2015).

Ofsted (Office for Standards in Education) (2014) *The Sexual Exploitation of Children: It Couldn't Happen Here, Could It?* (Reference no 140175). Available at: https://www.gov.uk/government/uploads/system/uploads/attachment_data/file/386598/The_20sexual_20exploitation_20of_20children_20it_20couldn_E2_80_99t_20happen_20here_2C_20could_20it.pdf (accessed 11 October 2015).

Ogloff, J.R.P., Cutajar, M.C., Mann, E. and Mullen, P. (2012) *Child Sexual Abuse and Subsequent Offending and Victimisation: A 45 Year Follow-Up Study. Trends & Issues in Crime & Criminal Justice No 440.* Canberra, Australia: Australian Institute of Criminology.

Olson, L.N., Daggs, J.L., Ellevoid, B.L. and Rogers, T.K.K. (2007) Entrapping the Innocent: Toward a Theory of Child Sexual Predators' Luring Communication. *Communication Theory,* 17(3), 231–51.

Oosterhuis, H. (2012) Sexual Modernity in the Works of Richard von Krafft-Ebbing and Albert Moll. *Medical History,* 56(2), 133–55.

Owusu-Bempah, K. and Howitt, D. (2000) *Psychology beyond Western Perspectives.* Leicester: British Psychological Society.

Pack, M. (2011) Discovering an Integrated Framework for Practice: A Qualitative Investigation of Theories Used by Social Workers Working as Sex Abuse Therapists. *Journal of Social Work Practice,* 25(1), 79–93.

Parton, N. and O'Byrne, P. (2000) *Constructive Social Work: Towards a New Practice.* Basingstoke: Palgrave Macmillan.

Patel, K. and Lord, A. (2001) Ethnic Minority Sex Offenders' Experiences of Treatment. *Journal of Sexual Aggression,* 7, 40–51.

Payne, M. (2014) *Modern Social Work Theory* (4th edn). Basingstoke: Palgrave Macmillan.

Peach, J. and Horner, N. (2007) Using Supervision: Support or Surveillance? In M. Lymbery and K. Postle (eds) *Social Work: A Companion To Learning.* London: Sage.

Peck, M. (2011) *Patterns of Reconviction Among Offenders Eligible for Multi-Agency Public Protection Arrangements (MAPPA): Ministry of Justice Research Series 6/11.* London: Ministry of Justice.

Percy, A. and Mayhew, P. (1997) Estimating Sexual Victimisation in a National Crime Survey: A New Approach. *Studies on Crime and Crime Prevention,* 6(2), 355–62.

Petrunik, M. and Deutschmann, L. (2007) The Exclusion Inclusion Spectrum in State and Community Response to Sex Offenders in Anglo-American and European Jurisdictions. *International Journal of Offender Therapy and Comparative Criminology,* 52: 499–519.

Phillips, C. (2010) White, Like Who? Temporality, Contextuality and Anti-Racist Social Work Education and Practice. *Critical Social Work,* 11(2), 71–88.

Phillips, C. (2012) *The Multicultural Prison: Ethnicity, Masculinity, and Social Relations Among Prisoners.* Oxford: Oxford University Press.

Pini, B. (2005) Interviewing Men: Gender and the Collection and Interpretation of Qualitative Data. *Journal of Sociology*, 41(2), 201–16.

Pithers, W.D. (1990) Relapse Prevention with Sexual Aggressors: A Method for Maintaining Therapeutic Gain and Enhancing External Supervision. In W.L. Marshall, D.R. Laws and H.E. Barbaree (eds) *Handbook of Sexual Assault: Issues, Theories and Treatment of the Offender* (pp 343–62). New York, NY: Plenum Press.

Plotnikoff, J. and Woolfson, R. (2000) *Where Are They Now? An Evaluation of Sex Offender Registration in England and Wales – Police Research Series Paper 126*. London: Home Office Policing & Reducing Crime Unit.

Pollack, S. (2010) Labelling Clients 'Risky': Social Work and the Neo-Liberal State. *British Journal of Social Work*, 40(4), 1263–78.

Powell, K.M. (2011) Working Effectively With At-Risk Youth: A Strengths-Based Approach. In M. Calder (ed) *Contemporary Practice With Young People Who Sexually Abuse: Evidence-Based Developments*. Lyme Regis: Russell House.

Prescott, D.S. (2009) *Building Motivation for Change in Sexual Offenders*. Brandon, VT: Safer Society Press.

Prison Reform Trust (2013) Information Booklet for People on Licence for a Sex Offence . Available at: http://www.prisonreformtrust.org.uk/Portals/0/Documents/sex%20offender%20information%20booklet.pdf (accessed 19 July 2014).

Purvis, M. (2010) *Seeking a Good Life: Human Goods and Sexual Offending*. Germany: Lambert Academic Press.

Purvis, M., Ward, T. and Willis, G. (2011) The Good Lives Model in Practice: Offence Pathways and Case Management. *European Journal of Probation*, 3(2), 4–28.

Quayle, E. (2015) Internet Risk Research and Child Sexual Abuse: A Misdirected Moral Panic? In V.E. Cree, G. Clapton and M. Smith (eds) *Revisiting Moral Panics* (pp 103–12). Bristol: The Policy Press.

Quinn, F.M. (1998) Reflection and Reflective Practice. In F.M. Quinn (ed) *Continuing Professional Development in Nursing*. Cheltenham: Stanley Thornes.

Quinsey, V.L., Rice, M.E. and Harris, G.T. (1995) Actuarial Prediction of Sexual Recidivism. *Journal of Interpersonal Violence*, 10(1), 85-105.

Quinsey, V.L., Khanna, A. and Malcolm, P.B. (1998) A Retrospective Evaluation of the Regional Treatment Centre Sex Offender Treatment Program. *Journal of Interpersonal Violence*, 13(5), 621–44.

Rainey, B. (2013) Human Rights and Sexual Offenders. In K. Harrison and B. Rainey (eds) *The Wiley-Blackwell Handbook of Legal and Ethical Aspects of Sex Offender Treatment and Management* (pp 18–37). Chichester: Wiley-Blackwell.

Rape Crisis South London (2011) *Reporting Sexual Offences: Research & Policy Bulletin 1*. London: Rape and Sexual Abuse Centre South London.

Reitzel, L.R. and Carbonell, J.L. (2006) The Effectiveness of Sexual Offender Treatment for Juveniles as Measured by Recidivism: A Meta-Analysis. *Sex Abuse*, 18(4), 401–21.

Renzetti, C.M. (1999) The Challenges to Feminism Posed by Women's Use of Violence in Intimate Relationships. In S. Lamb (ed) *New Versions of Victims: Feminists' Struggle with the Concept* (pp 42–56). New York, NY: New York University Press.

Rich, P. (2006) *Attachment and Sexual Offending: Understanding and Applying Attachment Theory to the Treatment of Juvenile Sexual Offenders.* Chichester:Wiley.

Robinson, A. (2011) *Foundations for Offender Management: Theory, Law and Policy for Contemporary Practice.* Bristol: The Policy Press.

Robinson, L. (1995) *Psychology for Social Workers: Black Perspectives,* London: Routledge.

Rohloff, A., Hughes, J., Petley, J. and Critcher, C. (2013) Moral Panics in the Contemporary World: Enduring Controversies and Future Directions. In C. Critcher, J. Hughes, J. Petley and A. Rohloff (eds) *Moral Panics in the Contemporary World.* London and New York, NY: Bloomsbury Academic.

Romero, J. and Williams, L. (1983) Group Psychotherapy and Intensive Probation Supervision with Sex Offenders: A Comparative Study. *Federal Probation*, 47, 36–42.

Rose, N. (1984) *The Psychological Complex: Psychology, Politics and Society in England, 1869–1939.* Abingdon: Routledge and Kegan Paul.

Rose, N. and Abi-Rached, J.M. (2013) *Neuro: The New Brain Sciences and the Management of the Mind.* Princeton University Press

Rozenberg, J. (2014) How a Local Authority Is Using the Law to Protect Girls from Sexual Exploitation. *The Guardian.* Available at: http://www.theguardian.com/law/2014/nov/19/local-authority-using-law-protect-girls-exploitation-birmingham (accessed 2 October 2015).

Ryan, G., Leversee, T. and Lane, S. (eds) (2010) *Juvenile Sexual Offending: Causes, Consequences and Correction.* Hoboken, NJ: John Wiley & Sons, Inc.

Saleebey, D. (2013) *The Strengths Perspective in Social Work Practice* (5th edn). Allyn and Bacon.

Salter, A.C. (1988) *Treating Child Sexual Offenders and Victims: A Practical Guide.* Newbury Park, CA, London and New Delhi: Sage.

Sample, L.L. and Kadleck, C. (2008) Sex Offender Laws: Legislators' Accounts of the Need for Policy. *Criminal Justice Policy Review*, 19(1), 40–62.

Sanday, P.R. (1979) *The Socio-Cultural Context of Rape.* Washington, DC: US Department of Commerce, National Technical Information Services.

Sanday, P.R. (2003) Rape-Free versus Rape-Prone: How Culture Makes a Difference. In C.B. Travis (ed) *Evolution, Gender, and Rape* (pp 337–62). Cambridge, MA: The MIT Press.

Sanday, P.R. (2007) *Fraternity Gang Rape: Sex, Brotherhood and Privilege on Campus* (2nd edn). New York, NY, and London: New York University Press.

Scheela, R.A. (2001) Sex Offender Treatment: Therapists' Experiences and Perceptions. *Issues in Mental Health and Nursing*, 22, 749–67.

Schippers, M. (2007) Recovering the Feminine Other: Masculinity, Femininity, and Gender Hegemony. *Theory and Society*, 36(1), 85–102.

Schober, J. (1993) Frameworks for Nursing Practice. In S.M. Hinchcliff, S.E. Norman and J. Schober (eds) *Nursing Practice and Health Care* (2nd edn). London: Edward Arnold.

Schön, D.A. (1983) *The Reflective Practitioner: How Professionals Think in Action*. London: Temple Smith.

Seager, J.A., Jellicoe, D. and Dhaliwal, G.K. (2004) Refusers, Dropouts, and Completers: Measuring Sex Offender Treatment Efficacy. *International Journal of Offender Therapy and Comparative Criminology*, 48, 600–12.

Segal, Z., Williams, J. and Teasdale, J. (2002) *Mindfulness-Based Cognitive Therapy for Depression: A New Approach to Preventing Relapse*. New York, NY: Guilford Press.

Sentencing Council (2013) Sexual Offences: Definitive Guideline (Effective from 1st April 2014). Available at: http://sentencingcouncil.judiciary.gov.uk/docs/Final_Sexual_Offences_Definitive_Guideline_content_(web).pdf (accessed 17 July 2014).

Sentencing Council (undated) *Sexual Offences: Note of approach when Sentencing Offenders under 18*. Available at: http://sentencingcouncil.judiciary.gov.uk/docs/Sexual_offences_-_note_of_approach_when_sentencing_offenders_under_18.pdf (accessed 17 July 2014).

Sentencing Guidelines Council (2009) *Overarching Principles: Sentencing Youths: Definitive Guideline*. Available at: http://www.sentencingcouncil.org.uk/wp-content/uploads/web_overarching_principles_sentencing_youths.pdf.

Sexual Violence Research Initiative (2014) Sexual Violence in Conflict and Post Conflict Settings. Available at: http://www.svri.org/emergencies.htm

Shaw, T.A., Herkov, J.M. and Greer, R.A. (1995) Examination of Treatment Completion and Predicted Outcome Among Incarcerated Sex Offenders. *The Bulletin of the American Academy of Psychiatry and the Law*, 23, 35–41.

Shlonsky, A. and Wagner, D. (2005) The Next Step: Integrating Actuarial Risk Assessment and Clinical Judgment into an Evidence-Based Practice Framework in CPS Case Management. *Children and Youth Services Review*, 27(4), 409–27.

Siegert, R.J., Ward, T., Levack, W.M. and McPherson, K.M. (2007) A Good Lives Model of Clinical and Community Rehabilitation. *Disability and Rehabilitation*, 29(20/21), 1604–15.

Silver, E. and Miller, L.L. (2002) A Cautionary Note on the Use of Actuarial Risk Assessment Tools for Social Control. *Crime and Delinquency*, 48(1), 138–61.

Silverman, J. and Wilson, D. (2002) *Innocence Betrayed: Paedophilia, the Media and Society*. Cambridge: Polity Press.

Simonelli, L.E., Ray, W.J. and Pincus, A.L. (2004) Attachment Models and Their Relationships with Anxiety, Worry, and Depression. *Counseling and Clinical Psychology Journal*, 1, 107–18.

Slater, C. and Lambie, I. (2011) The Highs and Lows of Working with Sexual Offenders: A New Zealand Perspective. *Journal of Sexual Aggression*, 17(3): 320–34.

Smale, G., Tuson, G., Biehal, N. and Marsh, P. (1993) *Empowerment, Assessment, Care Management and the Skilled Worker*, London: HMSO.

Smallbone, S., Marshall, W.L. and Wortley, R. (2008) *Preventing Child Sexual Abuse: Evidence, policy and practice*. Cullompton: Willan Publishing.

Smith, P., Gendreau, P. and Swartz, K. (2009) Validating the Principles of Effective Intervention: A Systematic Review of the Contributions of Meta-Analysis in the Field of Corrections. *Victims and Offenders*, 4(2), 148–69.

Soothill, K. and Walby, S. (1991) *Sex Crime in the News*. London: Routledge.

Stanford, S. (2011) Constructing Moral Responses to Risk: A Framework for Hopeful Social Work Practice. *British Journal of Social Work*, 41, 1514–31.

Stermac, L.E., Segal, Z.V. and Gillis, R. (1990) Social and Cultural Factors in Sexual Assault. In W.L. Marshall, D.R. Laws and H.E. Barbaree (eds) *Handbook of Sexual Assault: Issues, Theories, and Treatment of the Offender*. New York, NY: Plenum.

Stevenson, K., Davies, A. and Gunn, M. (2004) *Blackstone's Guide to the Sexual Offences Act 2003*. Oxford: OUP.

Stevenson, O. (2013) *Reflections on a Life in Social Work: A Personal and Professional Memoir*. Buckingham: Hinton House Publishers Ltd.

Surviving Therapist Abuse (2009) Don't Call it Consent: Being Groomed. Available at: http://www.survivingtherapistabuse.com/2009/08/dont-call-it-consent-being-groomed-for-sex/ (accessed 10 October 2015).

Terry, K.J. and Ackerman, A. (2008) Child Sexual Abuse in the Catholic Church: How Situational Crime Prevention Strategies Can Help Create Safe Environments. *Criminal Justice and Behavior*, 35(5), 643–57.

Thomas, T. (2004) Sex Offender Registers and Monitoring. In H. Kemshall and G. McIvor (eds) *Managing Sex Offender Risk* (pp 225–48). London and Philadelphia, PA: Jessica Kingsley.

Thomas, T. (2008) The Sex Offender 'Register': A Case Study in Function Creep. *Howard Journal*, 47(3), 227–37.

Thomas, T. (2011) *Sex Crime: Sex Offending and Society* (2nd edn). Abingdon: Routledge.

Thomas, T. and Thompson, D. (2013) New Civil Orders to Contain Sexual Offending – A Matter of 'Purposive Logic'?. *Criminal Law and Justice Weekly*, 177(43), access online by using title.

Thompson, S. and Thompson, N. (2008) *The Critically Reflective Practitioner*. Basingstoke: Palgrave Macmillan.

Thornhill, R. and Palmer, C.T. (2000) *A Natural History of Rape: Biological Bases of Sexual Coercion*. Cambridge, MA, and London: MIT.

Thornton, D. (2002). Constructing and Testing a Framework for Dynamic Risk Assessment. *Sexual Abuse: A Journal of Research and Treatment*, 14, 139–53.

Thornton, D. (2010) *Scoring Guide for Risk Matrix 2000.10/SVC*. London: Ministry of Justice.

Topping, C. (2009) Sex Offenders and Their Place Within the Prison Estate. *Insidetime: The National Newspaper for Prisoners*. Available at: http://insidetime.org/articleview.asp?a=490&c=sex_offenders_and_their_place_within_the_prison_estate (accessed 18 July 2014).

Tosh, J. (2011) The Medicalisation of Rape: A Discursive Analysis of 'Paraphilic Coercive Disorder' and the Psychiatrisation of Sexuality. *Psychology of Women Section Review*, 13(2), 2–12.

Travis, C.B. (ed) (2003) *Evolution, Gender, and Rape*. Cambridge, MA: The MIT Press.

Tsopelas, C., Tsetsou, S., Ntounas, P. and Douzenis, A. (2012) Female Perpetrators of Sexual Abuse of Minors: What Are the Consequences for the Victims? *International Journal of Law and Psychiatry*, 35, 305–10.

Tully, R.J., Chou, S. and Browne, K.D. (2013) A Systematic Review on the Effectiveness of Sex Offender Risk Assessment Tools in Predicting Sexual Recidivism of Adult Male Sex Offenders. *Clinical Psychology Review*, 33(2), 287–316.

Turnell, A. and Edwards, S. (1999) *Signs of Safety*. New York, NY: Norton.

Valentine, T.M. (2008) Language and Gender. In B.B. Kachru, Y. Kachru and S.N. Sridhar (eds) *Language in South Asia* (pp 429–49). Cambridge: Cambridge University Press.

Vrieze, S.I. and Grove, W.M. (2008) Predicting Sex Offender Recidivism: I. Correcting for Item Overselection and Accuracy Overestimation in Scale Development. II. Sampling Error-Induced Attenuation of Predictive Validity over Base Rate Information. *Law and Human Behavior*, 32, 266–78.

Waites, M. (2009) *The Age of Consent: Young People, Sexuality and Citizenship*. London: Palgrave.

Walby, S., Armstrong, J. and Strid, S. (2012) Intersectionality: Multiple Inequalities in Social Theory. *Sociology*, 46, 224–40.

Walters, D.R. (1978) *Physical and Sexual Abuse of Children: Causes and Treatment*. Bloomington, IN: Indiana University Press.

Wampold, B.E. (2011) Qualities and Actions of Effective Therapists. Available at: http://apa.org/education/ce/effective-therapists.pdf (accessed 21 October 2015).

Ward, T. (2000) Relapse Prevention: Critique and Reformulation. *Journal of Sexual Aggression*, 5(2), 118–33.

Ward, T. (2003) The Explanation, Assessment, and Treatment of Child Sexual Abuse. *International Journal of Forensic Psychology*, 1, 10–25.

Ward, T. and Beech, A. (2006) An Integrated Theory of Sexual Offending. *Aggression and Violent Behavior*, 11, 44–63.

Ward, T. and Beech, A. (2015) Dynamic Risk Factors: A Theoretical Dead-End? *Psychology Crime & Law*, 21(2), 100–13.

Ward, T. and Fisher, D.D. (2005) New Ideas in the Treatment of Sexual Offenders. In W.L. Marshall, Y. Fernandez, L. Marshall and G.A. Serran (eds) *Sexual Offender Treatment: Issues and Controversies*. Chichester: John Wiley & Sons Ltd.

Ward, T. and Gannon, T. (2006) Rehabilitation, Etiology, and Self Regulation: The Comprehensive Good Lives Model of Treatment for Sexual Offenders. *Aggression and Violent Behavior*, 11, 77–94.

Ward, T. and Hudson, S.M. (1998) The Construction and Development of Theory in the Sexual Offending Area: A Metatheoretical Framework. *Sexual Abuse: A Journal of Research and Treatment*, 10, 47–63.

Ward, T. and Maruna, S. (2007) *Rehabilitation: Beyond the Risk Paradigm*. London: Routledge.

Ward, T. and Rose, C. (2013) Punishment and the Rehabilitation of Sex Offenders: An Ethical Maelstrom. In K. Harrison and B. Rainey (eds) *The Wiley-Blackwell Handbook of Legal and Ethical Aspects of Sex Offender Treatment and Management* (pp 271–86). Chichester: John Wiley & Sons.

Ward, T. and Siegert, R.J. (2002) Toward an Comprehensive Theory of Child Sexual Abuse: A Theory Knitting Perspective. *Psychology, Crime, and Law*, 9, 319–51.

Ward, T., Polaschek, D. and Beech, A.R. (2006) *Theories of Sexual Offending*. Chichester: John Wiley.

Ward, T., Yates, P.M. and Willis, G.M. (2012) The Good Lives Model and the Risk Need Responsivity Model: A Critical Response to Andrews, Bonta, and Wormwith. *Criminal Justice and Behavior*, 39(1), 94–110.

Ware, J. and Mann, R.E. (2012) How Should 'Acceptance of Responsibility' Be Addressed in Sexual Offending Treatment Programs? *Aggression and Violent Behavior*, 17(4), 279–88.

Warner, K. (2004) Gang Rape in Sydney: Crime, the Media, Politics, Race and Sentencing. *The Australian and New Zealand Journal of Criminology*, 37(3), 344–61.

Wastell, D. and White, S. (2012) Blinded by Neuroscience: Social Policy, the Family and the Infant Brain. *Families, Relationships and Societies*, 1(3), 397–414.

Webb, S.A. (2006) *Social Work in a Risk Society: Social and Political Perspectives*. Basingstoke: Palgrave Macmillan.

Webb, S.A. (2009) Risk, Governmentality and Insurance: The Actuarial Recasting of Social Work, in H-U. Otto, A. Polutta, and H. Ziegler (eds) *Evidence-based Practice: Modernising the Knowledge Base of Social Work?* (pp 211-225). Barbara Budrich Publishers.

Webster, C., Mann, R., Carter, A., Long, J., Milner, R., O'Brien, M., Wakeling, H. and Ray, N. (2006) Inter-rater Reliability of Dynamic Risk Assessment with Sexual Offenders. *Psychology Crime & Law*, 12(4): 439–52.

Westwood, J. (2015) Unearthing Melodrama: Moral Panic Theory and the Enduring Characterisation of Child Trafficking. In V.E. Cree, G. Clapton and M. Smith (eds) *Revisiting Moral Panics* (pp 83–91). Bristol: Policy Press.

White, M. and Epston, D. (1990) *Narrative Means to Therapeutic Ends*. New York, NY: Norton.

White, S. (2013) Discourse and Reflexivity. In M. Gray and S.A. Webb (eds) *Social Work Theories and Methods* (pp 218–28). London: Sage.

Wijkman, M., Weerman, F., Bijleveld, C. and Hendriks, J. (2015) Group Sexual Offending by Juvenile Females. *Sexual Abuse: A Journal of Research and Treatment*, 27(3), 335–56.

Wilcox, D.T. (2013) Ethical Practice and the Use of the Polygraph in Working with Sex Offenders. In K. Harrison and B. Rainey (eds) *The Wiley-Blackwell Handbook of Legal and Ethical Aspects of Sex Offender Treatment and Management* (pp 251–70). Chichester: Wiley-Blackwell.

Williams, K.S. and Bierie, D.M. (2015) An Incident-Based Comparison of Female and Male Sexual Offenders. *Sexual Abuse: A Journal of Research and Treatment*, 27(3), 235–57.

Willis, G.M., Levenson, J.S. and Ward, T. (2010) Desistance and Attitudes Towards Sex Offenders: Facilitation or Hindrance? *Journal of Family Violence*, 25, 545–56.

Wilson, R.J. and McWhinnie, A.J. (2013) Putting the 'Community' Back in Community Risk Management of Persons Who Have Sexually Abused. *Journal of Behavioral Consultation and Therapy*, 8(Special Edition: Current Approaches and Perspectives in the Treatment of Adult and Juvenile Sexual Offending, ed P. Rich), 79–87.

Wilson, R.J., McWhinnie, A.J. and Wilson, C. (2008) Circles of Support and Accountability: An International Partnership in Reducing Sexual Offender Recidivism. *Prison Service Journal*, 178, 26–36.

Wilson, R.J.J., M.A., Picheca, A.J., Prinzo, M. and Cortoni, F. (2007). Circles of Support and Accountability: Engaging community volunteers in the management of high risk sexual offender. *Howard Journal of Criminal Justice*, 46, 1–15.

Wood, J. and Kemshall, H. (2007) The Operation and Experience of Multi-Agency Public Protection Arrangements. Home Office online report 12/2007.

Wood, R.M., Grossman, L.S. and Fichtner, C.G. (2000) Psychological Assessment, Treatment, and Outcome with Sex Offenders. *Behavioral Sciences & the Law*, 18(1), 23–41.

Yates, P.M. (2007) Taking the Leap: Abandoning Relapse Prevention and Applying the Self-Regulation Model to the Treatment of Sexual Offenders. In D. Prescott (ed) *Applying Knowledge to Practice: The Treatment and Supervision of Sexual Abusers*. Oklahoma City, OK: Wood 'n' Barnes.

Yates, P.M. (2009) Is Sexual Offender Denial Related to Sex Offence Risk and Recidivism? A Review and Treatment Implications. *Psychology, Crime & Law*, 15(2/3), 183–99.

Yates, P.M. (2013) Treatment of Sexual Offenders: Research, Best Practices, and Emerging Models. *International Journal of Behavioral Consultation and Therapy*, 8(3/4), 89–95.

Yates, P.M. and Ward, T. (2008) Good Lives, Self-Regulation, and Risk Management: An Integrated Model of Sexual Offender Assessment and Treatment. *Sexual Abuse in Australia and New Zealand: An Interdisciplinary Journal*, 1, 3–20.

Yates, P.M., Kingston, D.A. and Ward, T. (2009) *The Self-Regulation Model of the Offence and Re-Offence Process: A Guide to Assessment and Treatment Planning Using the Integrated Good Lives/Self-Regulation Model of Sexual Offending*. Victoria, BC: Pacific Psychological Assessment Corporation.

Yates, P.M., Prescott, D.S. and Ward, T. (2010) *Applying the Good Lives and Self-Regulation Models to Sex Offender Treatment*. Brandon, VT: Safer Society Press.

Index

Note: Page numbers in *italics* indicate figures and tables. Page numbers followed by *n* refer to end-of-chapter notes and page numbers in **bold** indicate major references.